German Grammar

Jenny Russ

TEACH YOURSELF BOOKS

For my mother,
who still battles with
German Grammar

For UK order queries: please contact Bookpoint Ltd, 39 Milton Park, Abingdon, Oxon OX14 4TD. Telephone: (44) 01235 400414, Fax: (44) 01235 400454. Lines are open from 9.00 – 6.00, Monday to Saturday, with a 24 hour message answering service. Email address: orders@bookpoint.co.uk

For U.S.A. & Canada order queries: please contact NTC/Contemporary Publishing, 4255 West Touhy Avenue, Lincolnwood, Illinois 60646–1975 U.S.A. Telephone: (847) 679 5500, Fax: (847) 679 2494.

Long-renowned as the authoritative source for self-guided learning – with more than 30 million copies sold worldwide – the *Teach Yourself* series includes over 200 titles in the fields of languages, crafts, hobbies, sports, and other leisure activities.

British Library Cataloguing in Publication Data
A catalogue record for this title is available from the British Library

Library of Congress Catalog Card Number: 98-65237

First published in UK 1998 by Hodder Headline Plc, 338 Euston Road, London NW1 3BH

First published in US 1998 by NTC/Contemporary Publishing, 4255 West Touhy Avenue, Lincolnwood (Chicago), Illinois 60646–1975 U.S.A.

The 'Teach Yourself' name and logo are registered trade marks of Hodder & Stoughton Ltd.

Typeset by Transet Limited, Coventry, England.
Printed in Great Britain for Hodder & Stoughton Educational, a division of Hodder Headline Plc, 338 Euston Road, London NW1 3BH by Cox & Wyman Ltd, Reading, Berkshire.

Impression number   10   9   8   7   6   5   4   3   2
Year   2004   2003   2002   2001   2000   1999

CONTENTS

Functional Grammar

1 **Asking for and giving personal information**
Say who you are • State your nationality • Say where
you are from • Say what your occupation is • Give
similar information about other people • Ask for

2 **Introducing and identifying people,
places and things**
Introduce yourself and other people • Greet people when
being introduced • Say goodbye • Identify people, places
and things • Ask questions in order to identify people,
places and things • Talk on the telephone • Write letters •

3 **Expressing existence and availability**
Ask if something exists or is available • State that
something exists or is available • Ask and answer

4 **Expressing location**
Enquire about and give information about location •
Enquire about and give information about distance

INTRODUCTION

This book is intended as a reference guide for those who, with or without the help of a teacher, wish to study the essentials of German grammar.

A particular feature of the book is the two-fold approach to the language, linking the communicative skills to the learning of grammar. The functional grammar consists of 21 units illustrating the various uses to which the language can be put – for example, giving instructions or talking about the recent past. The more traditional reference grammar deals with grammatical structures, such as the imperative or the perfect tense. A few points not covered in the functional grammar are to be found in the reference grammar.

The beginner will find that all terms are explained in the glossary at the start of the book, all structures are illustrated and all examples are translated into English. The more advanced student will be able to progress at a faster pace, either by working through any or all of the units in the functional grammar as necessary, or by starting at any given point in the reference grammar and cross-referencing to the relevant functional section, whenever illustration or further practice is required.

Details are given on the contents page at the beginning of the functional grammar of both the language uses and the grammatical structures covered. This means that each unit can be approached from either the functional or the structural perspective. Additionally, the provision of exercises at the end of each unit allows students to test their understanding of the material covered. Coupled with a regular fifteen minutes of learning grammar and vocabulary items per day, the student should quickly establish firm linguistic foundations.

HOW TO USE
THIS BOOK

The glossary is at the front of the book for easy reference whenever the explanation of a term is required.

Each of the 21 units in the functional grammar consists of the following five sections:

1. Preliminary Note
2. Grammar summary
3. Im Kontext (In context)
4. Machen wir weiter! (Let's continue!)
5. Jetzt sind Sie dran! (Now it's your turn!)

The following procedure is suggested for working through each unit: first, read through the box marked Aims, which gives details of the language uses or functions which are dealt with in the unit. Then read the box marked Grammar Content, which outlines the grammatical constructions and the language forms associated with these language functions.

You can then go on to read the Preliminary Note, which gives a brief explanation and some examples of the language you will encounter in this unit. English translations are given throughout to aid your understanding.

After you have worked through the examples and translations you should be ready to move on to the Grammar Summary. Read through this section carefully, checking that you understand all the explanations and examples. See if you can work out further examples of your own, if necessary referring back to the Preliminary Note at the beginning of the unit or to the Reference Grammar, to check that you understand the link between the particular usage of the language and the grammatical construction.

Now you will be in a position to study the passages Im Kontext, which illustrate how examples of such usage and constructions are used in a realistic context. Read through each passage, referring to the Grammar

Summary or the list of vocabulary as necessary. The serious student will want to keep his or her own vocabulary book, noting not only new words and their meanings but also each gender and plural. If possible, try to learn a few of these systematically each day.

When you are confident that you understand the language and can handle the structures covered you can move on to the fourth section, Machen wir weiter! The aim of this section is to expand further on the material covered and deal with allied areas.

Finally, there is the opportunity for you to test yourself by attempting the exercises in the section Jetzt sind Sie dran!

Those students who already have some knowledge of the language may choose to start with the Reference Grammar and, by means of cross-referencing, refer to the relevant examples in the Functional Grammar.

The author has taken the conscious decision to simplify the description of verbs, for simplicity's sake, referring merely to regular and irregular verbs. A comprehensive verb list is to be found in the Reference Grammar 10.7.

Viel Spaß und viel Erfolg! (*Have fun and every success!*)

Acknowledgements

I should like to record my thanks to Ian Small, Headmaster of Bootham School, York, and to the Bootham School Governing Committee for generously granting me a sabbatical term to write this book. I am equally grateful to my colleagues who covered for me during my absence.

Sincere thanks go to Alison Ralph, Ken Wood, Ralf Tobias, Susanne Schepers, and to Birgit Gunsenheimer. Grateful thanks go to Sarah Butler for being such a patient and pleasant editor. I also want to thank my two sons; Jamie and Thomas. I owe the biggest debt to my husband, Charles. He undertook so much of the unglamorous work, putting my text into the new spelling system and tidying up the manuscript – a real labour of love.

Jenny Russ
York

GLOSSARY OF TERMS

(items in bold italics have a separate entry in the glossary)

accusative is one of four **cases** in German. See also *nominative, dative* and *genitive*.

active voice – see *voice*

adjectival noun is a *noun* which changes its form like an *adjective*. See Reference grammar 5.2.

adjective is a word which gives us more information as to what a *noun* or *pronoun* is like. See Functional grammar 15 and Reference grammar 5.1.

adverb is a word or group of words which tells us more about a *verb*, *adjective*, or another *adverb*. It often tells us how something is done and answers the questions how? when? where? why?: langsam (*slowly*), leicht (*easily*), sehr (*very*). In German there is no clear adverbial ending such as -ly in English.

agreement is when adjectives change their ending to reflect the nature of the noun or pronoun they describe.

article – see *gender*

auxiliary verb is a 'helping verb' which is used with another verb to form different *tenses* or the passive *voice*, e.g. haben, sein, werden.

cardinal number is a number used to show quantity, or when counting e.g. fünf Tassen Tee, (*five cups of tea*) eins, zwei, drei, vier (*one, two, three, four*) as opposed to *ordinal numbers*.

case is when the form of the *definite* or *indefinite article* or other *determiner* changes according to context in a *sentence*. These changes are due to the fact that a so-called case system is still in use in German. It comprises four cases: *nominative, accusative, dative* and *genitive*. See Reference grammar 6.

clause is a group of words which contains a *subject* and a *verb*. A major or main clause can also form a sentence in its own right: Ich lachte laut (*I laughed loudly*). A minor or subordinate clause normally starts with a *subordinating conjunction*, e.g. weil (*because*), als (*when*), and cannot stand complete in its own right: als ich ihn sah (*when I saw him*). These two clauses can be combined to form a complex sentence: Ich lachte laut, als ich ihn sah (*I laughed loudly when I saw him*). A *co-ordinating conjunction*, und (*and*), aber (*but*), can join two equal clauses: Ich sah ihn, und ich lachte laut (*I saw him and I laughed loudly*), Ich sah ihn, aber ich sprach nicht mit ihm (*I saw him, but I didn't speak to him*).

colloquial is a style of language suitable for familiar speech, but not for formal writing

comparative is the form of the *adjective* or *adverb* which compares one thing or person with another, e.g. Er ist größer als ich (*he is taller than I am*). See Reference grammar 5.3. See also *superlative*.

compound noun is a word which is made up of two or more words, each of which could stand on its own. See Reference grammar 2.2.

compound tense is a *tense* which is formed using two verbal forms, e.g. ich habe geschlafen (*I have slept*) – see *perfect*, *pluperfect*, *future* and *future perfect*.

conditional is a *clause* normally starting with wenn (*if*). See Functional grammar, unit 21.

conjugation is the word used to describe the changes in a *verb* to denote a different *person*, *number* or *tense*.

conjunction is a word or group of words (apart from *relative pronouns*) used to join together two words, *phrases* or *clauses*, e.g. und (*and*) aber (*but*). If the conjunction joins two clauses which are of equal importance it is called a *coordinating* conjunction: und (*and*), aber (*but*), denn (*for*), oder (*or*), sondern (*but*, after a negative). These do not alter the word order in any way.

If a conjunction joins a major or main clause (which can stand alone and make sense) to a minor or subordinate clause, it is called a subordinating conjunction. In German the *subordinating* conjunction is preceded by a comma if it appears mid-sentence, and it sends the verb to the end of the clause: weil (*because*) so dass (*so that*), während (*whilst*), wenn (*if*, *whenever*), e.g. Ich komme heute nicht, weil es so stark regnet (*I'll not come today because it is raining so heavily*).

declension describes the way the *determiner* changes to show case: der Vater, den Vater, dem Vater, des Vaters.

definite article is the *determiner* der, die, das (*the*) which stands before the noun in the noun phrase, e.g. der Ingenieur (*the engineer*), die Kirche (*the church*), das Dorf (*village*).

demonstratives are *adjectives* or *pronouns* which point something out: dieser (*this*), jener (*that*), diese (*these*), jene (*those*).

determiner is the name given to the word which precedes the *noun*, for example the *definite article* (der, etc.), the *indefinite article* (ein, etc.), the negative *indefinite article* (kein etc.), *possessive adjectives* (mein, etc.), *demonstratives* (dieser, jener, etc.), and some numbers (zwei, etc.).

direct object refers to the person or thing which is directly affected by the action of the *verb*: der Mann erkennt *den* Dieb (*the man recognises the thief*). See Functional grammar 3.2.3. (Be careful! The direct object normally appears after the verb in English, but this is not always true in German.) See also *accusative case* and *indirect object*.

direct speech is the exact recording of words which someone has said or written. This is either preceded or followed by a reporting formula such as 'she said', 'he asked' and is enclosed in speech marks. In German the speech marks at the beginning of the quotation are often on the base writing line: „Hast du meine Uhr gesehen?" fragte er.

feminine -see *gender*

finite verb is any part of the verb apart from the *infinitive* and *present* and *past participles*, i.e. it is the parts of the verb which change according to *person*, *number* and *tense*. The finite verb is usually preceded by a *subject noun* or *pronoun*: der Mann liest (*the man is reading*), wir kaufen (*we are buying*).

future perfect is a compound tense made up of the appropriate part of the present tense of the auxiliary verb werden plus a past participle plus the *infinitive* of either haben (*to have*) or sein (*to be*): Sie werden es schon gekauft haben (they will already have bought it).

future tense is the way of expressing something that is yet to happen e.g. Die Hochzeit wird nächsten Juni stattfinden (*the wedding will take place next June*).

gender: All German nouns are grouped according to whether they are *masculine* (der), *feminine* (die) or *neuter* (das). See Functional grammar 1.2.4.

idiomatic is a particular usage of language which cannot necessarily be explained by grammar rules or translated directly into a foreign language, e.g. jemand auf den Arm nehmen (*to pull someone's leg*).

imperative is the *mood* of the *verb* used to give an order or command. See Functional grammar 13.2.2. See also *indicative mood* and *subjunctive mood*.

imperfect tense – see *preterite*

impersonal verb is a *verb* which is normally used only in the es form: Wie geht es dir? (*how are you?*) Es regnet (*it's raining*), Es gefällt mir hier (*I like it here*)

indefinite article is the *determiner* ein (masculine), eine (feminine), ein (neuter) (*a, an*) which precedes a *noun*, e.g. ein Berg (*a mountain*), eine Stadt (*a town*), and ein Haus (*a house*).

indefinite pronoun 'man' is used irrespective of gender. It is translated into English as '*one*', '*you*', '*they*' or '*people*'. See Functional grammar 8.4 and 19.4.

indicative mood is the normal form of the *verb* used to make statements or ask questions. See also *subjunctive* and *imperative* moods.

indirect object is the recipient or beneficiary of the activity of the *verb* and the *direct object*: See Functional grammar 14.2.

indirect speech (also known as reported speech) is the reported account by a third party of what has been said or asked, recording the gist of what was meant rather than the exact words. Because there is some uncertainty as to the accuracy of indirect speech, the *subjunctive mood* is used to record it. Speech marks are obviously not needed for indirect speech. Er sagte, er sei krank (*he said he was ill*).

infinitive is the form of the *verb* you always find in the dictionary: schlafen (*to sleep*), sparen (*to save*). In German this form usually ends in -en, (schlafen, sparen), sometimes in -n (wandern (*to hike*), wechseln (*to change*).

inflection describes the changes of form which take place in *nouns*, *adjectives*, *determiners* and *verbs* to show *number*, *person*, *case*, *tense*, *mood* or *voice*.

inseparable verb is a *verb* preceded by a *prefix* which always remains in front of the verb: der Arzt verschrieb mir Schlaftabletten (*the doctor prescribed me sleeping pills*). See also *separable verbs*.

interrogative forms are used to ask a question or to seek information. Wer? (*who?*), wen? (*who(m)?*), wessen? (*whose?*), welcher? (*which?*) was? (*what?*). Welcher? can also be an interrogative *adjective*. Wo? (*where?*) wohin? (*where to?*), woher? (*where from?*) are interrogative *adverbs*.

intransitive verb – see *transitive verb*

irregular verb is a *verb* whose forms cannot be predicted, and must therefore be checked in the verb lists and then learnt. These verbs usually undergo vowel change. See Reference grammar 10.7.

masculine noun – see *gender*

modal verb is a *verb* which can be used in conjunction with another verb to reflect the mood of the speaker, i.e. to express a wish, sense of obligation, volition, liking, ability or possibility, etc. See Functional grammar 7.2, 8.2 and 9.2.

mood is used to express a factual meaning see (*indicative* mood), a non-factual meaning (see *subjunctive* mood) or a command (see *imperative* mood).

negative is the means of expressing the idea of 'not a' or 'no' or 'nothing' (kein or nicht or nichts), e.g. Das ist keine Ausrede (*that's no excuse*), Das ist nicht richtig (*that's not right*).

neuter noun -see *gender*

noun is a word used for naming a person, der Mensch (*person*), place, die Stadt (*the town*), thing, der Tisch (*table*) or abstract idea, die Freiheit (*freedom*). See Functional grammar 1.2.4.

noun phrase is a group of words which is equivalent to a noun, e.g. der junge Arzt (*the young doctor*), ein regnerischer Tag (*a rainy day*).

number shows whether a *noun*, *pronoun* or *verb* is singular (referring to only one) or plural (more than one). Some nouns which are *plural* in English are *singular* in German: die Schere (*scissors*), die Brille (*glasses*), die Hose (*trousers*).

object – see either *direct object* or *indirect object*.

ordinal number is a number which shows a certain position within a sequence of numbers: *first*, *second*, *third*, etc. In German these inflect like ordinary adjectives e.g. der dritte Versuch (*the third attempt*), am ersten Januar (*on the first of January*).

passive – see *voice*

past participle is the form of the verb which, together with an *auxiliary verb*, haben or sein, forms the *compound tenses* of the *perfect* and *pluperfect* or the *passive voice*. See Functional grammar 18.2.1. It can also be used as an *adjective* with the appropriate adjectival ending: der gemähte Rasen (*the mown lawn*).

perfect tense is a *compound tense* made up of the *present tense* of either the *verb* haben (*to have*) or sein (*to be*) plus a *past participle* at the end of the *clause* or *sentence*. See Functional grammar 18.

person enables us to distinguish between the speaker, (the first person) the person(s) being addressed (the second person) and someone or something else (the third person).

Singular		*Plural*
1st person:	**ich** (*I*)	**wir** (*we*)
2nd person:	**du** (*you*, familiar)	**ihr** (*you*, familiar),
	Sie (*you*, polite)	**Sie** (*you*, polite)
3rd person:	**er**, **sie**, **es** (*he, she, it*)	**sie** (*they*)

personal pronouns – see *pronouns*

phrase is a group of words which does not contain a *finite verb* and is therefore not complete on its own, e.g. Mein neuer Chef (*my new boss*).

pluperfect tense is a *compound tense* made of the simple past tense of either haben (*to have*) or sein (*to be*), plus a *past participle* at the end of the **sentence** or **clause**: See Functional grammar 17.4.2.

plural – see *number*

possessive forms show ownership or possession. See Functional grammar 12.2.

prefix – see *verbal prefix*

preposition is a word (or words) showing the relationship in time or space between one thing or person and another. It often shows the position that a *noun* or *pronoun* is in. See Reference grammar 6.

present participle is the present form of the verb which in English ends in *-ing*, weinend (*crying*), schlafend (*sleeping*), sprechend (*talking*).
It is used less frequently in German than in English, but can be used as a adjective with the appropriate adjectival ending e.g. das schlafende Kind (*the sleeping child*).

present tense – see *tenses*

preterite, also known as the *imperfect* or *simple past tense*. See Functional grammar 17.2.

pronoun is a short word which stands instead of a *noun* or *noun phrase*. It is used to avoid repeating the noun, for example er replacing der Mann in Er kaufte ein Buch (*he bought a book*), sie instead of die Kinder in Sie spielten im Garten (*they played in the garden*). There are five main groups of pronoun:

1. *Personal pronouns*: ich (*I*), mich or mir (*me*), du, dich or dir (*you*), er (*he*), ihn, ihm (*him*), etc.
2. *Reflexive pronouns*: mich or mir (*myself*), dich or dir *yourself*, sich *himself, herself*, etc.
3. *Possessive pronouns*: meiner, meine, meins *mine* etc.
4. *Relative pronouns*: der, die, das *which, who, that*
5. *Demonstrative pronouns*: dieser, jener *this, that*

pronoun of address is a *personal pronoun* used to address someone. Du (*you*) is used to address a person with whom one is on familiar terms, ihr for more than one. Sie is a polite form used to address one or more persons known less well.

question – see *interrogative*

reflexive verbs express an action which is both carried out and received by the subject, e.g. Ich wasche mich (*I wash myself*). See Functional grammar 11.2.

relative clause normally starts with a *relative pronoun* der, die, das (*who, which, that*), e.g. Der Mann, der dieses Buch schrieb, ist Anthropologe (*the man who wrote this book is an anthropologist*). See Functional grammar 5.4.3.

reported speech see *indirect speech*

regular verbs have forms which follow a pattern and can be predicted by rules.

sentence is a group of words which makes full grammatical sense and contains at least a *subject* and a *finite verb*. In the written language it ends with either a full stop, exclamation mark or question mark.

separable verbs have an *infinitive* which begins with a *prefix*. This prefix moves to the end of the clause when the *verb* is used as a *finite verb* e.g. an/kommen (*to arrive*): Der Zug kommt pünktlich an (*the train is arriving on time*). See Reference grammar 9.3.

simple past – see *preterite*

singular – see *number*

stem is the part of the *regular verb* to which endings are added to indicate change of person or tense. See Functional grammar 5.2.1.

subject is the *noun* or *pronoun* which carries out or initiates the action of the *verb*, e.g. Der Arzt untersuchte meinen Onkel gestern (*the doctor examined my uncle yesterday*). To check whether someone or something is the *subject* of a *clause* or *sentence*, ask the question 'Who or what is doing the verb?' The answer (here: the doctor) is the subject and requires the *nominative* case. (Be careful! In English the subject normally appears immediately before the noun, but this does not always happen in German.)

subjunctive is the *mood* of the *verb* used when the content of the sentence is doubted or unlikely, as in indirect speech or when expressing unreal or hypothetical conditions, and often after the word wenn (*if*) in *conditional clauses*. See Reference grammar 11. See also *indicative* and *imperative moods*.

subordinating conjunction – see *conjunctions*

suffix is a part of a word which nevers occurs on its own, and is used to form new words. It is found at the end of the word, e.g. schön + heit → Schönheit (*beautiful* → *beauty*), -Milch + ig → milchig (*milk* → *milky*).

superlative is the form of an *adjective* or *adverb* which denotes the very highest or lowest level of quality, for example 'the biggest and best'. See Reference grammar 5.3.1. See also *comparative*.

tag question is a short phrase such as nicht wahr? gell? nicht? or oder? (*isn't it? aren't you? don't we?* etc.) which, added to a statement, changes it into a question.

tenses of the *finite verb* show you the time at which the action of the *verb* takes place. See Reference grammar 10.

transitive verb is a *verb* which needs a *direct object* to complete its meaning, e.g. Er kauft einen Hund (*he is buying a dog*). An *intransitive verb* needs only a subject to make sense, e.g. Der Lehrer kommt (*the teacher is coming*). (Be careful! Some verbs can be either *intransitive* or *transitive*, e.g. Ich fahre lieber (*I would prefer to drive*) and Ich fahre jetzt einen Mercedes (*I drive a Mercedes now*).

umlaut is the name for the symbol ¨ which can be placed above the vowels a, o or u. The addition of the umlaut alters the pronunciation of the vowel, e.g. Vater → pl. Väter (*father(s)*), Bruder → Brüder (*brother(s)*).

verbal prefix is a short element which can be attached to the **infinitive**, e.g. besuchen (*to visit*). See Reference grammar 9.3.

verb is a word or group of words which tells you what a person or thing (i.e. the subject of the *sentence*) is doing or being. Without a verb a sentence is incomplete. A verb can be used in various *tenses* e.g. I read, I was reading, I have read, I had read, I shall read, I shall have read.

voice is a way of using a verb actively or passively. Both forms have the same meaning but a different emphasis. See Reference grammar 13. The passive voice is used much less frequently than the active voice.

vowels In addition to the five vowel signs a, e, i, o, u, German also has ä, ö, and ü. Occasionally y is used as a vowel, as in der Zylinder (*top hat*), das Asyl (*asylum*).

weak nouns a group of unusual **masculine nouns** to which an -n or -en is added in every case apart from the **nominative singular**. See Reference grammar 2.4.

1 | ASKING FOR AND GIVING PERSONAL INFORMATION

Aims

In this unit you will learn how to:

■ Say who you are; ■ State your nationality; ■ Say where you are from; ■ Say what your occupation is; ■ Give similar information about other people; ■ Ask personal information about other people

Grammar content

■ Subject pronouns; ■ sein in the present tense; ■ Gender of nouns (nominative case); ■ Plural of nouns; ■ Nouns and adjectives indicating nationality; ■ Ask questions (interrogative sentences); ■ Negative sentences

1.1 Preliminary note

To ask and give personal information you will need the German equivalent of words like *I, you, he, she*, etc. These are known as pronouns. You will also need a verb. This shows an action or state, for example, *I cook, you buy, he is*, etc. In this unit we will learn the verb sein, which means 'to be'.

Saying who you are

Ich bin Hans Schmidt.	*I'm Hans Schmidt* (male).
Ich bin Inge Schneider.	*I'm Inge Schneider* (female).

Stating your nationality

Ich bin Deutscher.	*I'm German* (male).
Ich bin Deutsche.	*I'm German* (female).

Saying what your occupation is

Ich bin Arzt.	*I'm a doctor* (male).
Ich bin Ärztin.	*I'm a doctor* (female).

Saying where you come from

Ich bin aus Berlin.	*I'm from Berlin.*
Ich bin aus Deutschland.	*I'm from Germany.*

Giving information about other people

Er ist Lehrer.	*He's a teacher.*
Sie ist Lehrerin.	*She's a teacher.*
Er ist Schweizer.	*He is Swiss.*
Sie ist aus Zürich.	*She's from Zurich.*

Asking for personal information about other people

a) in a formal or polite way, using the polite pronoun Sie:

Sind Sie Deutscher?	*Are you German?* (male)
Sind Sie Architekt?	*Are you an architect?* (male)

b) familiarly, using the pronoun du:

Bist du Österreicherin?	*Are you Austrian?* (female)
Bist du aus Wien?	*Are you from Vienna?*

1.2 Grammar summary

1.2.1 Subject pronouns

To say *I, you, he, she*, etc. in German (as you would for the subject of the verb, i.e. the person or thing performing the action of the verb: *I* speak, *you* learn, *she* likes), we use the following set of words

Singular:		Plural:	
ich	*I*	wir	*we*
du	*you* (familiar)	ihr	*you* (familiar)
Sie	*you* (polite)	Sie	*you* (polite)
▪ er	*he*	sie	*they*
▪ sie	*she*		
es	*it*		

▪ these forms can also mean 'it' if replacing a der or die: der Tisch ist zu hoch (*the table is too high*) > er ist zu hoch (*it is too high*).

1.2.2 Familiar and polite forms of address

▪ You will notice that German uses familiar and polite forms of address. In general, the familiar forms (**du** and **ihr**) are used when addressing a child or children, members of one's family, a close friend (or friends), an animal (or animals) or God (in prayer and worship).

▪ The polite form **Sie** is used when addressing one or more person(s) whom you do not know or do not know well. In other words, the same form is used for both the singular and the plural polite form. The polite **Sie** is the only subject pronoun which is always written with a capital letter.

1.2.3 sein (to be) in the present tense

The verb **sein** is frequently used in German when giving personal information such as nationality or your occupation, and often for your place of origin and name. Here is the full form of sein in the present tense together with the appropriate subject pronouns:

Singular:		Plural:	
ich bin	*I am*	wir sind	*we are*
du bist	*you are* (familiar)	ihr seid	*you are* (familiar)
Sie sind	*you are* (polite)	Sie sind	*you are* (polite sing. or plural)
er ist	*he is*	sie sind	*they are*
sie ist	*she is*		
es ist	*it is*		

1.2.4 Gender of nouns (Reference Grammar 2.1)

A noun is a word for a person, a thing, a place, or even an idea. Apart from personal names, such as *Wilhelm, Berlin*, it can be preceded by either *the* or *a/an*, for example, *the* dog, *the* post office, *a* carrot, *an* egg.

All nouns in German begin with a capital letter and are *masculine, feminine* or *neuter*. Their gender is shown by the use of the definite article: **der** for masculine, **die** for feminine, or **das** for neuter, preceding the noun, but in dictionaries or course books it is sometimes shown by *m., f.* or *nt.* This form is known as the *nominative case* and is used after the verb **sein** and for the subject of the sentence.

Der, die or **das** are translated as 'the' in English. For full details of nouns see Reference Grammar 2. If you wish to say '*a/an*' instead of '*the*', then the indefinite article **ein** (for both masculine and neuter) and **eine** (for feminine) is used. As in English, the indefinite article is not needed when stating one's nationality, but unlike English, it is also not required when stating one's profession.

Gender of nouns indicating nationality and profession

Nouns which refer to people, such as those indicating nationality, profession or occupation, often show the masculine or feminine form in the noun itself, for example by adding a feminine ending such as -in:

Er ist Engländer.	*He is English.*
Sie ist Engländer**in**.	*She is English.*
Er ist Kellner.	*He is a waiter.*
Sie ist Kellner**in**.	*She is a waitress.*

NB For the sake of political correctness and brevity the following form with an internal capital letter I is sometimes found in some areas of journalism: **LehrerIn, SchülerIn**. This form stands for **der Lehrer** *and* **die Lehrerin, der Schüler** *and* **die Schülerin**. This usage is unofficial and is not recognised by the new spelling reform.

In nouns of nationality where the masculine form ends in -e, the final -e is replaced by -in in the feminine form:

Jens ist Däne.	*Jens ist Danish.* (male)
Jytte ist Dän**in**.	*Jytte is Danish.* (female)
Jozef ist Pole.	*Jozef is Polish.* (male)
Franya ist Pol**in**.	*Franya is Polish.* (female)

NB There are a few exceptions to the above, for example the German words **Arzt** (*doctor*), **Franzose**, (*Frenchman*) and **Koch** (*cook*). In these cases not only is -in added, but the vowel preceding the ending is changed by adding the umlaut sign (¨), for example: a → ä, o → ö, u → ü, i.e. **Ärztin, Französin, Köchin**. An umlaut can be put on the letters a, o or u (ä, ö, ü), and this alters the pronunciation. (Reference Grammar 1.2.2).

Er ist Koch.	*He is a cook.*
Sie ist Köch**in**.	*She is a cook.*

1.2.5 Plural of nouns (Reference Grammar 2.3)

As in English, most nouns in German can have singular and plural forms. In English most nouns form their plural by adding -s or -es, but there are a few exceptions such as *ox* → *oxen*, *mouse* → *mice* etc.

Unfortunately the formation of the plural in German is not so simple as in English, and it is always worth checking in a dictionary, where the plural is given in brackets after the noun, e.g. (-e), (-), (-n, or -nen), (¨), (¨-er), or (¨-e). The dash in these brackets represents the singular stem of the noun and the additional information is the plural ending, ¨ indicates an added umlaut. The plural ¨-er is chiefly used with neuter nouns, but **der Mann** (*man*) has the plural **Männer**.

der Ingenieur (-e)

Hans ist Ingenieur.	*Hans is an engineer.*
Hans und Otto sind Ingenieur**e**.	*Hans and Otto are engineers.*

NB In a mixed group of people the masculine form is used.

der Mechaniker (-)

Klaus ist Mechaniker.	*Klaus is a mechanic.*
Klaus und Ilse sind Mechaniker.	*Klaus and Ilse are mechanics.*

die Krankenschwester (-n)

Inge ist Krankenschwester.	*Inge is a nurse.*
Inge und Beate sind Krankenschwester**n**.	*Inge and Beate are nurses.*

die Studentin (-nen)

Karin ist Studentin in München.	*Karin is a student in Munich.*
Karin und Dagmar sind Studentin**nen** in München	*Karin and Dagmar are students in Munich.*

der Vater (⸚)

Johann ist Vater.	*Johann is a father.*
Johann und Reinhard sind Väter.	*Johann and Reinhard are fathers.*

der Arzt (-ᷓe)

Helmut ist Arzt.	*Helmut is a doctor.*
Helmut und Norbert sind Ärzte.	*Helmut and Norbert are doctors.*

A few words denoting nationality or a profession form their plurals in German by adding **-s**, e.g. **der Israeli(s)**, **der Pakistani(s)**:

David ist Israeli.	*David is an Israeli.*
David und Menachem sind Israelis.	*David and Menachem are Israelis.*

(The -er is pronounced almost like ay in English 'say'.)

1.2.6 Asking questions (interrogative sentences)

It is possible to form questions in German in several ways:

■ Reversing the order subject-verb (i.e. by starting the sentence with the verb):

Sind Sie Amerikaner?	*Are you American?*
Bist du Schotte?	*Are you Scottish?*

This form is normally answered with a **ja** (*yes*) or **nein** (*no*).

■ Using a special question word, known as an interrogative. Most of the German question words (interrogatives) begin with w, the most common being:

wie?	*how?*
Wie ist das Klima in Ägypten?	*What is the climate like in Egypt?*
wo?	*where?*
Wo ist Namibia, bitte?	*Where is Namibia, please?*
was?	*what?*
Was ist die Hauptstadt von Bulgarien?	*What is the capital of Bulgaria?*
wann?	*when?*
Wann ist der Nationaltag in der Schweiz?	*When is Switzerland's National Day* (literally, 'When is the National Day in Switzerland?')
warum?	*why?*
Warum sind Sie in Ulm?	*Why are you in Ulm?*

■ In informal speech one can form a question simply by making a statement followed by a phrase or word such as nicht wahr? (literally, *not true?*), or oder? (literally, *or?*), or, in Southern Germany and Switzerland, gell or gelt? (*right?*) and making one's voice rise at the end of the sentence. The words oder? and gelt? are colloquial, and gell/gelt is not usually written. In English these are rendered by the so-called tag questions where the pronoun of the sentence is repeated in a question.

Sie sind Schwede, **nicht wahr**?	*You're Swedish, aren't you?*
Sie ist katholisch, **oder**?	*She's Catholic, isn't she?*
Ihr seid evangelisch, **gell**?	*You're Protestant, aren't you?*

1.2.7 Negative sentences

If you want to negate the verb in a sentence you use the word nicht (*not*):

Ich bin nicht aus Russland.	*I am not from Russia.*
Er ist nicht Amerikaner.	*He is not American.*

If you want to negate the noun, i.e. say 'not a, no' in a sentence, you use kein or one of its forms:

Er ist kein Deutscher.	*He is not a German.*
Sie ist keine Mutter.	*She is not a mother.*
Es ist kein Geschenk.	*It's not a present.*

1.3 Im Kontext

Study these conversations between people who have just met and are getting to know each other. The first exchange is formal, using the polite pronoun Sie, and the second is informal, using du.

A)	**Professor**	Sind Sie Spanierin?
	Professorin	Ja, ich bin Spanierin, und Sie?
	Professor	Ich bin Türke. Ich bin aus Ankara.
	Professorin	Ich bin aus Madrid.

Spanierin *Spaniard (female)*		**Türke** *Turk (male)*

B)	**Schüler**	Grüß dich! Wie heißt du? (NB ß is pronounced as **ss**)
	Schülerin	Ich heiße Heidi, und du?
	Schüler	Ich heiße Karl Schmidt. Kommst du aus Köln?
	Schülerin	Nein, ich komme nicht aus Köln. Ich komme aus Bonn.

der Schüler	school boy
Grüß dich!	(chiefly South German) *Hello!*
die Schülerin	school girl
ich heiße	I am called
Kommst du?	Are you coming?
aus Köln	from Cologne

Look at this piece of writing which gives personal information:

Ich heiße Andreas Bauer. Ich bin Deutscher. Ich komme aus Kiel und ich bin Medizinstudent.

1.4 Machen wir weiter! *Let's continue!*

Asking someone's name in a formal way

Wie heißen Sie? *What is your name?* (literally, 'How are you called?')

Ich heiße Inge.   *I am (called) Inge.*

Saying what your occupation is

When giving your occupation or profession, German does not use the equivalent of the English word a, as in 'I'm a student':

Ich bin Student.   *I am a student.*
Er ist Dirigent.   *He is a conductor.* (of an orchestra)

The exception to this is when you want to use an adjective before the noun:

Ich bin **ein armer** Student.   *I am a poor student.*
Er ist **ein berühmter** Dirigent.   *He is a famous conductor.*

Saying where you come from

You can use either the appropriate form of the verb **sein** (*to be*) or kommen (*to come*):

Ich **bin** aus Indien.   *I come from India.*
Woher **kommst** du?   *Where do you come from?*

Er **ist** aus Japan.
Woher **kommen** Sie?

He comes from Japan
Where do you come from?

Translating 'where' into German

In the old days the words 'whither' and 'whence' were common in English to express the idea of Where are you going to? and Where have you come from? Nowadays they are usually considered old-fashioned and we tend to use the word where (sometimes with a preposition) to convey both of these ideas, as well as the static idea of where something is to be found.

In German the following distinctions are made:

wo? (*where?*) is used to express the static idea as in:

Wo wohnen Sie?
Wo ist Ihr Auto?

Where do you live?
Where is your car?

woher? (*where .... from? whence?*)

Woher kommst du?

Where do you come from?

wohin? (*where ... to? whither?*)

Wohin fahren sie?

Where are they going to?

Asking for and giving information about status or rank, religion or political affiliation.

Ich bin der Chef hier!
Er ist Oberleutnant.
Sind Sie evangelisch?
Ist sie Feministin?

I'm the boss here!
He is a first lieutenant.
Are you Protestant?
Is she a feminist?

Asking for and giving information about marital status

Sind Sie verheiratet oder ledig?
Ich bin geschieden.

Are you married or single?
I am divorced.

1.5 Jetzt sind Sie dran! *Now it's your turn!*

Aufgabe A

Read through the questions and answers below and link the most appropriate answer to each question:

Fragen (*questions*)

1 Ist er aus Zürich?
2 Bist du Studentin?
3 Ist Marie Polin?
4 Sind Sie katholisch?
5 Wie heißen Sie?
6 Woher kommen Sie?
7 Bist du verheiratet?
8 Seid ihr aus Dänemark?
9 Ist Fritz Student in Halle?
10 Sie sind kein Deutscher, oder?

Antworten(*answers*)

A Ich komme aus Indien.
B Nein, ich bin evangelisch.
C Nein, ich bin Österreicher.
D Nein, er ist aus Basel.
E Ja, wir sind Dänen.
F Ich heiße Otto Braun.
G Nein, ich bin Lehrerin.
H Nein, er ist Student in Erfurt.
I Nein, ich bin geschieden.
J Nein, sie ist Französin.

Antworten *(answers):*

1 D; 2 G; 3 J; 4 B; 5 F; 6 A; 7 I; 8 E; 9 H; 10 C

Aufgabe B

Fill in the following gaps using one each of the following words:

> ■ wohin? *where (to)?* ■ wo? *where?* ■ woher? *where from?*
> ■ wie? *how?* ■ warum? *why?*

1 _____ wohnen Sie?
2 _____ ist das Klima in Südafrika?
3 _____ kommst du?
4 _____ fahren Sie?
5 _____ sind Sie in Ulm?

Antworten *(answers):*

1 Wo? 2 Wie? 3 Woher? 4 Wohin? 5 Warum?

2 | INTRODUCING AND IDENTIFYING PEOPLE, PLACES AND THINGS

Aims

In this unit you will learn how to:

■ Introduce yourself and other people; ■ Greet people when being introduced; ■ Say goodbye; ■ Identify people, places and things; ■ Ask questions in order to identify people, places and things; ■ Write letters; ■ Pass on greetings

Grammar content

■ The verb **wissen**; ■ The verb **kennen**; ■ The demonstratives **dieser** and **jener**; ■ The interrogative **welcher**?

2.1 Preliminary note

Introducing yourself

In Unit 1 we learned that one can introduce oneself simply by saying:

Ich heiße Eva Rohweder.	*I am called Eva Rohweder.*

There are many other ways of introducing yourself, for example:

Darf ich mich vorstellen? Mein Name ist Eva Rohweder.	*May I introduce myself? My name is Eva Rohweder.*
Mein Vorname ist Eva.	*My first name is Eva.*
Mein Nachname ist Rohweder.	*My family name is Rohweder.*
Ich bin die Sekretärin von Dr. Müller.	*I am Dr. Müller's secretary.*

Ich bin Christiane Frenz, geb. (geborene) Pflegge.	*I am Christiane Frenz, née Pflegge.*

Less formal ways of introducing yourself

Ich bin (der) Henning	*I'm Henning.*
Ich bin (die) Beate.	*I'm Beate.*

Note: In colloquial speech the definite article can be used with names, but it should never be written.

Ich bin die Freundin von Arno.	*I'm Arno's girlfriend* (literally, 'I'm the girlfriend of Arno').

Introducing other people

Das (hier) ist mein Mann.	*This is my husband.*
Das ist meine Frau.	*This is my wife.*
Das sind meine Kinder.	*These are my children.*
Kennen Sie schon Frau Lieske?	*Do you already know Mrs. Lieske?*
Kennen Sie sich schon?	*Do you already know each other?*
Ich möchte Ihnen Fräulein König vorstellen.	*I should like to introduce Fräulein König (to you).*
Darf ich (Ihnen) meinen Mann vorstellen?	*May I introduce my husband (to you)?*

Greeting people when being introduced

Guten Morgen, Herr Tobias!	*Good morning, Mr. Tobias!*
Guten Tag, Frau Honig!	*Hello, Mrs. Honig!*
Grüß dich, Klaus! Hi, Klaus!	*Hello there, Klaus!*
Guten Abend!	*Good evening!*

Regional variations

Grüß Gott! is used widely in Southern Germany and Austria as a greeting at any time of the day, or simply as *hello!*

Grüezi! (singular) or **Grüezi mitenand!** (plural) is used in Switzerland as a greeting at any time of the day, or as an informal *hello!* or *hi!* This is not found in writing.

Servus! is used in Austria and Southern Germany for both *hello* and *goodbye*.

Moin! Moin! is the North German equivalent of **Morgen!** but it is heard throughout the day in parts of North Germany.

Guten Appetit! *Bon appetit!* Said at the beginning of a meal.

Mahlzeit! (*meal*) is an informal greeting used around mealtimes, meaning *Enjoy your meal!*

Formal farewells

Auf Wiedersehen!	*Goodbye! (Looking forward to seeing you again.)*
Auf Wiederschauen!	*Goodbye!* (used in Southern Germany and Austria)
Gute Nacht!	*Good night!* (used only late at night)

Saying goodbye

There are many ways of saying goodbye to friends:

Tschüs(s)!	*Bye, cheerio!* (colloquial)
Tschau! Ciao!	*Bye, cheerio!*
Ade! (Stressed on the e)	*Farewell!* (In the south-west of Germany)
Servus!	*Hello! or Goodbye!* (Particularly in southern Germany and Austria)

The following phrases use the preposition bis (*until*)

Bis bald!	*See you soon!*
Bis morgen!	*See you tomorrow!*
Bis Donnerstag!	*See you on Thursday!*

Asking questions leading to the identification of people, places and things

(Wie ist Ihr) Vorname?	*What is your first name?*
Wie ist Ihr Nachname?	*What is your surname?*
Wie ist Ihr Mädchenname?	*What is your maiden name?*
Wie heißen Sie mit Vornamen und Familiennamen?	*What is your first name and surname?*
Sind Sie Frau Müller? Ja, das bin ich.	*Are you Frau Müller? Yes, I am.*

Wer ist der Herr da?	*Who is the gentleman there?*
Wie heißt er? Ich weiß nicht.	*What's he called? I don't know.*
Welcher Herr ist der Chirurg?	*Which gentleman is the surgeon?*
Der Herr da.	*The gentleman there.*
Welche Dame kommt aus Finnland?	*Which lady comes from Finland?*
Die Dame dort drüben.	*The lady over there.*

Questions and answers to identify places

Was ist der nächste Halt, bitte?	*What is the next stop, please?*
Odeonsplatz.	*Odeon Square.*
Was ist die Hauptstadt von	*What is the capital of Egypt?*
Ägypten? Kairo.	*Cairo.*
Was ist unser Ziel heute?	*What is our destination today?*
Königswinter am Rhein.	*Königswinter on the Rhine.*

Questions and answers to identify things, using welcher? 'which?'

Welches Buch ist sein neuestes?	*Which book is his latest. That one*
Das da.	*there.*
Welche Gruppen spielen heute	*Which (music) groups are playing*
Abend? Die eine aus Berlin und	*this evening? (The) one from*
die andere aus Cottbus.	*Berlin and (the) one from Cottbus.*
Welches Hemd ist reduziert?	*Which shirt is reduced? The red*
Das rote.	*one.*

Questions and answers to identify things using was?

Was ist der Grund für diesen	*What is the reason for this strike?*
Streik? Zu wenig Lohn.	*Too little pay.*
Was ist das? Das ist eine Art	*What is that? That's a (sort of)*
Obst aus Südafrika.	*fruit from South Africa.*
Was ist das Problem? Der	*What is the problem? The engine*
Motor ist defekt.	*is broken.*

The use of dieser (this) to identify things

Dieser Kaffee aus Kenia ist	*This coffee from Kenya is very*
sehr stark.	*strong.*
Diese Farbe ist viel zu grell.	*This colour is much too garish.*

| Dieses Buch ist wirklich spannend. | *This book is really exciting.* |
| Diese Filme sind nicht für Kinder. | *These films are not for children.* |

2.2 Grammar Summary

2.2.1 The verbs wissen and kennen (to know)

There are two German verbs which can be translated as *to know*. **Wissen** means *to know intellectually or factually*, possibly denoting knowledge gained by study or learning.

| Wissen Sie, wie er heißt? | *Do you know what he is called?* |
| Ich weiß nicht. | *I don't know* |

The noun from this verb is **die Wissenschaft**, *science*.

Wissen has the following forms in the present tense :

Singular	Plural
ich weiß *I know, I do know*	**wir wissen** *we know*
du weißt *you know*	**ihr wisst** *you know*
Sie wissen *you know* (polite)	**Sie wissen** *you know* (polite)
er weiß *he knows*	**sie wissen** *they know*
sie weiß *she knows*	
es weiß *it knows*	

Kennen means *to be acquainted with*.

| Ich kenne deinen Vater. | *I know your father.* |

Kennen is an example of a regular verb, and the full form in the present tense is as follows:

Singular	Plural
ich kenne *I know, I do know, I am acquainted with*	**wir kennen** *we know*
du kennst *you know*	**ihr kennt** *you know*
Sie kennen *you know* (polite)	**Sie kennen** *you know* (polite)
er kennt *he knows*	**sie kennen** *they know*
sie kennt *she knows*	
es kennt *it knows*	

Now look at the the following examples using kennen:

Kennen Sie einander?	*Do you know each other?*
Ja, wir kennen uns gut.	*We know each other well.*

2.2.2 The formation of dieser (this) as a demonstrative and welcher? which? as an interrogative

You will notice that the demonstrative **dieser** and the interrogative **welcher**? end almost in the same way as the definite article **der**. Look at the following chart, which compares the three words in the nominative case:

Masculine	*Femine*	*Neuter*	*Plural*
the:			
de**r**	die	das	die
this/these:			
dies**er**	diese	dies**es**	diese
which?			
welch**er**?	welch**e**?	welch**es**?	welch**e**?

Jener (that) which has the same endings as **dieser**. **Jener** tends to be used in more literary contexts.

2.3 Im Kontext

Study the following brief encounters. The first exchange is formal, the second is familiar.

2.3.1

Herr Fuchs	Guten Tag, Pastor Fischer! Darf ich Ihnen meine Frau vorstellen? Sie ist Sprachtherapeutin.
Pastor Fischer	Guten Tag, Frau Fuchs, Es freut mich, Sie kennen zu lernen. Meine Frau ist auch Sprachtherapeutin!
Frau Fuchs	Guten Tag, Pastor Fischer. Ich freue mich auch. Wie geht es Ihnen?
Pastor Fischer	Sehr gut, danke. Und Ihnen?
Frau Fuchs	Auch gut, danke. Wo ist Ihre Frau?
Pastor Fischer	Das ist die Dame in Schwarz da drüben.

Frau Fuchs   Ach, wie schön! Und wer ist die Dame neben ihr?
Pastor Fischer   Ich weiß nicht. Ich kenne sie nicht.

die Sprachtherapeutin	*speech therapist* (female)
Wie geht es Ihnen?	*How are you?* (polite)
Sehr gut, danke!	*Very well, thanks!*
auch	*also*
Ihre Frau	*your wife*
da drüben	*over there*
neben ihr	*next to her*

2.3.2

Christel   Grüß dich, Willi!
Willi   Grüß dich, Christel! Wie geht's dir?
Christel   Furchtbar. Ich bin müde. Und dir?
Willi   Mir geht's prima, danke! Hier ist meine Freundin, Anita.
Christel   Ach, grüß Gott, Anita. Bis bald!

Wie geht's dir?	*How are you?* (familiar)
furchtbar	*dreadful*
müde	*tired*
mir geht's prima	*I feel fantastic*
meine Freundin	*my girlfriend*

2.4 Machen wir weiter!

Beginning and ending a letter

Look at the following examples of the formulae used to start and finish formal letters:

Sehr geehrte Damen und Herren   *Dear Sir or Madam*

N.B. in German the plural form is used, the equivalent of *Very honoured Ladies and Gentlemen.*

Sehr geehrter Herr Debus   *Dear Mr. Debus*
Sehr geehrte Frau Wagner   *Dear Mrs. or Ms. Wagner*

N.B. **Fräulein** is used only to address the young.

Mit freundlichen Grüßen	*Yours sincerely, yours faithfully*
Mit bestem Gruß	*With best wishes*

N.B. You may find that in more formal situations the form **Hochachtungsvoll** is used for *Yours faithfully* but this tends to be used less frequently nowadays.

Formulae to start informal letters:

Lieber Hanno	*Dear Hanno*
Liebe Karin	*Dear Karin*
Liebe Familie Lange	*Dear Lange family*
Ihr Lieben!	*Dear all* (literally, 'You dears')

Finishing an informal letter

Mit herzlichen Grüßen	*With best wishes*
Viele liebe Grüße	*Many good wishes*
Alles Gute	*All the best*

2.5 Jetzt sind Sie dran!

Aufgabe A

Look at the following snippets and link up one from each column to form a greeting

1	Grüß	A	Wiederhören
2	Guten	B	grüßen
3	Darf ich meine Sekretärin	C	Willkommen
4	Auf	D	mitenand
5	Einen schönen Gruß	E	vorstellen
6	Ich soll von Mutti	F	Tag, Herr Müller
7	Es freut mich,	G	bald
8	Herzlich	H	an Ihre Frau
9	Bis	I	dich, Inge
10	Grüezi	J	Sie kennen zu lernen

Antworten

1I; 2F; 3E; 4A; 5H; 6B; 7J; 8C; 9G; 10D

Aufgabe B

Insert the appropriate verb form from the box below into each of the following gaps:

1 Ich ... die Frau von Karl
2 Mein Vorname ... Hans
3 Ich ... Dr. Schleiffenbaum gut
4 ... du Studentin, Christel?
5 ... Sie, wie er heißt?
6 ... Sie einander?
7 Wir ... aus Wien
8 Wie ... du?
9 Ich ... Max Schulz
10 Dorothea und Waltraud ... Krankenschwestern

> ■ bist ■ kenne ■ sind ■ heißt ■ bin ■ ist ■ heiße
> ■ kommen ■ kennen ■ wissen

Antworten (Answers):

1 Ich bin die Frau von Karl. *I am Karl's wife.*
2 Mein Vorname ist Hans. *My first name is Hans.*
3 Ich kenne Dr. Schleiffenbaum gut. *I know Dr. Schleiffenbaum well.*
4 Bist du Studentin, Christel? *Are you a student, Christel?*
5 Wissen Sie, wie er heißt? *Do you know what he is called?*
6 Kennen Sie einander? *Do you know each other?*
7 Wir kommen aus Wien. *We are from Vienna.*
8 Wie heißt du? *What are you called?*
9 Ich heiße Max Schulz. *I'm called Max Schulz.*
10 Dorothea und Waltraud sind Krankenschwestern. *Dorothea and Waltraud are nurses.*

3 | EXPRESSING EXISTENCE AND AVAILABILIY

Aims

In this unit you will learn how to:

■ Ask if something exists or is available; ■ State that something exists or is available; ■ Ask and answer questions regarding quantity

Grammar content

■ **sein**; ■ **existieren**; ■ **es gibt**; ■ **bestehen**; ■ **haben**; ■ Indefinite articles in the accusative case; ■ More words used to ask a question (interrogatives) **Wer?**; ■ **Wieviel?**; ■ **Wie viele?**; ■ **Was?**; ■ Compound nouns

3.1 Preliminary Note

To ask if something exists you *either* use the appropriate question form of the verb **sein** (see Unit 1)

Ist hier eine Steckdose?	*Is there an electric socket here?*
Ist hier ein Hotel?	*Is there an hotel here?*

or use **gibt es?**, the German equivalent of the English expression *is there?* or *are there?* The latter can be used for both the singular and plural forms.

Gibt es ein Hotel in Ohlsdorf?	*Is there a hotel in Ohlsdorf?*
Gibt es Restaurants in der Nähe?	*Are there (any) restaurants nearby?*
Es gibt einen gotischen Dom in Köln, oder?	*There's a Gothic Cathedral in Cologne, isn't there?*

(Notice the form **einen** in this sentence. This is because **Dom** is a masculine noun. For fuller details see Grammar Summary.

Es gibt keine Hotels in Wellingdorf, nicht wahr?	*There aren't any hotels in Wellingdorf, are there?*
Wie viele Deutsche gibt es?	*How many Germans are there?*

Stating something exists using sein and existieren

To reply to questions about existence you can use the appropriate form of either **sein** or **existieren**:

Ein Arzt ist schon da.	*A doctor is already there.*
Ein Elektriker ist hier.	*An electrician is here.*
Ein Testament existiert wohl.	*A will does presumably exist.*
Kein Frauengesetz existiert dort.	*There's no women's law in existence there.*

Stating that something exists using es gibt

Es gibt einen Fernsehraum.	*There's a T.V. lounge.*
Es gibt eine Garage.	*There's a garage.*
Es gibt ein Tischtenniszimmer.	*There's a table-tennis room.*

Stating existence using the verb bestehen (to exist, to be in existence)

Die Universität zu Kiel besteht schon seit 1665.	*The University in Kiel has been in existence since 1655.*
Es besteht die Hoffnung, dass er noch lebt.	*There is hope that he is still alive.*

Stating lack of availability using es gibt

Es gibt can be used in the same way with the negative form, as follows:

Es gibt keinen Parkplatz.	*There isn't a car park.*
Es gibt keine Sonnenterasse.	*There's not a (no) sun terrace.*
Es gibt kein Restaurant.	*There isn't a restaurant.*
Es gibt keine Doppelzimmer.	*There aren't any double rooms.*

Asking about availability using the verb haben

Haben Sie ein Zimmer frei?	*Have you a room (free)?*
Hast du ein Taschentuch, bitte?	*Have you got a handkerchief, please?*
Hat das Hotel eine Sauna?	*Does the hotel have a sauna?*
Hat das Zimmer einen Balkon?	*Has the room got a balcony?*
Hat er ein Telefon?	*Has he got a telephone?*

Stating availability using the verb haben

Ja, ich habe ein Zimmer frei.	*Yes, I do have a room available (free).*
Er hat den Flugschein.	*He has the air ticket.*
Wir haben einen Tisch frei.	*We have a table available (free).*
Die Schule hat zwei Tennisplätze.	*The school has two tennis courts.*

Stating lack of availability using haben

Similarly, **haben** can be used to show the lack of availability:

Das Gasthaus hat keinen Parkplatz.	*The guesthouse has no car park.*
Die Wohnung hat kein Bad.	*The flat has no bathroom.*
Ich habe heute keine Zeit.	*I've no time today.*
Wir haben keine Tische frei.	*We haven't any tables free.*

Enquiring about availability using gibt es?

Gibt es keinen Parkplatz?	*Isn't there a car park?*
Gibt es eine Apotheke in der Nähe?	*Is there a chemist's round here?*
Gibt es da keine Toiletten?	*Aren't there any toilets there?*
Gibt es noch Fisch?	*Is there any fish?* (literally, 'Is there still fish?')

Swiss German usage

Note that in Swiss High German and parts of South West Germany the phrase **hat es?** or **es hat** is used in place of **gibt es?** or **es gibt**, for example:

Hat es noch Wein? Nein, es hat nur noch Bier.	*Is there still (some) wine? No, there is only beer.*

3.2 Grammar Summary

3.2.1 Use of the cases (Reference Grammar 6)

You will have noticed that the form of the definite and indefinite article changes according to the context. These changes are due to the fact that a so-called 'case system' is used in the German language. Once you have mastered it, you will be able to use the German language accurately and with confidence.

In English there are few remnants of the case system still to be found in present-day usage, only the distinction between *I* and *me*, *he* and *him*, *she* and *her*, etc. and the occasional use of *whom*. There are, however, four cases in constant use in German: the nominative, the accusative, the dative and the genitive – and we have already come across the first two of these.

3.2.2 The nominative case as seen in Unit 1

The *nominative case* (i.e. the form of the noun you find in a dictionary) is used with **sein** (*to be*), as well as for the subject of a sentence):

Singular				*Plural*
	Masculine	Feminine	Neuter	*m, f, n.*
the:	**der**	**die**	**das**	**die**
a/an:	**ein**	**eine**	**ein**	[–]

3.2.3 The accusative case

You have already learned that the indefinite article (**ein**) and definite article (**der**) for masculine nouns change to **einen** and **den** after the expression **es gibt** and after the verb **haben**, e.g. **Wir haben einen Tisch frei** (*we have a table free*). However, the forms of the articles in front of feminine (**eine** and **die**) and neuter nouns (**ein** and **das**) do NOT change.

The *accusative case* is used for the direct object of the sentence. To find the direct object of a sentence ask, 'Who or what is affected by the action of the verb?'. The pronoun or noun which forms the answer to this question is the direct object, for example:

I know the man.
Ask the question 'Whom (or what) do I know?'
The answer (*the man*) is the direct object.
Hence: Ich kenne **den** Mann.

		Singular		*Plural*
	Masculine	Feminine	Neuter	*m, f, n.*
the:	**den**	**die**	**das**	**die**
a/an:	**einen**	**eine**	**ein**	[–]

■ The accusative case is also used after the prepositions:

durch (*through*)
für (*for*)
gegen (*against, towards, to*)
ohne (*without*)
um (*round, around, about*)
wider (*against, contrary to*)
bis (*until, till*).

N.B. If the preposition **entlang** (*along*) follows the noun, for example: **Er geht die Straße entlang,** *He goes along the street* then the noun requires the accusative case. (See Unit 4 for an example of how **entlang** can be used with the dative.)

■ The accusative case is also used after the following prepositions if motion is implied:

in	*into*
an	*onto, on the side of, against*
auf	*onto, on, on the top of*
über	*over, above*
unter	*under, underneath, below*
hinter	*behind, at the back/rear of*
vor	*in front of*
zwischen	*between, among*
neben	*beside, next to*

(See unit 4 for details of when these same prepositions require the dative case.)

The negative (*no, not a*) is formed by putting **k** before **einen, eine, ein**, producing **keinen, keine, kein** for the singular accusative case. The plural form is **keine**:

		Singular		Plural
	Masculine	Feminine	Neuter	*m, f, n.*
nominative:	**kein**	**keine**	**kein**	**keine**
accusative:	**keinen**	**keine**	**kein**	**keine**

3.2.4 The verb haben (to have)

Here is the full form of the present tense .

Singular	Plural
ich habe *I have, I am having, I do have*	wir haben *we have etc.*
du hast *you have, etc.* (familiar)	ihr habt *you have* (familiar) *etc.*
Sie haben *you have, etc.* (formal)	Sie haben *you have* (formal) *etc.*
er hat *he has etc.*	sie haben *they have etc.*
sie hat *she has, etc.*	
es hat *it has, etc.*	

3.3 Im Kontext

3.3.1 Study this conversation between a tourist and a hotel receptionist:

Tourist	Guten Tag!
Empfangsdame	Guten Tag! Haben Sie eine Reservierung?
Tourist	Nein, leider nicht. Haben Sie ein Zimmer frei?
Empfangsdame	Für wie viele Gäste?
Tourist	Für zwei.
Empfangsdame	Wir haben leider keine Doppelzimmer mehr, aber es gibt noch zwei Einzelzimmer.
Tourist	Was kosten sie?
Empfangsdame	50 DM pro Zimmer.

Tourist	Gibt es noch ein Hotel in der Nähe?
Empfangsdame	Jawohl! Gleich hier um die Ecke durch das Tor, dann die Straße entlang. Aber sie haben keine Zimmer frei.
Tourist	Also gut! Wir nehmen die Einzelzimmer hier. Aber nur für eine Nacht, bitte!

die Empfangsdame	*hotel receptionist*
leider	*unfortunately*
Gäste	*guests, visitors*
für	*for*
aber	*but*
Doppelzimmer	*double rooms*
mehr	*more*
noch	*still*
Einzelzimmer	*single rooms*
Was kosten sie?	*What do they cost?*
pro Zimmer	*per room*
noch ein	*another*
in der Nähe	*in the vicinity, nearby*
gleich hier um die Ecke	*just round the corner*
durch das Tor	*through the gateway*
die Straße entlang	*along the street*
sicher	*certainly*
nur für eine Nacht	*only for one night*

3.3.2 Read this text describing the facilities available at a hotel:

Das Hotel 'Vier Jahreszeiten' hat vier Sterne. Es hat zweiundzwanzig Doppelzimmer, zwölf Einzelzimmer und zehn Suites. Jedes Zimmer hat ein Bad, eine Dusche, einen Fernseher, ein Telefon und einen Anrufbeantworter. Es gibt vier Restaurants (der Koch kommt aus Frankreich!) und zwei Bars. Außerdem haben wir einen Konferenzsaal, ein Fitnesscenter und einen Friseursalon. Weiterhin bieten wir ein Spielzimmer mit Kindermädchen für die kleinen Gäste. Es gibt auch einen Garten und eine Sonnenterrasse. Bei uns haben Sie jeden Komfort. Sie werden bei uns sicher sehr zufrieden sein!

3.4 Machen wir weiter!

3.4.1 *German as a 'verb second' language*

You will notice in the passage above that the verb in a normal sentence is normally the second idea – not necessarily the second word. **Das Hotel**

Jahreszeiten	*seasons*
Sterne	*stars*
das Zimmer	*the room*
das Bad	*the bath*
die Dusche	*the shower*
der Fernseher	*the television set*
außerdem	*in addition, as well*
der Anrufbeantworter	*answerphone*
der Konferenzsaal	*conference room*
der Friseursalon	*hairdressing salon*
weiterhin	*furthermore, on top of that*
bieten	*to offer*
das Spielzimmer	*playroom*
das Kindermädchen	*nanny*
die kleinen Gäste	*the young guests, children*
jeden Komfort	*every comfort*
sicher	*certainly, sure to be*
Sie werden bei uns zufrieden sein	*You'll be very contented with us (in our hotel)*

'**Vier Jahreszeiten**' is one idea, as is also **Jedes Zimmer** and so they are followed immediately by the verb. If you start the sentence with a word or a group of words (known as a phrase) other than those which usually come before the verb, the verb is still the second idea, for example in the sentences beginning **Außerdem haben wir ...** and **Bei uns haben Sie ...**

3.4.2 Asking and answering questions regarding quantity

Preliminary note: To ask questions relating to quantity, as in *How much information is there? How many newspapers are there?* we need to use **wieviel** (*how much?*) or **wie viele**? (*How many?*)

Wie viele Zeitungen gibt es?   *How many newspapers are there?*
Wie viele Informationen gibt es?   *How much information is there?*

(Note that in German 'information' is often used in the plural.)

Wie viele Esszimmer hat das Hotel?   *How many dining rooms does the hotel have?*

To reply to a question like that you will need a phrase such as

ein bisschen *a little*	**nichts** *nothing*
viel *a lot*	**keine** *none*
genug *enough*	

or a number, for example: (eins, (or einen or eine) (*one*), fünf (*five*)). For further numbers see Reference grammar 8.1.

You will also need the German equivalent of words such as

einige *some*	**Nicht genug!** *Not enough!*
(irgend) welche *any*	**niemand** *nobody*
keine *none*	**etwas** *something*
jemand *somebody*	**nichts** *nothing*

Wie viel Taschengeld bekommt er?	*How much pocket money does he get?*
Zu viel!	*Too much!*
Wie viele Angestellte gibt es bei Siemens?	*How many employees has Siemens?*
Viele.	*Lots.*

3.4.3 Compound nouns

Ein kleiner Scherz *(a little joke, bit of fun)*

Children have great fun trying to invent the longest compound noun possible. Can you recognise any of the component parts of this record-breaking compound noun?

der Donaudampfschifffahrtsgesellschaftskapitänskajütenschlüssel

You can find all the following words in this one compound noun:

die Donau *the Danube*	die Gesellschaft *company, society*
der Dampf *steam*	der Kapitän *captain*
das Schiff *ship*	die Kajüte *cabin*
die Fahrt *journey*	der Schlüssel *key*
(die Schiff-Fahrt *shipping*)	

Starting almost from the end of the word we can work out that it means: *the cabin key of the captain of the Danube Steam Shipping Company*.

In the exercise below we will encounter several examples of compound nouns, for example **das Schlafzimmer, das Fahrrad, das Puppenhausmuseum, der Fahrplan, das Schwimmbad, das Kaffeehaus**, in which two or more components are joined together to form one noun.

If we examine the last example, **das Kaffeehaus**, we see that it is made up of the two nouns: **der Kaffee** and **das Haus**. You will notice that the compound noun takes the same gender as the *last* component in the compound noun. We could, if we wished, develop this compound noun even further by adding (**die**) **Musik** onto the end, giving us **die Kaffeehausmusik** (*palm court music*.)

3.5 Jetzt sind Sie dran!

Aufgabe A

Use the chart in 3.2.3 to fill in the following gaps, using the appropriate form of *a*, *the* or *not a*: (The vocabulary at the bottom will help you to find the correct form)

1 Haben Sie ...... Bleistift da?
2 Gibt es ... Fön im Schlafzimmer?
3 Er hat ... Fahrrad parat.
4 Nürnberg hat ... Puppenhausmuseum
5 Wir haben ...... Tisch frei
6 Jedes Zimmer hat ...... Telefon
7 Herr Meier hat ...... neue Sekretärin
8 Habt ihr ... Fahrplan gerade zur Hand?
9 ... Schwimmbad steht Ihnen zur Verfügung.
10 Gibt es ... Kaffeehaus in der Nähe?

---

der Bleistift *pencil*
der Fön *hairdryer*
das Fahrrad *bicycle*
das Puppenhausmuseum *doll's house museum*
der Tisch *table*
das Telefon *telephone*

die Sekretärin *secretary*
der Fahrplan *timetable*
das Schwimmbad *swimmig pool*
zur Verfügung stehen *to be at your disposal*
das Kaffeehaus *cafe, coffee shop*

Antworten

1. Haben Sie einen Bleistift da? 2. Gibt es einen Fön im Schlafzimmer?
3. Er hat ein Fahrrad parat. 4. Nürnberg hat ein Puppenhausmuseum. 5. Wir haben
einen Tisch frei. 6. Jedes Zimmer hat ein Telefon. 7. Herr Meier hat eine neue
Sekretärin. 8. Habt ihr einen Fahrplan gerade zur Hand? 9. Das Schwimmbad steht
Ihnen zur Verfügung. 10. Gibt es ein Kaffeehaus in der Nähe?

Aufgabe B

Re-write the following sentences, starting with the given word or phrase.
This has the effect of shifting the emphasis onto the first word:

1 Wir spielen Tennis am Dienstag. *We play tennis on Tuesday.*
Am Dienstag ....

2 Otto fährt immer mit dem Taxi. *Otto always travels by taxi.*
Immer ....

3 Anita besucht ihre Mutter jeden Tag. *Anita visits her mother every day.*
Jeden Tag ....

4 Mein Mann und ich denken oft an Hans. *My husband and I often think
of Hans.*
Oft ....

5 Sie essen nie Rindfleisch. *They never eat beef.*
Nie ....

6 Ich muss jetzt gehen. *I must go now.*
Jetzt ....

7 Inge hat meistens keine Zeit zum Lesen. *Inge mostly no time for
reading.*
Meistens ....

8 Wir essen abends kalt. *We have a cold meal in the evening.*
Abends ....

9 Bundeskanzler Kohl fährt im Sommer an den Wolfgangssee.
Chancellor Kohl goes to Lake Wolfgang in the summer.
Im Sommer ....

10 Er macht dort eine Kur. *He 'takes a cure' there.*
Dort ....

Anworten

1. Am Dienstag spielen wir Tennis. 2. Immer fährt Otto mit dem Taxi.
3. Jeden Tag besucht Anita ihre Mutter. 4. Oft denken mein Mann und ich an
Hans. 5. Nie essen sie Rindfleisch. 6. Jetzt muss ich gehen. 7. Meistens hat Inge
keine Zeit zum Lesen. 8. Abends essen wir kalt. 9. Im Sommer fährt
Bundeskanzler Kohl an den Wolfgangsee. 10. Dort macht er eine Kur.

4 | EXPRESSING LOCATION

Aims

In this unit you will learn how to:

■ Enquire about and give information about location; ■ Enquire about and give information about distance

Grammar content

■ wo? ■ auf welchem? in welchem? ■ wie weit? ■ The verbs **liegen**, **sich befinden**, **stehen**, **warten**, **bleiben**; ■ Prepositions to express location and distance; ■ dative case

4.1 Preliminary Note

■ To ask the location of a place, facility or object, simply start the question with **Wo?** (*where?*) and follow it with the verb you wish to use, and the place, facility or object, e.g. Wo ist das Kino? *Where is the cinema?*

■ If you wish to be slightly more specific and ask 'on which?' or 'in which?' then start the sentence with **Auf welchem? / Auf welcher?** (*on which?*) or **In welchem / In welcher?** (*in which?*).

■ To enquire about distance start the sentence with **Wie weit ist?** (*How far is?*)

■ To give information regarding location, e.g *It's in the Market Square, It's at the railway station* we often use the verb **sein** (*to be*) or **liegen** (*to be situated*), **bleiben** (*to stay*), **stehen** (*to stand*), occasionally **sich befinden** (*to be found*) or **warten** (*to wait*).

■ We also need to use a word (known as a preposition) which shows the position or location of the thing (noun). Most prepositions cause the definite article (**der, die, das** or **die** (pl.)) or the indefinite article (**ein, eine, ein**) or the possessive adjective (**mein, meine, mein, meine** (pl.)) to change its form. (For fuller details on prepositions see 3.2.3 and 4.2.3., also Reference Grammar 6.)

Enquiring about location

Look at the following questions regarding location:

Wo ist die Apotheke, bitte?	*Where is the chemist's please?*
Wo sind die Gemälde von Dürer?	*Where are the Dürer paintings?*
Wo liegt Schleswig?	*Where is Schleswig situated?*
Wo finde ich ein Telefon, bitte?	*Where can I find a telephone, please?*
In welchem Aktenschrank befindet sich der Brief?	*In which filing cabinet is the letter to be found?*
In welcher Handtasche ist dein Pass?	*In which handbag is your passport?*
In welchem Büro arbeitest du?	*In which office do you work?*

Giving information about location

Now have a look at these examples of location and their English translations before going on to the Grammar Summary. Note that the form **an dem** can be, and regularly is, contracted to **am**. In fact it must be contracted if the article is not stressed. (This obviously refers only to the masculine and neuter forms.)

Die Apotheke ist an dem (am) Marktplatz.	*The chemist's is on the Market Square.*
Das nächste Telefon ist an der Post.	*The nearest phone is at the post office.*
Die Bushaltestelle ist an dem (am) Rathaus.	*The bus stop is at the Town Hall.*
Ich arbeite in einem Bierkeller.	*I work in a beer cellar.*
Sie arbeitet in einer Bank.	*She's working in a bank.*
Er schläft fest in seinem Bett.	*He is fast asleep in his bed.*
Es gibt zu viele Autos in unseren Städten.	*There are too many cars in our towns.*

The location of towns and areas

To give information about the location of towns the verb **liegen** is often used. This information can involve the points of the compass or more specific geographic locations:

Schleswig liegt in Norddeutschland.	*Schleswig is in North Germany.*
München liegt in Süddeutschland.	*Munich is in South Germany.*
Die Insel Rügen liegt im Nordosten.	*The island of Rügen is in the North East.*
Karlsruhe liegt im (in dem) Südwesten.	*Karlsruhe is in the South West (NB **im** is the contracted form of **in + dem**, similar to am.)*
Oberammergau liegt in den Alpen.	*Oberammergau is in the Alps.*
Berlin liegt an der Spree.	*Berlin is on the (River) Spree.*
Königswinter liegt an dem (am) Rhein.	*Königswinter is on the Rhine.*

Questions about distance

To enquire how far it is to a particular amenity within a neighbourhood, for example the post office, the university, the football stadium, you can ask:

Wie weit ist der Flughafen von hier?	*How far is the airport from here?*
Wie weit ist es zum Flughafen?	*How far is it to the airport?*

If you wish to ask how far it is to a town or country, you ask:

Wie weit ist Kiel von hier?	*How far is Kiel from here?*
Wie weit ist es nach Kiel?	*How far is it to Kiel?*

Various expressions of distance:

Der Flughafen ist weit entfernt.	*The airport is far away.*
Bonn ist nicht weit entfernt.	*Bonn is not far away.*
Potsdam ist ungefähr 30 Kilometer von Berlin entfernt.	*Potsdam is approximately 30 kilometres from Berlin.*

4.2 Grammar Summary

4.2.1 The dative case (Reference Grammar 6.3)

In the examples above, **der**, **die**, **das**, or the plural **die** as we met them in unit 1 (the nominative case) underwent a change – under the influence of the preposition **an** or **in** – to **dem, der, dem** or **den**. The latter are examples of the dative case.

At this point we realise how important it is to learn the gender with each new word (i.e. whether it is **der, die, das** in the dictionary), as it changes its form when used in different cases.

4.2.2 The cases

The charts below show the cases we have learned so far:

	Singular			*Plural*
	Masculine	Feminine	Neuter	*m, f, n.*
the:				
nominative	**der**	**die**	**das**	**die**
accusative	**den**	**die**	**das**	**die**
dative	**dem**	**der**	**dem**	**den**
a/an				
nominative	**ein**	**eine**	**ein**	–
accusative	**einen**	**eine**	**ein**	–
dative	**einem**	**einer**	**einem**	–
this/these:				
nominative	**dieser**	**diese**	**dieses**	**diese**
accusative	**diesen**	**diese**	**dieses**	**diese**
dative	**diesem**	**dieser**	**diesem**	**diesen‡**
which?:				
nominative:	**welcher?**	**welche?**	**welches?**	**welche?**
accusative:	**welchen?**	**welche?**	**welches?**	**welche?**
dative:	**welchem?**	**welcher?**	**welchem?**	**welchen?‡**

‡ See 4.4.1.

4.2.3 Prepositions which always require the dative case

The dative case is used after the following prepositions:

aus	*out of, from*
außer	*except for, apart from*
bei	*at, at the house of, with*

mit	*with*
nach	*after, to – a town or country*
seit	*since, for – a length of time*
von	*from*
zu	*to* (a local amenity)
gegenüber	*opposite*
entlang	*along* (when used before the noun)

bei with, at the house of, at:

> Er wohnt bei seiner Freundin.   *He lives with his girlfriend.*

gegenüber *opposite*:

> Er wohnt dem Gefängnis gegenüber.   *He lives opposite the prison*

(N.B. **gegenüber** can appear either before or after the noun.)

Prepositions which require the dative case when they show location or position

The nine prepositions which we came across in Unit 3 take the *dative* case if they show location, position or a static condition:

in	*in*
an	*on, on the side of*
auf	*on, on top of*
über	*over, above*
unter	*under*
hinter	*behind*
vor	*in front of*
zwischen	*between*
neben	*next to, beside*

an *on, on the side of*:

> Ihr zweites Zuhause ist an der Küste. *Her second home is on the coast.*

auf *on*:

> Die Buchhandlung ist auf der rechten Seite.   *The bookshop is on the righthand side.*

unter *under*:

> Der Koffer ist unter dem Bett.   *The case is under the bed.*

hinter *behind/at the back of*:

Die Taxis stehen hinter den
  Telefonzellen.

The taxis are (standing) *behind the
  telephone boxes.*

vor *in front of*:

Die Toiletten sind vor dem Café.

The toilets are in front of the cafe.

zwischen *between*:

Die Bank ist zwischen der
  Kirche und der Post.

*The bank is between the
  church and the post office.*

neben *next to*:

Das Reisebüro ist neben dem Dom.

*The travel agency is next to the
  cathedral.*

For examples of this usage see Reference Grammar 6.

Remember that these prepositions require the accusative case when they
show motion or movement from one place to another. (See 3.2.3)

4.3 Im Kontext

4.3.1 *Looking for a bank*

Tourist   Entschuldigung! Gibt es eine Bank hier in der Nähe?
Polizist Ja, klar. Es gibt eine am Marktplatz.
Tourist   Wo ist der Marktplatz, bitte?
Polizist Gar nicht weit von hier, nur zwei Minuten zu Fuß. Er ist direkt
              hinter dem Bahnhof dort drüben.
Tourist   Vielen Dank!
Polizist Nichts zu danken!

klar (*colloquial)	*of course*
direkt	*directly*
der Bahnhof	*the railway station*
Vielen Dank.	*Many thanks.*
Nichts zu danken.	*It's a pleasure.*

4.3.2 Eine Stadtrundfahrt *(A guided tour of the town)*

Meine Damen und Herren. Unsere Stadttour von Leipzig beginnt hier am Augustusplatz vor dem restaurierten Mende-Brunnen. Links sehen Sie das Gewandhaus und rechts das Opernhaus. Davorne ist das Hochhaus der Universität (Man nennt es hier den Weisheitszahn!) Wir fahren jetzt entlang der Schillerstraße am Ägyptischen Museum vorbei. In wenigen Minuten erreichen wir die Thomaskirche, in der Johann Sebastian Bach Thomaskantor war. Seine Grabstätte befindet sich seit 1950 in der Kirche. Vor der südlichen Seite der Kirche sehen wir das Bach-Denkmal. Nach dieser Tour können Sie ein Bier in Auerbachs Keller trinken. Er ist gar nicht weit vom Markt entfernt. Das berühmte Messegelände liegt außerhalb der Stadtmitte. Am besten fahren Sie mit einem Linienbus dorthin.

---

restauriert *restored*
der Brunnen *fountain, well*
das Gewandhaus *famous concert hall in Leipzig, housing a magnificent organ*
das Opernhaus *the opera house*
davorne *in front* (of it)

das Hochhaus der Universität *university skyscraper*
der Weisheitszahn *wisdom tooth* (used figuratively here)
Das Ägyptische Museum *the Egyptian Museum*
vorbei/fahren an + *dative *to drive past*
in wenigen Minuten *in a few minutes*
erreichen *to reach*

in der ... *in which ...* (note that the verb is sent to the end of this relative clause. For more details, see Functional Grammar 5.4.3)
der Kantor *choirmaster, cantor*
die Grabstätte *grave, tomb*
südlich *southern*
das Denkmal *statue, monument*
Auerbachs Keller *Auerbach's Cellar* (famous restaurant mentioned in Goethe's play **Faust**)
berühmt *famous*
das Messegelände *exhibition centre*
außerhalb + *genitive *outside of* (See Reference Grammar 6.4)
der Linienbus *public service bus*
dorthin/fahren *to go (to) there*

4.4 Machen wir weiter!

4.4.1 Dative plural

In the dative plural the noun itself must end in -n. If the plural naturally ends in **-n** there is no need to add another one. Look at the following examples:

Wir fahren mit den Kinder*n*
nach Frankreich.

We are travelling to France with the children.

The plural of **das Kind** is **die Kinder**. Because the plural form **Kinder** is in the dative case – it comes after the preposition **mit** – an additional **-n** must be added.

Ich wandere gern in den Bergen.   *I like hiking in the mountains.*

The plural of **der Berg** is **die Berge**. This plural noun is in the dative case, which is used after the preposition **in** when the latter shows position.

Das ist ein Bild von meinen   *That is a picture of my brothers.*
Brüdern.

The plural of **der Bruder** is **die Brüder**. (See also 12.4.5)

Viele Plastiken von Barlach befinden   *Many of Barlach's sculptures are*
sich in den Kirchen von   *to be found in North Germany's*
Norddeutschland.   *churches.*

The plural of **die Kirche** is **die Kirchen**, so no additional **-n** needs to be added to show that it is in the dative plural.

4.4.2 Personal pronouns

In later units we will come across examples of the personal pronouns in these three cases. You may well be interested to see them in chart form here, and compare them with their English equivalents.

		Singular			
Person 1st.		2nd.			3rd.
N ich (*I*)	du (*you*)	Sie (*you*)	er (*he*)	sie (*she*)	es (*it*)
A mich (*me*)	dich (*you*)	Sie (*you*)	ihn (*him*)	sie (*her*)	es (*it*)
D mir ((*to*) *me*)	dir ((*to*) *you*)	Ihnen ((*to*) *you*)	ihm ((*to*)*him*)	ihr ((*to*)*her*)	ihm ((*to*)*it*)

	Plural		
Person 1st.		2nd.	3rd.
N wir (*we*)	ihr (*you*)	Sie (*you*)	sie (*they*)
A uns (*us*)	euch (*you*)	Sie (*you*)	sie (*them*)
D uns ((*to*) *us*)	euch ((*to*) *you*)	Ihnen ((*to*) *you*)	ihnen ((*to*) *them*)

4.5 Jetzt sind Sie dran!

Aufgabe A

Join the following sentence halves together:

1	Hamburg liegt	A	zum Flughafen?
2	Ich arbeite in	B	am Rhein
3	Der ICE kommt	C	von Griechenland
4	Bonn liegt	D	in Norddeutschland
5	Athen ist die Hauptstadt	E	am Marktplatz
6	Wie weit ist es	F	die Hauptstadt von Island
7	Die Bushaltestelle ist	G	auf Gleis 4 an
8	Reykjavik ist	H	einer Bank
9	Er wandert gern	I	arbeiten Sie?
10	In welchem Büro	J	in den Bergen

Antworten

1D, 2H, 3G, 4B, 5C, 6A, 7E, 8F, 9J, 10 I

Aufgabe B

Rewrite the following sentences replacing the underlined nouns with the appropriate pronoun:

Zum Beispiel: Die Frau hat nur einen Sohn > **Sie** hat nur einen Sohn. Refer to the chart in 4.4.2 for help.

1 <u>Frau Müller</u> ist sehr krank. > ... ist sehr krank.
2 <u>Die Schulkinder</u> sind sehr faul. > ... sind sehr faul.
3 <u>Hans Schmidt</u> arbeitet in einem Hotel. > ... arbeitet in einem Hotel.
4 Wir fahren mit <u>Hans und Lotte</u> nach Hamburg. > Wir fahren mit ... nach Hamburg.
5 Frau Braun besucht <u>den Arzt</u>. > Frau Braun besucht ...
6 Heinrich wohnt bei <u>Oma</u> > Heinrich wohnt bei ...
7 <u>Meine Mutter</u> hat am neunten Oktober Geburtstag. > ... hat am neunten Oktober Geburtstag.
8 <u>Seine Eltern</u> sind sehr nett. > ... sind sehr nett.
9 Inge spielt Tennis mit <u>Fritz</u>. > ... spielt Tennis mit ...
10 Der Brief ist für <u>den Chef</u>. > Der Brief ist für ...

krank	*ill*
faul	*lazy*
arbeiten	*to work*
Oma	*grandmother*
Geburtstag haben	*to have one's birthday*
Eltern, die	*parents*
Brief, der	*letter*
Chef, der	boss

Antworten

1. Sie ist sehr krank. 2. Sie sind sehr faul. 3. Er arbeitet in einem Hotel.
4. Wir fahren mit ihnen nach Hamburg. 5. Frau Braun besucht ihn.
6. Heinrich wohnt bei ihr. 7. Sie hat am neunten Oktober Geburtstag.
8. Sie sind sehr nett. 9. Sie spielt Tennis mit ihm. 10. Der Brief ist für ihn.

5 | TALKING ABOUT THE PRESENT

Aims

In this unit you will learn how to:

■ Talk about something which is happening now; ■ Talk about something which is true as of now, but not necessarily at this specific time; ■ Describe a regular or habitual activity; ■ Express universal truths and well-known facts; ■ Present information about the past in a dramatic present form

Grammar content

■ The present tense of regular verbs; ■ The present tense of irregular verbs; ■ Relative clauses; ■ Separable verbs

5.1 Preliminary Note

1 You would naturally choose the present tense to talk about an activity, action, state of affairs or event which is happening just now, for example: *It's snowing. He's arriving. The train is just leaving.*

2 You would also use the present tense to describe an activity, action, state of affairs or event which is true as of now, but is not necessarily happening at this specific moment, for example: *I'm reading a novel by Böll. My son's studying medicine. They understand the problem.*

3 The present tense would also be your natural choice to describe a regular or habitual action or activity that you do or are doing, for example: *I read the newspaper every morning. He works every Saturday. You always look half-starved. They go to the mosque on Fridays.*

4 The present is also used for expressing universal truths and proven facts, for example: *Children love chips and icecream. Blood is thicker than water. Time heals. Practice makes perfect, The earth is round.*

5 The so-called dramatic present is sometimes used either to bring historical narrative to life or to present an incident from the past more vividly, for example: *And then the Vikings simply come up the river and set fire to the whole settlement. I get out of the car and see water streaming out from under the front door.*

Talking about something which is true or is happening just now

Es ist heute kalt.	*It's cold today.*
Sie ist wirklich krank.	*She's really ill.*
Schh! Das Baby schläft.	*Shh! The baby's asleep.*

Talking about something which is theoretically happening or true now, but not necessarily at this precise moment

Ich komme gleich.	*I'm on my way /I'm coming immediately.*
Mein Sohn studiert Medizin.	*My son's studying medicine*
Sie sucht ihren idealen Mann.	*She's looking for her ideal man.*
Wir lernen kochen.	*We're learning to cook.*

Describing a regular activity or habitual action which is ongoing

Ich arbeite samstags.	*I work on Saturdays.*
Er liest die Zeitung jeden Morgen.	*He reads the newspaper every morning.*
Er trinkt.	*He drinks, he's a regular drinker.*
Renate isst jeden Tag Nudeln.	*Renate eats pasta every day.*
Freitags gehen sie in die Moschee.	*They go to the mosque on Fridays.*

Expressing universal truths and proven facts

Kinder essen gern Pommes frites.	*Children love eating chips.*
Blut ist dicker als Wasser.	*Blood is thicker than water.*

Presenting information about the past in a dramatic present form

Und dann kommen die Wikinger und brennen die Siedlung nieder.	*Then the Vikings come and burn the settlement down.*
Ich steige aus dem Auto und sehe Wasser aus der Haustür strömen.	*I get out of my car and see water streaming out of the front door.*

5.2 Grammar Summary

5.2.1 The present tense of regular verbs

English has various ways of expressing the present tense, such as: *I cook*, *I am cooking* or *I do cook*. German has only one form to translate these three: **Ich koche**.

This verb **kochen** (*to cook*) consists of the stem **koch-** plus various endings, which are shown below in bold. This provides the pattern for several other verbs in the present tense, in that the various forms of the verb all have the same endings as below and therefore can be worked out.

Several other verbs which also follow this pattern in the present tense are, for example:

kaufen *to buy*	sparen *to save*
lernen *to learn*	spielen *to play*
klopfen *to knock*	studieren *to study*
machen *to make or to do*	suchen *to look for*
malen *to paint*	verkaufen *to sell*
sagen *to say*	wohnen *to live*

Singular

ich koch**e** *I cook, I am cooking, I do cook*
du koch**st** *you cook, you are cooking, etc.*
Sie koch**en** *you cook, you are cooking, etc.*
er koch**t** *he cooks, he is cooking, etc.*
sie koch**t** *she cooks, she is cooking, etc.*
es koch**t** *it cooks, it is cooking, etc.*

Plural

wir koch**en** *we cook, we are cooking, etc.*
ihr koch**t** *you cook, you are cooking, etc.*
Sie koch**en** *you cook, you are cooking, etc.*
sie koch**en** *they cook, they are cooking, etc.*

Have another look at the examples on the preceding pages and check that
the endings are the same as those marked in italics in the box above.

How to find the stem of the verb

If we subtract the endings from the infinitive (the verb form which we find
in the dictionary with the meaning *to cook, to play, to pay*, etc., (kochen,
spielen, bezahlen, etc) we are left with the so-called stem of the verb,
koch-, **spiel-**, **bezahl-**, etc.

If the stem of regular verb ends in **d**, **t**, e.g. **reden** (*to speak*), **arbeiten** (*to
work*), or a combination of **m** or **n** preceded by another consonant, e.g.
atmen (*to breathe*), **regnen** (*to rain*), an **e** is added before the endings of
the **du**, **er**, **sie**, **es** and **ihr** forms in the present tense, for ease of
pronunciation, for example:

arbeiten, *to work*

Mein Vater arbeitet bei Bosch.   *My father works for Bosch.*

atmen, *to breathe*

Oma atmet sehr langsam.   *Grandma's breathing very slowly.*

finden, *to find*

Er findet seine Fahrkarte nicht.   *He can't find his ticket.*

öffnen, *to open*

Die alte Frau öffnet ihre Haustür   *The old lady isn't opening her*
nicht.   *front door.*

senden, *to send, transmit*

CNN sendet rund um die Uhr.   *CNN broadcasts round the clock.*

arbeiten *to work*

Singular	*Plural*
ich arbeite *I work, am working*	wir arbeit**en** *we work, are working*
du arbeit**est** *you work, are working*	ihr arbeit**et** *you work, are working*
Sie arbeit**en** *you work, are working*	Sie arbeit**en** *you work, are working*
er arbeit**et** *he works, is working*	sie arbeit**en** *they work, are working*
sie arbeit**et** *she works, is working*	
es arbeit**et** *it works, is working*	

5.2.2 The present tense of irregular verbs (Reference Grammar 9.1.2 and 10.7)

Although we noticed some slight variations in the endings of the regular verbs above to ease pronunciation, the stem was always based on the infinitive form.

Other verbs, however, change their stem vowel in the second (**du**) and third (**er, sie, es**) person singular, so that these forms are different from the stem and thus also from the infinitive. We cannot work these out, but have to refer to a verb list, such as that in Reference Grammar 10.7, to be sure of the correct form.

Look at the vowel changes in the following verbs.

fahren   *to go, to travel*
ab/fahren *to depart, set off*

Fährst du gleich ab?	*Are you setting off straight away?*
Nein, ich fahre erst morgen.	*No. I'm not going until tomorrow.*
Der Zug fährt um 12 Uhr von Gleis 5 ab.	*The train departs from platform 5.*

fangen *to catch*

Unsere Katze fängt zu gerne Mäuse.	*Our cat likes catching mice too much.*

schlafen *to sleep*

Das Mädchen schläft nicht gut.	The girl doesn't sleep well.

geben *to give*

aus/geben *to spend*

Meine Tochter gibt sehr viel Geld für Kosmetika aus.	*My daughter spends a lot of money on cosmetics.*
Der Chef gibt mir keinen Tag frei.	*The boss doesn't give me a day off.*

(Do you remember the expression **es gibt** from Unit 3? It is the third person singular of this verb, **geben**.)

essen *to eat*

Du isst viel zu wenig.	*You're eating far too little.*
Er isst Lachs so gern.	*He loves eating salmon so much.*

lesen *to read*

Liest du Focus?	*Do you read Focus?*
Meine Frau liest den Spiegel jede Woche.	*My wife reads the Spiegel each week.*

sehen *to see*

aus/sehen *to look*

Siehst du den Baum da?	*Can you see the tree there?*
Er sieht sehr müde aus.	*He looks very tired.*

laufen *to run* (In Northern Germany **laufen** is also used for *to go*, *to walk*.)

Der Vertreter läuft aus dem Büro.	*The company representative runs out of the office.*
Läufst du oft in die Stadt?	*Do you often walk into town?*

Remember that only the **du** and **er**, **sie**, **es** forms change. All the other forms are predictable and have the same vowel as the stem , for example:

Ich fahre nicht gern Rad.	*I don't like cycling.*
Wir fahren heute nach Schwerin.	*We're going to Schwerin today.*
Lesen Sie nichts?	*Don't you read anything?*
	(Literally, 'Do you read nothing?')

5.3 Im Kontext:

5.3.1 Read the following article in which Ilse explains why she always returns to the same Greek island for her holidays:

Meine Freunde und Kollegen wechseln ihr Urlaubsziel von Jahr zu Jahr. Ich selbst fahre seit zwölf Jahren auf die gleiche Insel, die kaum jemand kennt, in Griechenland. Wollt ihr wissen, warum ich immer wieder hinfahre?

Ich kenne die Kinder des Dorfes, ich kenne die schwarzgekleideten Großmütter, ich kenne die Wirte. Wenn ich ankomme, freuen sich alle, und ich habe das Gefühl im Urlaub nach Hause zu kommen. "Fährst du schon wieder nach Griechenland?" spotten meine Freunde. "Willst du nichts anderes kennen lernen? Die Welt ist groß …" Ich weiß es besser. Diese Insel, die ich jedes Jahr besuche, ist mein Platz an der Sonne.

---

die Freunde *friends*
die Kollegen *colleagues*
wechseln *change*
das Urlaubsziel *holiday destination*
von Jahr zu Jahr *from year to year*
ich selbst *I myself*
Ich fahre seit zwölf Jahren zu … *For twelve years I have been going/travelling to …*
die gleiche Insel *the same island*
kaum jemand *scarcely anybody*
immer wieder *again and again, time after time*
hin/fahren *to go/travel there*
die Kinder des Dorfes *the children of the village* (See 12.4.4)

die schwarzgekleideten Großmütter *the grandmothers dressed in black*
der Wirt *the landlord*
Wenn ich ankomme, freuen sich alle. *Whenever I arrive, everyone is pleased.*
das Gefühl *the feeling*
nach Hause kommen *to come home*
schon wieder *yet again*
spotten *to mock*
nichts anderes *nothing else*
die Welt *the world*
besser *better*
mein Platz an der Sonne *my place in the sun*

5.4 Machen wir weiter!

5.4.1 Relative clauses (Reference Grammar 15.2)

Have another look at the sentences:

Ich fahre seit zwölf Jahren auf die gleiche Insel, **die** kaum jemand kennt.	*For twelve years I have been going to the same island, which scarcely anyone knows.*

and

Diese Insel, **die** ich jedes Jahr besuche, ist mein Platz an der Sonne.	*This island which I visit every year is my place in the sun.*

In these sentences **die** (*which*) is a relative pronoun, and it introduces the relative clause, **die kaum jemand kennt** or **die ich jedes Jahr besuche**.

You will notice that the relative pronoun **die** is preceded by a comma, and that it sends the verb to the end of the clause, which also ends with a comma if the sentence continues.

First of all, have a look at the chart of relative pronouns, and then study the following examples of relative clauses. See if you can work out how they relate back to the main clause.

Relative pronouns				
		Singular		*Plural*
	masculine	feminine	neuter	m, f, n.
nominative	der	die	das	die
accusative	den	die	das	die
dative	dem	der	dem	denen
genitive	dessen	deren	dessen	deren

Der Wein, der aus diesem Gebiet kommt, ist lieblich.	*The wine which comes from this region is sweet.*

The relative pronoun here is in the nominative case, because it is the subject of the relative clause in which it stands. To check this, replace the pronoun with the noun to which it refers, viz. '*The wine comes from this region*'. *The wine* is clearly the subject of this sentence. The relative pronoun is masculine singular, because it is referring or relating back to **der Wein** in the main clause.

Der Wein, **den** wir trinken, ist herb.	*The wine which we are drinking is dry.*

The relative pronoun, **den**, is in the accusative case, because it is the direct object of the verb in the relative clause. The pronoun is masculine singular, because it is referring back to **der Wein**.

Der Wein, mit dem wir diese Weinprobe beenden, ist eine Spätlese.	*The wine with which we are concluding this wine tasting is a late vintage.*

The relative pronoun is in the dative case, because it is straight after the preposition mit. It is masculine singular, because it is referring back to der Wein.

Viele Weinsorten, **die** wir exportieren, sind für die Deutschen zu süß.	*Many of the wines which we export are too sweet for the Germans.*

Die Weinreben, aus **denen** wir diesen Wein machen, wachsen in den Weingärten um Rüdesheim.	*The vines from which we make this wine grow in the vineyards around Rüdesheim.*

The same relative pronoun can also be translated as *who* or *whom* if referring to a person:

Die Dame, die jetzt redet, ist Professorin für Tiefbau.	*The lady* who *is speaking at the moment is the civil engineering professor.*
Die Dame, **die** ich meine, ist Professorin für Hochbau.	*The lady* (whom) *I mean is the structural engineering professor.*

You will realise that we sometimes omit the relative pronoun in English, but this never happens in German.

Die Dame, mit **der** ich verabredet bin, ist die neue Professorin für Jura.	*The lady* (with) whom *I have arranged to meet, is the new Law Professor.*
Die Damen, die morgen ankommen, sind alle aus China.	*The ladies who are arriving tomorrow are all from China.*

5.4.2 *Separable verbs*

In this unit we have come across several so-called separable verbs , for example **ab/fahren, ab/trocknen, fern/sehen, aus/sehen/ nieder/brennen**. A prefix, such as **ab-, an-, aus-, ein-, fern-, nieder-**, is to be found at the beginning of the infinitive form of a separable verb. It will be followed by / to show that it is separable. This prefix changes the meaning of the basic verb , for example:

fahren = *to travel, to go*	**ab**/fahren = *to depart, to set off*
kommen = *to come*	**an**/kommen = *to arrive*
geben = *to give*	**aus**/geben = *to spend* (money)
sehen = *to see*	**aus**/sehen = *to look (like)*
	fern/sehen = t*o watch TV*

When a separable verb is used as a finite verb, (i.e. as a working verb in a main clause) the prefix splits from the rest of the verb and goes to the end of the clause:

ab/fahren:

Der Zug **fährt** um 12 Uhr **ab**.	*The train leaves at 12 o'clock.*

aus/geben:

Er **gibt** sehr viel Geld **aus**.   *He spends a lot of money.*

5.5 Jetzt sind Sie dran! *Now it's your turn!*

Aufgabe A

Choose one of the verb forms from the box below to complete these sentences:

1 Inge ... gerade nach Hannover.
2 Seit dem Unfall (*accident*) ... ich keinen Alkohol mehr.
3 Heute ... es schön. Die Sonne ...
4 Der Zug aus Köln ... um 12 Uhr auf Gleis 2 an.
5 Das Baby ... in dem Kinderwagen.
6 Was ... Sie da? Einen Roman (*novel*)?
7 Am Samstagabend ... wir immer in einem Restaurant.
8 ... ihr schon für die Englandreise, oder habt ihr schon genug Geld?
9 Fritz und Hanno ... Jura (*law*) an der Universität Marburg.
10 Was ... du jetzt?
11 Der Schüler ... schon zwanzig Minuten an der Bushaltestelle.
12 Wie lange ... Otto schon Klavier?

■ machst ■ scheint ■ essen ■ spielt ■ studieren ■ wartet
■ fährt ■ spart ■ trinke ■ ist ■ kommt ■ lesen ■ schläft ■ habt

---

Antworten

1 Inge fährt gerade nach Hannover. *Inge is travelling to Hanover now.*
2 Seit dem Unfall trinke ich keinen Alkohol mehr. *Since the accident I no longer drink any alcohol.*
3 Heute ist es schön. Die Sonne scheint. *Today it's nice. The sun is shining.*
4 Der Zug aus Köln kommt um 12 Uhr auf Gleis 2 an. *The train from Cologne arrives at Platform 2 at 12.00 pm.*
5 Das Baby schläft in dem Kinderwagen. *The baby is sleeping in the pram.*
6 Was lesen Sie da? Einen Roman? *What are you reading there? A novel?*
7 Am Samstagabend essen wir immer in einem Restaurant. *On Saturday evening we always eat in a restaurant.*

8 Spart ihr für die Englandreise, oder habt ihr schon genug Geld? *Are you saving up for the trip to England, or do you already have enough money?*

9 Fritz und Hanno studieren Jura an der Universität Marburg. *Fritz and Hanno are studying law at the University of Marburg.*

10 Was machst du jetzt? *What are you doing now?*

11 Der Schüler wartet schon zwanzig Minuten an der Bushaltestelle. *The pupil has already waited twenty minutes at the bus stop.*

12 Wie lange spielt Otto schon Klavier? *How long has Otto been playing the piano?*

Aufgabe B

Complete the following sentences by changing the infinitive in brackets into a finite verb:

Zum Beispiel:

Ich (gehen) ... in die Stadt. *I'm going into town.*

Ich gehe in die Stadt.

1 (Kommen) ... du mit? *Are you coming with us?*
2 Mein Mann (nehmen) ... Zucker in den Tee. *My husband takes sugar in his tea.*
3 (Sehen) ... du den Mann da? *Do you see the man there?*
4 Der Chef (fahren) ... oft nach Berlin. *The boss often travels to Berlin.*
5 Wir (fern/sehen) ... abends ... *We watch TV in the evening.*
6 Der Zug (ab/fahren) ... um 12 Uhr ... *The train departs at 12 o'clock.*
7 Wir (ein/kaufen) ... am liebsten bei Aldi ... *We like shopping most at Aldi.*
8 Jakob (an/kommen) ... heute Nachmittag ... *Jakob arrives this afternoon.*
9 Man (aus/geben) ... zu Weihnachten zu viel Geld ... *One spends too much money at Christmas.*
10 Ich (ein/schlafen) ... sofort ... *I go to sleep immediately.*

Antworten

1. Kommst du mit? 2. Mein Mann nimmt Zucker in den Tee. 3. Siehst du den Mann da? 4. Der Chef fährt oft nach Berlin. 5. Wir sehen abends fern. 6. Der Zug fährt um 12 Uhr ab. 7. Wir kaufen am liebsten bei Aldi ein. 8. Jakob kommt heute Nachmittag an. 9. Man gibt zu Weihnachten zu viel Geld aus. 10. Ich schlafe sofort ein.

6 | EXPRESSING LIKES AND DISLIKES

Aims

In this unit you will learn how to:

■ Express likes and dislikes; ■ Ask questions about likes and dislikes

Grammar content

■ Various verbs followed by gern; ■ The verbs **mögen, gefallen, lieben** and **schätzen**; ■ Pronouns in the accusative and dative

6.1 Preliminary Note

Expressing likes using the word gern

The German word **gern** is particularly useful.

■ Used on its own, often in the form **gerne**, in response to a question asking if you would like to do something, it means *with pleasure, willingly, readily.*

■ When used after a verb, **gern** expresses the idea of *enjoying* the action portrayed. Look at the following examples, using the different forms of the verb **spielen** (to play):

Ich spiele gern Fußball.	*I enjoy/like playing football.*
Er spielt gern Gitarre.	*He likes/enjoys playing the guitar.*
Wir spielen gern zusammen.	*We like playing together.*

Enquiring about likes using gern

Spielt sie gern Klavier?	*Does she like playing the piano?*
Sie spielen gern Golf, ja?	*You like playing golf, don't you?*

Expressing dislikes

The word **ungern** can be used in the above examples to change the meaning to: *I cook with reluctance, He swims very reluctantly, They don't like playing chess.*

Ich koche ungern.	*I don't like cooking.*
Er schwimmt sehr ungern.	*He swims very reluctantly.*

It is also possible to use **nicht gern** to express dislike, as in these sentences:

Er geht nicht gern in die Schule.	*He doesn't like going to school.*
Wir spielen nicht gern Tischtennis.	*We don't like playing table tennis.*

Expressing and enquiring about likes

The verb **mögen** is also used to express liking and is followed sometimes by an infinitive at the end of the clause, sometimes by a noun or pronoun (See 6.2.2 for the full verb):

Ich mag gern Turnen.	*I enjoying doing gym.*
Du magst Blumenkohl, nicht?	*You like cauliflower, don't you?*

Expressing likes using the verb gefallen (to please)

This irregular verb is often used with the impersonal pronoun **es** (*it*) plus a personal pronoun in the *dative* case: **mir** (*me, to me*), **dir** (*you, to you*), **ihm** (*him, to him*), **ihr** (*her, to her*), **ihm** (*it, to it*), **uns** (*us, to us*), **euch** (*you, to you*), **Ihnen** (*you, to you*), **ihnen** (*them, to them*) (see chart in Unit 4, 4.4.2, also Reference Grammar 4), for example:

Es gefällt ihm hier nicht.	*He doesn't like it here.*
Es gefällt ihr, wie er spricht.	*She likes the way he speaks.*

The impersonal pronoun **es** can, of course, be replaced by a noun of your choice, for example:

Wien gefällt ihm besonders gut.	*He particularly likes Vienna.*
Die deutsche Sprache gefällt mir gut.	*I like the German language.*

Enquiring about likes using the verb gefallen

You can also use this verb to ask how somebody likes something:

Gefällt Ihnen das Hotelzimmer?	*Do you like the hotel room?*
Wie gefällt dir der Film?	*How do you like the film?*

The verb Lust haben (to feel like doing, to be in the mood to)

Hast du Lust, Eis zu essen?

Do you feel like (eating) an icecream?

Wir haben heute keine Lust zu arbeiten.

We don't feel like working today.

The verb lieben (to love)

This regular German verb is not so widely used as its English or French counterparts. It is mostly used with reference to people or pets:

Sie liebt ihr Patenkind sehr.

She loves her god child very much.

Er liebt seine Katze so.

He loves his cat so dearly.

Compound nouns using Lieblings- (favourite)

Compound nouns using **Lieblings-** (*favourite*) are much more widely used than the verb **lieben**, for example:

Seine Lieblingsfarbe ist Purpur.

His favourite colour is purple.

Ihre Lieblingsgruppe ist Um Mitternacht.

Her favourite (pop) group is Round Midnight.

Mein Lieblingsfach war immer Chemie.

My favourite subject was always chemistry.

Expressing a high regard using the verb schätzen

You can express a high regard for someone by using the regular verb **schätzen** (*to value, to think highly of*) as in the following examples:

Sie schätzt ihren Pfarrer sehr.

She holds her vicar/minister in high regard.

Thomas schätzt seinen Physiklehrer sehr.

Thomas thinks very highly of his physics teacher.

6.2 Grammar Summary

Look at the following examples,which show how very many other verbs can be used with **gern** to express the idea of enjoying or liking doing something.

6.2.1 Verbs with gern

haben (*to have*)

gern haben (*to like*) (for full verb forms see 3.2.4)

Ich habe ihn sehr gern.	*I like him a lot.*
Sie hat Rockmusik sehr gern.	*She likes rock music very much.*

sein (*to be*), (for full verb forms see 1.2.3)

Das Kind ist gern bei seiner Oma.	*The child likes it at his grandma's.*

Regular verbs

hören (*to hear*)

Was für Musik hören Sie gern?	*What sort of music do you enjoy listening to?*

malen (*to paint*)

Er malt sehr gern.	*He enjoys painting very much.*

reisen (*to travel*)

Reist du auch gern?	*Do you also like travelling?*

For further details about the formation of the regular verbs see Unit 5.2.1

Irregular verbs

lesen (*to read*)

Liest du gern?	*Do you enjoy/like reading?*

fahren (*to drive, to travel*)

Er fährt sehr gern schnell.	*He likes driving fast.*

For further details about the formation of the regular verbs, see Unit 5.2.2

6.2.2 The verb mögen

Here is the full form of the verb **mögen** (to like)

Singular:		*Plural:*	
ich mag	*I like*	wir mögen	*we like*
du magst	*you like*	ihr mögt	*you like*
er mag	*he likes*	Sie mögen	*you like*
sie mag	*she likes*	sie mögen	*they like*
es mag	*it likes*		

Note: The verb **mögen** is one of the six so-called modal verbs. It is sometimes followed by an infinitive at the end of the clause , for example: **Ich mag nicht daran denken**, 'I don't like *to think* about it'. Sometimes this second verb does not appear in actual speech or writing, but it is still implied in the thought. (For details of the others see Units 8 and 9.)

In speech you will regularly come across the subjunctive form of this verb: **ich möchte** (*I should like*) used as an idiom. (See also 7.1.3)

6.3 Im Kontext

6.3.1 Read this letter from a German girl to a new penfriend abroad.

Liebe Anna,

Ich bin deine neue Brieffreundin. Ich bin vierzehn Jahre alt und ich wohne in Pockau. Ich habe einen Bruder und eine Schwester. Wir haben einen Hund. Er heißt Raudi. Ich liebe ihn sehr.

Ich schwimme gern. Ich spiele sehr gern Tennis und es gibt einen Tennisplatz hier in der Nähe. Ich höre gern Musik, besonders Popmusik. Pur ist meine Lieblingsgruppe. Was machst du gern? Was für Musik hörst du gern?

Ich mag die Schule nicht sehr und ich lerne nicht gern Mathe. Geschichte finde ich gar nicht interessant und Erdkunde ist einfach langweilig! Aber ich finde Kunst echt toll und Turnen gefällt mir gut. Hast du Lust, nach Deutschland zu kommen? Schreib mir bitte bald.

Deine Waltraud

deine neue Brieffreundin *your new penfriend*	**interessant** *interesting*
der Hund *dog*	**Geschichte** *history*
besonders *especially*	**Erdkunde** *geography*
die Lieblingsgruppe *favourite pop group*	**langweilig** *boring*
die Schule *school*	**Kunst** *art*
Mathe *maths*	**echt toll** *really super*
gar nicht *not at all*	**Turnen** *P.E., gymnastics*
	Schreib mir bitte bald. *Please write (to me) soon.*

6.3.2 Now read this magazine interview with a famous Swiss personality:

Interviewerin	Grüezi, Norbert Eichler! Wie wunderbar, dass Sie mit uns sprechen! Sie haben sicher nicht sehr viel Freizeit. Aber was haben Sie als Hobby?
N.E	Naja, im Winter fahre ich leidenschaftlich gern Ski und im Sommer wandere ich sehr gern im Berner Oberland. Curling gefällt mir auch sehr. Ich liebe die Natur.
Interviewerin	Sie sind also sehr sportlich. Was machen Sie noch?
N.E	Ich schätze meine Familie sehr. Abends spielen wir sehr gern zusammen, Elfer raus, Mensch ärgere dich nicht, Uno usw. Manchmal auch Skat oder Schach. Ich koche auch gern, wenn möglich Schweizer Spezialitäten wie Geschnetzeltes, Raclette oder Fondue.
Interviewerin	Vielen Dank für das Gespräch, Norbert! Viel Spaß beim Skifahren!

---

die Freizeit *free time, leisure*
im Winter *in the winter*
Skifahren *to go skiing*
leidenschaftlich *passionate(ly)*
im Sommer *in the summer*
wandern *to hike, to ramble*
das Berner Oberland *the Bernese Oberland*
die Natur *nature*
Elfer raus! *All the elevens out! (a card game)*
Mensch ärgere dich nicht! *Ludo*

manchmal *sometimes*
Skat *a card game*
Schach *chess*
Schweizer *Swiss*
die Spezialität *speciality*
Geschnetzeltes *slivers of meat served in a cream sauce*
Raclette *a Swiss cheese dish*
Vielen Dank *many thanks*
das Gespräch *the conversation*
Viel Spaß beim Skifahren! *Have fun skiing!*

6.4 Machen wir weiter! *Let's continue!*

6.4.1 The use of accusative personal pronouns

Each time we have used a verb we have come across a personal pronoun (**ich, du, er, sie, es, wir, ihr, Sie, sie**) which is used as a subject in the nominative case.

The accusative personal pronouns are **mich, dich, ihn, sie, es, uns, euch, Sie, sie** (*me, you, him, her, it, us, you, them*). We can use them in a sentence such as *I like him very much* or *He doesn't like it at all*, where they function as direct objects.

Look at the following questions and answers to illustrate the use of these. (In speech these questions could obviously be answered with a *yes* (ja) or *no* (nein), but the full answers illustrate the use of the pronouns very clearly.)

Mag er den Lehrer? Ja, er mag **ihn** sehr.	*Does he like the teacher. Yes, he likes him a lot.*
Du magst den Film nicht, oder? Doch, ich mag **ihn** sehr.	*You don't like the film, do you? Oh yes, I like it a lot.*

(You use **doch** instead of **ja**, when a negative answer is expected, but it turns out to be positive.)

Magst du die Königin? Oh ja. Ich mag **sie** sehr.	*Do you like the Queen? Yes, indeed. I like her very much.*
Isst du gern Eis? Nein, ich finde **es** zu kalt.	*Do you like eating icecream? No, I find it too cold.*
Wie finden Sie Annas Eltern? Ich finde **sie** zu streng.	*What do you think of Anna's parents? I find them too strict.*

6.5 Jetzt sind Sie dran!

Aufgabe A

Imagine that you are visiting a family in Vienna, who want to know your likes and dislikes so that they can plan the programme for your stay.

Using the icons and vocabulary in the box below to help you, form a sentence as your reply to the questions which follow:

☺	besonders gut + gefallen	✋	gern + a verb
✊	nicht gern + a verb	☹	gar nicht + gefallen
☻	nicht sehr interessant. + finden		

---

der or **das Gulasch** *goulasch*
die moderne Kunst *modern art*
das Kaffeehaus *coffee shops*
das Museum (plural: **die Museen**) *the museum*

der Prater *permanent funfair by the River Danube in Vienna*
die Oper *the opera*
die blaue Donau *The Blue Danube*

Zum Beispiel (*for example*):

1 Mögen Sie Gulasch? 👍 Ja, ich mag *or* (ich esse) gern Gulasch.
2 Schwimmen Sie gern? 👎
3 Wie finden Sie Jazz? 😐
4 Hören Sie gern die Musik von Strauß? 👍
5 Gefällt Ihnen die moderne Kunst? 😟
6 Wie gefallen Ihnen die Kaffeehäuser von Wien? ☺
7 Besuchen Sie gern Museen? 👎
8 Wie gefällt Ihnen der Prater? 😟
9 Wie finden Sie die Oper? 😐
10 Gefällt Ihnen die blaue Donau? ☺

Antworten

1 Ich mag gern Gulasch *or* Ich esse Gulasch gern.
2 Nein, ich schwimme nicht gern.
3 Ich finde Jazz nicht sehr interessant.
4 Ich höre die Musik von Strauß gern.
5 Die moderne Kunst gefällt mir gar nicht.
6 Die Kaffeehäuser von Wien gefallen mir besonders gut.
7 Ich besuche nicht gern Museen.
8 Der Prater gefällt mir gar nicht.
9 Ich finde die Oper nicht sehr interessant.
10 Die blaue Donau gefällt mir besonders gut.

Aufgabe B

Re-read the magazine interview in 6.3.2 and decide whether the following statements are **richtig** (*true*) or **falsch** (*false*). If they are false, write out the correct answer.

1 Sein Vorname ist Herbert.
   R F _____
2 Norbert Eichler kommt aus der Schweiz.
   R F _____
3 Er fährt nicht gern Ski.
   R F _____
4 Im Sommer wandert er gern in den Alpen.
   R F _____
5 Er liebt die Natur.
   R F _____
6 Er ist nicht sportlich.   ·
   R F _____

7 Norbert schätzt seine Familie sehr.

R F _____

8 Abends spielen sie Curling.

R F _____

9 Er kocht gern.

R F _____

10 Geschnetzeltes, Raclette und Fondue sind deutsche Spezialitäten.

R F _____

Antworten

1. Falsch. Sein Vorname ist Norbert. 2. Richtig. 3. Falsch. Er fährt leidenschaftlich gern Ski. 4. Falsch. Im Sommer wandert er gern im Berner Oberland. 5. Richtig. 6. Falsch. Er ist sehr sportlich. 7. Richtig. 8. Falsch. Abends spielen sie *Elfer raus*, *Mensch ärgere dich nicht*, *Uno* usw. 9. Richtig. 10. Falsch. Geschnetzeltes, Raclette und Fondue sind Schweizer Spezialitäten.

7 | EXPRESSING WANTS AND PREFERENCES

Aims

In this unit you will learn how to:

■ Express wants and preferences; ■ Ask questions about wants and preferences

Grammar content

■ The verb **wollen**; ■ The idiomatic use of **möchten**; ■ The use of **lieber** to express preference; ■ The verb **vor/ziehen**; ■ Other ways of expressing preferences

7.1 Preliminary note

7.1.1 Expressing wants using wollen

The verb **wollen** is used when you wish to express what you want to do in fairly strong terms, for example, *I want to stay here*. This is a direct way of speaking but is not necessarily impolite.

Ich will unbedingt Kaffee trinken.   *I really want to drink some coffee.*
Sie will ein Auto kaufen.   *She wants to buy a car.*

Enquiring about wants using the verb wollen

Willst du auch nach Spanien fahren? *Do you also want to go to Spain?*
Will er nicht bei Hans übernachten? *Doesn't he want to stay at Hans'?*

7.1.2 The use of the conjunction dass with wollen

Notice the way that German uses the conjunction **dass** to express the following:

Ihr Mann will, dass sie zu Hause bleibt.	*Her husband wants her to stay at home* (literally, 'her husband wants that she stay at home').
Mein Sohn will nicht, **dass** ich zu laut spreche.	*My son doesn't want me to talk too loudly.*

You will notice that **dass** is a conjunction which sends the verb to the end of the clause. For further examples of such conjunctions, see 10.2.1.

7.1.3 Expressing polite requests using the idiomatic forms ich möchte etc.

ich möchte (*I should like*)

It is possible to express likes and preferences in a more subtle and certainly polite way using the verb forms **ich/er/sie/es möchte, du möchtest, ihr möchtet, wir/Sie/sie möchten**. This is in fact the simple past subjunctive form of the verb **mögen** (see unit 6). In this context it is simply used as an idiom, and you do not need to understand how it is formed.

You are very likely to be asked in a cafe or a restaurant **Was möchten Sie?** (*What would you like?*) Another verb is implied in this question (most probably *to order*), but it is not always said.

Look at the following examples of this verb:

Ich möchte bitte Käsekuchen.	*I should like cheesecake, please.*
Wir möchten bezahlen, bitte!	*We'd like to pay, please.*

Enquiring politely about wants, using the idiomatic forms of möchten

Möchtest du Tee, Hans?	*Would you like tea, Hans?*
Möchtet ihr Apfelsaft?	*Would you like apple juice?*

7.1.4 Expressing preferences using lieber or am liebsten

You can express what you prefer doing by using the same structures as above, replacing **gern** with **lieber**, for example:

Sie möchte **lieber** keinen Alkohol trinken.	*She would prefer to drink no alcohol.*
Er spielt **lieber** Handball.	*He prefers playing handball.*
Wir trinken **lieber** Bier.	*We prefer (we'd prefer) to drink beer.*
Ich würde **lieber** in die Schweiz fahren als nach Schweden.	*I'd prefer to go to Switzerland rather than Sweden.*
Er bleibt **am liebsten** zu Hause.	*He likes staying at home best of all.*

Asking questions about preferences, using lieber

| Du hörst **lieber** CDs, oder? | *You prefer listening to CDs, don't you?* |
| Essen Sie **lieber** rote Grütze als Eis? | *Would you prefer (to eat) fresh red fruit pudding rather than ice-cream?* |

7.2 Grammar Summary

The verb **wollen** is another one of the six *modal verbs*. The formation of **wollen** is similar to that of **mögen** in Unit 6, 6.2.2, in that there is no ending in the first and third person singular, and there is a vowel change from the singular to the plural.

The full form of **wollen** is as follows:

wollen *to want to*			
Singular		*Plural*	
ich will	*I want to*	wir wollen	*we want to*
du willst	*you want to*	ihr wollt	*you want to*
er will	*he wants to*	Sie wollen	*you want to*
sie will	*she wants to*	sie wollen	*they want to*
es will	*it wants to*		

N.B. You will have noticed that the *I, he, she* and *it* forms of **wollen** look like the English future tense. You must resist the temptation to translate it in this way. **Ich will** means *I want to*, in the same way that the response in the 1662 Prayer Book version of the Church of England marriage ceremony presumably means *I will* in the sense that *I want to*, rather than *I have the intention of doing so in future!*

7.3 Im Kontext

7.3.1 In a restaurant.

Herr Schneider	Die Speisekarte, bitte.
Kellner	Jawohl. Ich bringe sie gleich.
Herr Schneider	Danke.

Herr Schneider and his wife call the waiter and order their meal.

Herr Schneider	Ich möchte gern eine Gulaschsuppe und nachher den Fisch, bitte.
Kellner	Wie mögen Sie ihn? Gebraten oder gegrillt?
Herr Schneider	Lieber gegrillt. Das ist gesund und schmeckt besser.
Kellner	Gut. Und was möchten Sie, gnädige Frau?
Frau Schneider	Zuerst möchte ich am liebsten den Thunfischsalat und dann das Hähnchen, bitte. Aber gibt es nur Pommes frites als Beilage? Ich esse sie nicht gern.
Kellner	Es gibt auch Salzkartoffeln heute Abend und Blumenkohl, Bohnen und Salat.
Frau Schneider	Ich möchte gern den Salat aber sind Eier in der Mayonnaise? Ich bin allergisch gegen Eier.
Herr Schneider	Gut, mein Schatz, was möchtest du am liebsten trinken?
Frau Schneider	Lieber keinen Alkohol; vielleicht nur eine Flasche Mineralwasser.
Herr Schneider	Und ich trinke ein Glas Weißwein.
Kellner	Ist in Ordnung. Einen Moment, bitte. Es kommt gleich.

---

die Gulaschsuppe *goulasch soup*
nachher *afterwards*
der Fisch *fish*
gebraten *baked/fried*
gegrillt *grilled*
gesund *healthy*
es schmeckt besser *it tastes better*
zuerst *first of all*
der Thunfischsalat *tuna salad*
das Hähnchen *chicken*
nur *only*
Pommes frites *chips*
als Beilage *as an accompaniment*

Salzkartoffeln *boiled potatoes*
(literally 'salt potatoes')
heute Abend *this evening*
der Blumenkohl *cauliflower*
die Bohnen (pl.) *beans*
der Salat *salad*
das Ei *egg*
allergisch gegen *allergic to*
der Schatz *darling* (literally,
'treasure')
eine Flasche Mineralwasser *a
bottle of mineral water*

7.4 Machen wir weiter!

7.4.1 Making polite requests using the verb form hätten

A level of politeness can be achieved by using the past subjunctive of the verb **haben** in the following way:

Meine Frau hätte gern eine Kaltschale.
My wife would like a cold sweet soup (often cherry).

Wir hätten gern ein Zimmer mit Bad.
We'd like a room with a bath.

7.4.2 Expressing preferences using the separable verb vor/ziehen

Ich ziehe Beethoven den Beatles vor. *I prefer Beethoven to the Beatles.*
Sie zieht Wein dem Bier vor. *She prefers wine to beer.*

Vorsicht! *Be careful!* This word order is an exception and is not true of other constructions which have two nouns after the verb, such as:

Der Lehrer schenkt dem Schüler das Buch.
The teacher gives the book to the boy.

Here, the indirect object in the dative case precedes the direct object in the accusative case.

Der Chef gibt seiner Sekretärin einen Kuss.
The boss gives his secretary a kiss.

Der Mann kauft seinem Sohn ein Fahrrad.
The man buys his son a bicycle.

If you wish to check an indirect object, try rephrasing the English version, prefacing what you think is the indirect object with either *to the* or *for the*. If the result sounds natural, even if a little stilted, for example, *The boss gives a kiss to his secretary. The mother sings a lullaby to the baby. The man buys a bicycle for the boy.* this noun phrase is the indirect object and will require the dative case. For full details about word order, see Reference Grammar 14.

7.4.4 *Expressing wishes using* sich etwas wünschen *(to wish for something, to want something)*

Ich wünsche mir einen gutbezahlten Beruf.	*I wish for a well-paid job.*
Was wünschst du dir zum Geburtstag?	*What would you like for your birthday?*
Sie wünscht sich einen reichen Mann.	*She'd like a rich husband.*

(See 11.2.3 for more reflexive verbs)

Enquiring about wishes using wünschen

Ich wünsche dir vor allem Gesundheit und ein langes Leben.	*I wish you above all health and a long life.*
Wir wünschen Ihnen alles Gute zum Neuen Jahr.	*We wish you all the best for the New Year.*

7.5 Jetzt sind Sie dran!

Aufgabe A

Meine Traumfrau (*the woman of my dreams*)

You are looking for a partner at an introduction agency and are being asked about your interests and preferences. Answer each of the questions you are asked, using the personal details in the box:

> You are called *Willi Winkelmann*, are 30 years old and live in Zurich, Switzerland. You are divorced and have a dog. You enjoy playing the guitar and prefer classical music to pop music. Of course you enjoy drinking beer, but do not like wine. Your favourite food is boiled knuckle of pork with pickled cabbage, but unfortunately you are allergic to fish. You don't like hotels but prefer camping, particularly in Greece and Spain. The woman of your dreams is a kind blonde who loves dogs, likes drinking beer and enjoys fresh air.

Interviewer	Guten Tag! Wie heißen Sie bitte?
Willi Winkelmann	Ich heiße Willi Winkelmann.
Interviewer	Gut, und wie alt sind Sie, Herr Winkelmann?

Willi Winkelmann	Ich ....
Interviewer	Wo wohnen Sie?
Willi Winkelmann	Ich ....
Interviewer	Sind Sie verheiratet?
Willi Winkelmann	Nein, ...
Interviewer	Haben Sie Haustiere (*pets*)?
Willi Winkelmann:	Ja, ...
Interviewer	Was machen Sie gern in Ihrer Freizeit? (*free-time*)
Willi Winkelmann	Ich ....
Interviewer	Hören Sie gern Popmusik?
Willi Winkelmann	Ich ....
Interviewer	Trinken Sie viel (*much*)?
Willi Winkelmann	Ich ....
Interviewer	Was ist Ihr Lieblingsessen?
Willi Winkelmann	Mein ....
Interviewer	Haben Sie irgendwelche Allergien (*Any allergies*)?
Willi Winkelmann	Ich bin ....
Interviewer	Übernachten Sie gern in Hotels?
Willi Winkelmann	Nein, ich ....
Interviewer	Wo zelten Sie am liebsten (*where do you most like camping*)?
Willi Winkelmann	In .... und in ....
Interviewer	Wie ist Ihre Traumfrau?
Willi Winkelmann	Sie ist ...... liebt ...... und frische Luft, ... gern Bier, kurz gesagt (*in short*) eine nette Blondine.
Interviewer	Wunderbar! Ich habe hier die Adresse von einer bestimmten (*certain*) Rosi Rösti. Sie ist eine schöne Blondine (*pretty blond*), die Luft und Liebe sucht (*who's looking for air and love*) und auch ein Herz für Tiere hat (*also loves animals*, literally, 'has a heart for animals') Sie ist sicher Ihre Traumfrau!

geschieden *divorced*	**das Eisbein mit Sauerkraut**
Gitarre spielen *to play the guitar*	*boiled knuckle of pork with pickled*
die Popmusik *pop music*	*cabbage*
klassische Musik *classical music*	**allergisch gegen** *allergic to*
das Bier *beer*	**zelten** *to camp*
der Wein *wine*	**Griechenland** *Greece*
	Spanien *Spain*

Antworten

Gut, und wie alt sind Sie, Herr Winkelmann? Ich bin dreißig Jahre alt.
Wo wohnen Sie? Ich wohne in Zürich in der Schweiz.
Sind Sie verheiratet? Nein, ich bin geschieden.
Haben Sie Haustiere? Ja, ich habe einen Hund.
Was machen Sie gern in Ihrer Freizeit? Ich spiele gern Gitarre.
Hören Sie gern Popmusik? Ich ziehe die klassische Musik der Popmusik vor.
Trinken Sie viel? Ich trinke gern Bier, aber ich mag keinen Wein.
Was ist Ihr Lieblingsessen? Mein Lieblingsessen ist Eisbein mit Sauerkraut.
Haben Sie irgendwelche Allergien? Ich bin allergisch gegen Fisch.
Übernachten Sie gern in Hotels? Nein, ich zelte lieber.
Wo zelten Sie am liebsten? In Griechenland und in Spanien.
Wie ist Ihre Traumfrau? Sie ist sympathisch, liebt Hunde und frische Luft, trinkt
   gern Bier, kurz gesagt, eine nette Blondine.

Aufgabe B

German friends have sent you details about a young girl who would like
an au pair job in England. Can you translate the information into English
for a family who are looking for an au pair?

Anneliese will ein Jahr lang in England bleiben. Die Schule gefällt ihr gar
nicht, und sie studiert sehr ungern. Aber ihre Mutter will, dass sie Englisch
lernt. Sie würde am liebsten in einer Großstadt wie London oder
Manchester wohnen, und sie möchte gern bei einer Familie mit
Kleinkindern wohnen. Sie hört gern Musik und zieht englische Popmusik
der deutschen Popmusik vor. Sie ist keine Vegetarierin, aber sie isst lieber
kein Fleisch. Sie hätte gern ein Einzelzimmer, und sie will auf gar keinen
Fall Hausarbeit machen.

Übersetzung (*translation*):

Anneliese wants to stay in England for a year. She doesn't like school and
doesn't like studying. But her mother wants her to learn English. She
would most prefer to live in a city like London or Manchester, and she
would like to live with a family with toddlers. She enjoys listening to
music and prefers English pop music to German pop music. She isn't a
vegetarian but she prefers not to eat meat. She would like to have a single
room and really doesn't want to do any housework.

8 | EXPRESSING PERMISSION AND ABILITY

Aims

In this unit you will learn how to:

■ Make statements about permission and ability; ■ Ask questions about permission and ability

Grammar content

■ The verb **dürfen** and **können**; ■ The indefinite pronoun **man**

8.1 Preliminary note

In this unit we will learn two more verbs which are similar to **mögen** (see 6.2.2) and **wollen** (see 7.2). In fact, there are numerous ways of translating these verbs, but we are mainly going to restrict ourselves to the areas of permission, ability and obligation.

Making statements about permission

In order to express permission the verb **dürfen** is often used. This infinitive form is normally translated as *to be allowed to, to be permitted to*, but depending on the context the individual parts of the verb are also rendered in the following ways: *I may, I can, I am allowed to, I am permitted to*.

Ich darf keine Butter essen.   *I am not allowed to eat butter.*

Asking questions about permission

You will have noticed in the above examples that **dürfen** is normally followed by another infinitive at the end of the clause, for example: **Ihr dürft schon gehen** but, as we noted with **wollen** and **mögen**, the infinitive is not always stated, even though it is implied.

Darf ich Sie nach Hause bringen?	*May I/can I take you home?*

NB. German uses the verb 'to bring' whereas English uses 'to take'.

Darf er im Krankenhaus rauchen?	*Can he/is he allowed to smoke in hospital?*
Dürfen wir Sie um das Geld bitten?	*Can/may we ask you for the money?*

8.2 Grammar Summary

8.2.1 Here is the full form of the verb dürfen

Singular	Plural
ich darf *I may/can, am permitted to*	wir dürfen *we may, etc.*
du darfst *you may, etc.*	ihr dürft *you may, etc.*
er darf *he may, etc.*	Sie dürfen *you may, etc.*
sie darf *she may, etc.*	sie dürfen *they may, etc.*
es darf *it may, etc.*	

In shops you will often hear the question: **Was darf es sein?** *What is it to be? What can I do for you? How can I help you?* You would not use the verb **dürfen** in your reply, but rather a phrase such as **Ich möchte ...** or **Haben Sie ...?**

Note:

Dürfen changes its meaning when used in the negative form. (See 9.4.1)

8.2.2 Granting permission using können

Können is used to express permission in the same way as *can* in English.

Du kannst bei uns übernachten.	*You can spend the night with us.*
Ihr könnt gerne heute Abend ins Kino gehen.	*You can go to the cinema this evening with pleasure.*

Selbstverständlich können Sie hier rauchen.	*Of course you can smoke here.*

8.2.3 Is it expressing permission or ability?

Before looking in detail at the verb **können** (*to be able to*), we must explain some of the overlap that exists between this verb and **dürfen**, and indeed between their English counterparts. Literally, **können** is used to show ability, for example 'My three-year old daughter *can* already swim, I *can* easily sing the alto part, they *can* fix it tomorrow'. These sentences clearly show the ability to perform an action.

But in spoken language, **können**, as well as its English counterpart, is also used to express or enquire about permission.

As we saw above in the examples, **dürfen** is sometimes translated as *Can I take you home? You can get up tomorrow*, in the sense of *Am I allowed to take you home? You have permission to get up tomorrow*. **Dürfen** gives a polite tone to the language, but **können** is very often used in its place. Thus you will hear the following examples in speech:

Kann ich Sie nach Hause bringen?	*Can I take you home?*
Kann ich rauchen?	*Can I smoke?*

In these examples **dürfen** and **können** have a very similar meaning and can be interchanged, affecting only the level of politeness of the language.

8.2.4 Expressing ability with können

Können expresses ability in various ways. It can simply mean that someone is either old enough, big enough, clever enough or strong enough to do something. It can also suggest that they know or understand how to do something, or have the right or power to do it.

Ich kann schlecht hören.	*I hear with difficulty* (literally, 'I can hear badly').
Du kannst gut Rad fahren.	*You can ride (a bicycle) well.*
Alina kann fließend Russisch (sprechen).	*Alina can speak fluent Russian.*
Wir können morgen kommen.	*We can come tomorrow.*
Sie können schon Auto fahren, oder?	*You can already drive a car, can't you?*

Können can also be used without being followed by an infinitive, although a second verb is implied, as in:

Ich kann nicht weiter.	*I can't (go) any further/I can't go on.*
Er kann kein Deutsch.	*He can't (speak) German.*
Sie kann das schon.	*She can already (do it).*

8.2.5 Asking questions about ability

Questions about ability can be asked either by inverting the verb or by using one of the words we learned in Unit 1.

Kannst du Schach spielen?	*Can you play chess?*
Können sie nicht länger warten?	*Can't they wait any longer?*
Wie kann ich Ihnen helfen?	*How can I help you?*
Wer kann kochen?	*Who can cook?*

8.2.6 Here is the full form of the verb **können**:

Singular	*Plural*
Ich kann *I can/am able to*	wir können *we can/are able to*
du kannst *you can/are able to*	ihr könnt *you can/are able to*
er kann *he can/is able to*	Sie können *you can/are able to*
sie kann *she can/is able to*	sie können *they can/are able to*
es kann *it can/is able to*	

8.3 Im Kontext:

8.3.1 An interview for a job

Der Chef   Guten Morgen, Frau Braun! Sie dürfen gerne Platz nehmen. Darf ich fragen: Warum wollen Sie bei uns arbeiten?

Frau Braun   Also, ich kann fließend Französisch sprechen, und ich kann sowohl auf Französisch als auch auf Deutsch Geschäftsbriefe schreiben.

Der Chef   Sie können auch Englisch, oder?

Frau Braun   Nein, leider nicht. Aber mein Mann und ich wollen es lernen.

Der Chef   Möchten Sie etwas fragen?

Frau Braun Darf man im Büro rauchen?
Der Chef Aber ja. Wir können alle nicht ohne Zigaretten arbeiten.
Können Sie gleich bei uns anfangen?

fließend Französisch *fluent French*	**das Büro** *the office*
sowohl ... als auch *both ... and*	**rauchen** *to smoke*
auf Französisch *in French*	**ohne** *without*
auf Deutsch *in German*	**die Zigarette** *the cigarette*
der Geschäftsbrief *business letter*	**gleich** *immediately*
leider nicht *unfortunately not*	**anfangen** *to begin, start*
etwas fragen *to ask something/anything*	

Machen wir weiter!

Some other expressions which suggest permission given:

ruhig *feel free to, you're welcome to* (– normally means 'calm, quiet')

Du kannst den Rest des Essens ruhig mitnehmen.

Feel free to take the rest of the food with you.

ohne weiteres *it's quite all right, it's no problem*

Er kann **ohne weiteres** hereinkommen.

It's quite all right for him to come in.

von mir (uns) aus *as far as I am/we are concerned*

Von uns aus kannst du nach dem Faschingsball bei Trudi schlafen.

As far as we are concerned, you can sleep at Trudi's after the Carnival Ball

schon *of course, it's all right* (no exact English equivalent)

Du kannst schon gehen.

You can go.

8.4 The indefinite pronoun man

The indefinite pronoun **man**, which translates into English as *one* or *you* is often found with one of these modal verbs. Look at the following:

Man darf hier rauchen.   *You can smoke here.*
Man kann nur hoffen.   *One can only hope.*
Man muss in der Schlange warten.   *You have to wait in the queue.*

Man soll nicht gleich nach dem   *You shouldn't go swimming*
Essen schwimmen.   *straight after a meal.*
Kann man hier Briefmarken kaufen?   *Can you buy stamps here?*

8.5 Jetzt sind Sie dran!

Aufgabe A

In der Jugendherberge (*in the Youth Hostel*)

You have arrived in a Youth Hostel with a group of teenagers and are being told the house rules by the warden (**Herbergsvater**). Read the passage and answer the questions.

Ihr dürft bis 22 Uhr fernsehen und bis 20 Uhr die Waschmaschine benutzen. Es kann sein, dass jemand von euch Klavier spielen kann. Wenn ja, dürft ihr gern das Klavier bis 21 Uhr im Aufenthaltsraum benutzen. Zwischen 20 und 22 Uhr darf man in der kleinen Küche Tee, Kaffee, usw. kochen aber bitte, niemand darf die große Küche benutzen. Frühstück gibt es von 6-8 Uhr morgens. Darf ich euch jetzt bitten, eure Rucksäcke in eure Schlafzimmer zu bringen.

1 What three things are you allowed to do in the evening?
2 What is nobody allowed to do?
3 What final request does the Youth Hostel warden make?

Answers:

1.a) watch television until 10.00 pm b) use the washing machine until 8.00 pm c) play the piano until 9.00 pm 2. use the large kitchen 3. to take their rucksacks to their rooms.

Aufgabe B

Der Ausflug (*excursion*)

Tante Inge has a young godchild, Renate. While Renate's mother is in hospital she takes her and her friend Anna to the zoo for the day. In the following excited conversation fill in each gap with the appropriate form of either **dürfen** or **können**:

Anna   … wir die Tiere füttern? (*dürfen*)
Tante Inge   Ihr … sicher einige Tiere füttern aber nicht alle. (*dürfen*)
Renate   … ich ein Eis haben, bitte? (*dürfen*)

Anna (aufgeregt)	Oh, ich … einen Elefanten sehen! (können) … du ihn auch sehen, Renate? (*können*)
Renate	… der Elefant unser Brot essen? (*dürfen*)
Tante Inge	Wie bitte? Ach, es ist hier so laut! Ich … dich nicht hören, Renate! (*können*) Ich frage den Zoowärter. Entschuldigen Sie, … Sie uns sagen (*können*), ob wir den Elefanten füttern …? (*dürfen*)
Zoowärter	Selbstverständlich.
Renate	Tante Inge, … ich bitte Mutti anrufen und ihr alles erzählen? (*dürfen*)

die Tiere *animals*		**so laut** *so loud, so noisy*	
füttern *to feed*		**fragen** *to ask*	
einige *some*		**der Zoowärter** *zoo keeper*	
ein Eis *an ice-cream*		**entschuldigen** *to excuse*	
aufgeregt *excitedly*		**selbstverständlich** *but of course*	
der Elefant *elephant* (*accusative*		**an/rufen** *to telephone*	
den Elefanten, weak noun, see		**erzählen** *to tell, relate*	
Reference Grammar 2.4)			

Antworten

Anna	Dürfen wir die Tiere füttern?
Tante Inge	Ihr dürft sicher einige Tiere füttern, aber nicht alle.
Renate	Darf ich ein Eis haben, bitte?
Anna (aufgeregt)	Oh, ich kann einen Elefanten sehen! Kannst du ihn sehen, Renate?
Renate	Darf der Elefant unser Brot essen?
Tante Inge	Wie bitte? Ach, es ist hier so laut! Ich kann dich nicht hören, Renate! Ich frage den Zoowärter. Entschuldigen Sie, können Sie uns sagen, ob wir den Elefanten füttern dürfen?
Zoowärter	Selbstverständlich.
Renate	Tante Inge, darf ich bitte Mutti anrufen und ihr alles erzählen?

9 | EXPRESSING OBLIGATION AND NECCESSITY

9.1 Preliminary Note

The verb **sollen** can be translated into English in many different ways, but its main use is to express moral obligation in the sense of *I am obliged to, I should, I am supposed to, I am expected to, I am to.*

It is interesting to note that the Ten Commandments are expressed by means of **sollen**: **Du sollst nicht töten** can be translated as *Thou shalt not kill,* or *You ought not to kill, you are obliged not to kill, You shouldn't kill* or *You are not supposed to kill.* This verb strongly expresses moral obligation but it still allows you to decide whether to obey or not.

Look at the following examples and their translations:

Ich soll schöne Grüße von Antje bestellen.	*I am to pass on Antje's best wishes.*
Sie soll zum Arzt gehen.	*She should go to the doctor.*
Wir sollen nicht zu lange bleiben.	*We oughtn't to stay too late.*

To obey or not to obey, that is the question!

In fact, German uses two forms of **sollen** to show how obedient you really are! Look at the following sentences using the two forms of **sollen** and their English translations, and see if you can work out the difference in their meanings:

Ich soll keine Schokolade essen.	*I am not supposed to eat any chocolate* (and so I wouldn't dream of it).
Ich sollte nicht so viel Schokolade essen.	*I ought not to eat so much chocolate* (but I like it so much, who cares!).
Der Hund soll draußen warten.	*The dog should wait outside* (so I'll tie him up outside).
Der Hund sollte aber draußen warten.	*The dog ought to wait outside* (It's unhygienic to bring it in here!)
Sie sollen schon um 8 Uhr da sein.	*They're supposed to be there by 8 o'clock* (and I expect they will be).
Sie sollten um 8 Uhr da sein.	*They were supposed to be there at 8 o'clock* (so where on earth are they?)

In some situations these two forms can be interchangeable, as in the following example:

Sie soll(te) zum Arzt gehen.	*She ought to go to the doctor's.*

Some of the examples above used the subjunctive version of **sollen**, i.e. sollten. For more details about its use and formation see Unit 21.

9.2 Grammar Summary

9.2.1 Now look at the full verb form of **sollen** (You will notice that, unlike the other modal verbs we have come across, **sollen** has the same vowel in the singular as in the plural. It is, however, similar to the other five modal verbs in that the first and the third person singular have no ending.)

Singular	Plural
ich soll *I ought to/am obliged to/should*	wir sollen *we ought to*, etc.
du sollst *you ought to*, etc.	ihr sollt *you ought to*, etc.
er soll *he ought to*, etc.	Sie sollen *you ought to*, etc.
sie soll *she ought to*, etc.	sie sollen *they ought to*, etc.
es soll *it ought to*, etc.	

9.2.2 Expressing compulsion or necessity using müssen

To a certain extent there is an overlap in the usage of the verbs **müssen** and **sollen**, in that **müssen** can sometimes express obligation in the sense of *I must*, *I have to*; but **müssen** is normally used to express compulsion or necessity rather than obligation. Look at the following examples using **müssen** to work out the possible meanings of the verb:

Ich muss mal zum Klo gehen (colloquial).	*I must go/I've got to go to the loo.*
Du musst fleißig arbeiten.	*You must/you've got to work hard.*
Er muss jeden Tag zwölf Tabletten nehmen.	*He has to take twelve pills every day.*

You can use this verb in questions in the same way we have learned in previous units:

Was muss ich jetzt machen?	*What do I have to do now?*
Müssen wir noch einkaufen?	*Do we still have to go shopping?*
Warum müssen Sie so früh gehen?	*What do you have to go so early?*

9.2.3 Expressing lack of necessity using müssen

When used with a negative, **müssen** expresses the idea of lack of necessity, as the following examples show :

Ich muss nicht abnehmen.	*I don't need to lose weight.*
Sie muss heute nicht in die Schule gehen.	*She doesn't have to go to school today.*
Sie müssen nicht länger bleiben.	*You don't have to stay any longer.*

9.2.4 Here is the full form of the verb **müssen**

Singular	*Plural*
ich muss *I must, I have to, I've got to*	wir müssen *we must,* etc.
du musst *you must,* etc.	ihr müsst *you must,* etc.
er muss *he must,* etc.	Sie müssen *you must,* etc.
sie muss *she must,* etc.	sie müssen *they must,* etc.
es muss *it must,* etc.	

9.3 Im Kontext:

9.3.1 *Enquiring about a visa to go to Russia*

Beamter   Grüß Gott! Wie kann ich helfen?

Reisende   Muss ich ein Visum für diese Reise nach Russland haben, bitte?

Beamter   Ja. Sie brauchen nur dieses Formular auszufüllen, und Sie müssen es an die russische Botschaft schicken. Sie können dann einen Monat da bleiben. Sie dürfen aber nicht länger bleiben. Wann wollen Sie dorthin fahren?

Reisende   Im Juni. Soll ich das Formular hier ausfüllen?

Beamter   Nein. Ich darf das nicht abfertigen. Man muss das in der Botschaft stempeln lassen. Übrigens brauchen Sie drei Fotos und einen Scheck. Sie sollen das alles wegschicken. Aber Sie dürfen nicht zu lange warten. Es dauert sehr lange, ein Visum zu bekommen.

Reisende   Vielen Dank für Ihre Hilfe.

Beamter   Gern geschehen.

9.4 Machen wir weiter! *Let's continue!*

9.4.1 Nicht dürfen *in the sense of must not*

We have already learned that the verb **dürfen** expresses permission. However, when it is used in the negative, it means *must not*, expressing a prohibition.

helfen *to help*	**hier** *here*
das Visum *visa*	**stempeln lassen** *to have*
diese Reise *this journey, trip*	*something stamped*
das Formular ausfüllen *to fill in*	**übrigens** *by the way, incidentally*
the form	**das Foto** *photo*
die russische Botschaft *the*	**der Scheck** *cheque*
Russian Embassy	**das alles** *all that*
ab/fertigen *to process, clear*	**weg/schicken** *to send away*
schicken *to send*	**zu lange** *too long*
der Monat *month*	**es dauert** *it takes (time)*
da *there*	**Vielen Dank für Ihre Hilfe.**
bleiben *to stay*	*Many thanks for your help.*
nicht länger *not any longer*	**Gern geschehen.** *You're*
im Juni *in June*	*welcome/It's a pleasure.*

Compare the examples on page 88 using **müssen** with these below, which use the negative form of **dürfen**:

Ich darf nicht zu viel essen.	*I must not eat too much.*
Man darf im Restaurant nicht rauchen.	*You mustn't smoke in the restaurant.*
Sie dürfen nichts sagen.	*You mustn't say anything.*

9.4.2 *The verb* brauchen *(to need to)*

Another verb which is used in a similar way to a modal verb is **brauchen** (to need to). This is a regular verb and its forms follow the pattern of **spielen** or **kochen** in 5.2.1).

Look at the following sentences and compare them with those above:

Ich brauche nicht länger (zu) warten.	*I don't need to wait any longer.*
Das brauchst du nicht (zu) wiederholen.	*You don't need to repeat that.*
Er braucht nicht nach Prag (zu) fahren.	*He doesn't need to go to Prague.*

You will notice the **zu** in brackets. Unlike the traditional modal verbs **brauchen** really needs the word **zu** to express the idea I don't need to. In modern usage it has been influenced by the modal verbs and so the **zu** is often omitted, for example:

Er braucht nicht zur Bank gehen.	*He doesn't need to go to the bank.*
Man braucht einen gültigen Paß aber kein Visum.	*You need a valid passport but no visa.*

In this respect **brauchen** can be considered to be an honorary modal verb but it also has other usages, for example when it simply means 'to need' or 'to require'.

9.5 Jetzt sind Sie dran!

Aufgabe A (See Reference Grammar 9.2)

You are visiting a relative in hospital. She has had a stroke and her speech is confused. Can you make full sense of what she is saying by incorporating the correct form of the modal verb into each sentence? The modal verb is given in brackets at the end. Remember you will also have to put the finite verb into the infinitive.

1 Ich sehe nicht gut (**können**) *I cannot see well.*
2 Ich stehe nicht alleine (**können**) *I cannot stand on my own.*
3 Ich bleibe im Bett (**müssen**) *I have to stay in bed.*
4 Ich nehme diese Tabletten dreimal am Tag (**müssen**) *I have to take these tablets three times daily.*
5 Ich rauche nicht (**dürfen**) *I'm not allowed to smoke.*
6 Ich trinke keinen Alkohol (**dürfen**) *I am not allowed to drink alcohol.*
7 Ich esse nicht soviel Schokalade (**sollen**) *I am not supposed to eat so much chocolate.*
8 Ich mache jeden Tag Krankengymnastik (**sollen**) *I ought to do physiotherapy every day.*
9 Ich gehe sofort nach Hause (**wollen**) *I want to go home straightaway.*
10 Ich schlafe jetzt (**wollen**) *I want to sleep now.*

Antworten

1 Ich kann nicht gut sehen.
2 Ich kann nicht alleine stehen.
3 Ich muss im Bett bleiben.
4 Ich muss diese Tabletten dreimal am Tag nehmen.
5 Ich darf nicht rauchen.
6 Ich darf keinen Alkohol trinken.
7 Ich soll nicht soviel Schokolade essen.
8 Ich soll jeden Tag Krankengymnastik machen.
9 Ich will sofort nach Hause gehen.
10 Ich will jetzt schlafen.

Aufgabe B

Berufsberatung (*careers advice*)

You are looking for a job and need to tell the careers adviser what your expectations are. Complete the folowing sentences by filling the gaps with the appropriate part of the modal verb given in brackets at the end of the sentence.

1 Ich ... im Freien arbeiten (*wollen*)
2 Die Arbeit ... interessant sein (*sollen*)
3 Ich ... jeden Tag arbeiten (*können*)
4 Ich ... nichts Schweres heben (*dürfen*)
5 Ich ... Geld verdienen (*müssen*)

Antworten

1 Ich will im Freien arbeiten. *I want to work in the open air.*
2 Die Arbeit soll interessant sein. *The work should be interesting.*
3 Ich kann jeden Tag arbeiten. *I can work every day.*
4 Ich darf nichts Schweres heben. *I am not allowed to lift anything heavy.*
5 Ich muss viel Geld verdienen. *I must earn a lot of money.*

10 ASKING FOR AND GIVING OPINIONS

10.1 Preliminary Note

The aim of this unit is to teach you how to ask people what they think about something or somebody and to give opinions regarding what you or others think.

Asking for and giving opinions

Using the verb finden

The simplest way to ask for and give opinions is to use the verb **finden** (*to find*). Look at the following questions and anwers:

Wie findest du seinen Sohn?	*What do you think of his son?* (Literally, 'How do you find his son?').
Sehr frech!	*Very cheeky!*
Wie finden Sie Augsburg?	*What do you think of Augsburg?*
Sehr interessant!	*Very interesting.*
Nicht schlecht.	*Not bad.*

Using the verb glauben (to believe)

Glaubst du, dass er das machen kann?	*Do you believe/think that he can do it?*
Ich glaube schon.	*I believe so/I think so.*
Glauben Sie, dass er heute kommt?	*Do you think that he will come today?*
Ich glaube kaum.	*I scarcely think so.*

Using the verb denken (to think)

Although this verb means *to think*, it is used much less frequently than its English counterpart, and is often replaced by **glauben** or **meinen**.

Ich denke nicht, dass er mich vermisst.	*I don't think he's missing me.*
Sollen wir bleiben? Was denken Sie?	*Should we stay? What do you think?*
Sie denkt, ich habe genug Geld dazu.	*She thinks I have enough money for it.*

Using the verb meinen

Meinen is used very frequently to ask for and give opinions, and can be translated *to think, to believe, to reckon, to mean*.

Was meinen Sie zu diesem Vorschlag?	*What do you think of this suggestion?*
Was meint sie zu dieser Sache?	*What does she think about this matter?*
Was meinst du (dazu)?	*What do you think (about it)?*
Meint ihr, dass das vernünftig ist?	*Do you think that's sensible?*

There are many possible answers to the above questions but the following are frequently used:

Ich meine ja.	*I think so.*
Ich meine nein.	*I don't think so.*
Ich meine nicht.	*I think not.*
Ich meine, wir sollen ihn annehmen.	*I think we ought to accept it.*

Using the noun Meinung

The noun **die Meinung** is closely connected to the above verb, and is used very often to ask for or express opinions.

Was ist Ihre Meinung dazu?	*What's your opinion about that?*
Welche Meinung haben Sie dazu?	*What opinion do you have on the matter?*
Meiner Meinung nach sollten wir weitermachen.	*In my opinion we ought to continue.*
Ich bin der Meinung, dass wir weitermachen sollten.	*I am of the opinion that we ought to continue.*
Das ist auch meine Meinung!	*That's just what I think!*

10.2 Grammar Summary

10.2.1 Constructing a more complex sentence using the conjunction dass

A sentence can consist of one or more clauses and a conjunction. The latter is a linking word that joins two clauses together to form one sentence. **Dass** is an example of a so-called subordinating conjunction and is very similar to the English word *that* in a sentence such as 'I think *that* dangerous dogs should wear a muzzle', 'He firmly believes *that* she should resign'. (Note that in colloquial English usage *that* is often left out.) You will notice in the following examples that **dass** sends the verb to the end of the clause and that there is a comma in front of it:

Glauben Sie, **dass** er **kommt**?	*Do you think that he will come?*
Ich meine, **dass** wir gleich abfahren **sollten**.	*I think we ought to set off straight away.*
Sie denkt, **dass** wir das leicht **schaffen**.	*She thinks that we will manage it easily.*

Other conjunctions follow this same pattern, for example

weil *because*
wenn *if, when, whenever*
ob *whether*
obwohl *although*
als *when, when talking about the past*

Ich kaufe das Auto doch nicht, **weil** es zu teuer **ist**.	*I won't buy the car because it's too expensive.*
Er kommt nicht, **wenn** es **regnet**.	*He won't come if it's raining.*

Sie möchte wissen, **ob** es morgen **schneit**.	*She would like to know whether it will snow tomorrow.*
Sie wollen Ski fahren, **obwohl** es wenig Schnee **gibt**.	*They want to ski, even though there's little snow.*
Wir bestiegen den Eiffel-Turm, **als** wir in Paris **waren**.	*We climbed the Eiffel Tower when we were in Paris.*

(For further details on subordinating conjunctions, see Reference Grammar 15)

10.2.2 Idiomatic use of die Meinung and die Überzeugung

In the examples shown in this unit we see the noun **die Meinung** used in various cases :

1. In the example **Das ist meine Meinung**, that's my opinion, the nominative case is used because it follows the verb **sein**.

2. **Meiner Meinung nach** ist das ungerecht, *in my opinion that is unjust* (literally, 'according to my opinion'): the preposition **nach** puts **Meinung** into the dative case (even though it occurs after the noun in this example).

3. The genitive case is used in the example:

Ich bin der Meinung, dass wir weitermachen sollen, *I am* of the *opinion that we should continue.*

Die Überzeugung (*conviction*) can be used in the same ways, e.g. **Meiner Überzeugung nach** soll man Atomkraft verbieten, *I am convinced that atomic power should be banned.*

10.2.3 Some other examples of expressing strongly held opinions or firm convictions:

überzeugt sein *to be convinced*

Ich bin davon überzeugt, dass Kinder schon mit fünf Jahren in die Schule gehen sollen.	*I'm convinced that children ought to go to school at five (years of age).*
Er ist fest davon überzeugt, dass man vegetarisch essen soll.	*He's firmly convinced that one ought to eat a vegetarian diet.*

halten von *to think about*

Was halten Sie von dem neuen Direktor?	*What do you think of/make of the new headteacher?*
Ich halte nicht sehr viel von Frau Schmidt, aber ich schätze ihren Mann sehr.	*I don't think much of Mrs. Smith but I value/regard her husband highly.*

auf dem Standpunkt stehen *to take the view that*

Er steht auf dem Standpunkt, dass Kinder unter 16 Jahren spätestens um zehn Uhr zu Hause sein sollten.	*He takes the view that children under 16 should be home by 10 o'clock at the latest.*

10.3 Im Kontext

10.3.1 Read the following interview with an author who specialises in writing **Jugendliteratur** (*literature for young people*).

Interviewer Also, Frau Asbach, warum schreiben Sie für Jugendliche und nicht für Erwachsene?

F.A Ich bin der festen Meinung, dass unsere Jugend über ihre Geschichte Bescheid wissen sollte, und auch dass sie Verständnis für die heutigen Probleme haben sollen. Dann wird sie, glaube ich, nicht die gleichen Fehler wie ihre Eltern machen.

Interviewer Wie finden Sie unsere Jugend?

F.A Im allgemeinen, durchaus nett. Aber ich meine, dass alle jungen Leute ein Ziel brauchen. Leider haben viele kein Ziel. Das ist das Problem.

Interviewer Sie haben sicher recht. Herzlichen Dank!

Jugendliche *young people, youth*	**die gleichen Fehler machen** *to make the same mistakes*
Erwachsene *adults*	
die Jugend *youth*	**im Allgemeinen** *in general*
Bescheid wissen *to know about*	**durchaus nett** *thoroughly/perfectly nice*
die Geschichte *history*	
das Verständnis *understanding, sympathy*	**das Ziel** *goal*
	brauchen *to need*
heutig *today's, of today*	**recht haben** *to be right*
das Problem *the problem*	**Herzlichen Dank!** *Many thanks!*

10.4 Machen wir weiter

10.4.1 The use of dazu, darüber, dafür, dagegen, etc.

In some of the examples in this unit we came across **da-** words such as **dazu**, **darüber**, **dafür** and **dagegen** in the sense of *with it, about it, for it, against it*. These are prepositional compounds, and are normally used when referring to a thing rather a person (for a person personal pronouns are used; see 6.4.1 and Reference Grammar 4). This compound form is made up of the preposition you wish to use, e.g. **in, an, mit, über**, preceded by **da**. If the preposition starts with a vowel, e.g. **über**, a linking **r** is required in the middle: **darüber**, **darin**, (*in it*) **daran** (*on it*), **darunter** (*under it*) for ease of pronunciation. In the spoken language these can be shortened to **drüber**, **drin**, **dran**, **drunter**. This is similar to the old-fashioned English usage of *thereafter*, *thereupon*.

Look at the following examples:

Ich bin **dazu** bereit.	*I am prepared **for that** (for it).*
Er ist **damit** einverstanden.	*He is in agreement **with it**.*
Sie ist **davon** nicht überzeugt.	*She is not convinced **about it**.*
Wir wollen lieber nicht **daran** denken.	*Let's (preferably) not think **about it**.*

Note: A question form of this compound can be constructed by substituting **wo-**, (or **wor-** before a preposition beginning with a vowel) for **da**, giving, for example:

Woran denken Sie?	*What are you thinking **about**?*
Womit schreibst du?	*What are you writing **with**?*
Wovon (**Worüber**) redet ihr?	*What are you talking **about**?*

Note also: In German the **wo-** or **wor-** can never be separated from the preposition – something which is possible in English.

10.5 Jetzt sind Sie dran!

Aufgabe A

Rewrite the following sentences, replacing the bold phrases with a compound beginning with **da(r)-**:

1 Er fährt immer **mit dem Fahrrad**. *He always goes by bike.*
   Er fährt immer ......
2 Ich denke ungern **an den Unfall**. *I don't like thinking about the accident.*
   Ich denke ungern ......
3 Die Lampe steht dicht **neben dem Fernseher**. *The lamp is right next to the television.*
   Die Lampe steht dicht ......
4 Der Kellner stellt das Glas Wasser **auf den Tisch**. *The waiter puts the glass onto the table.*
   Der Kellner stellt das Glas Wasser ......
5 Meine Tante findet ihr Sparbuch **unter dem Bett**. *My aunt finds her bankbook under the bed.*
   Meine Tante findet ihr Sparbuch ......
6 Die Mülltonne ist **hinter der Garage**. *The dustbin is behind the garage.*
   Die Mülltonne ist ......
7 Der Gärtner pflanzt Frühlingsblumen **zwischen den Bäumen**. *The gardener plants spring flowers between the trees.*
   Der Gärtner pflanzt Frühlingsblumen ......
8 Wir essen Pizza **nach dem Film**. *We are going to eat some pizza after the film.*
   Wir essen Pizza ......
9 Er spricht gar nicht **über sein Problem**. *He doesn't talk about his problem at all.*
   Er spricht gar nicht ......
10 Es ist ein Hundertmarkschein **in dem Umschlag**. *There is DM 100 note in the envelope.*
   Es gibt einen Hundertmarkschein ......

Antworten

1. Er fährt immer damit. 2. Ich denke ungern daran. 3. Die Lampe steht dicht daneben. 4. Der Kellner stellt das Glas Wasser darauf. 5. Meine Tante findet ihr Sparbuch darunter. 6. Die Mülltonne ist dahinter. 7. Der Gärtner pflanzt Frühlingsblumen dazwischen. 8. Wir essen Pizza danach. 9. Er spricht gar nicht darüber. 10. Es ist ein Hundertmarkschein darin.

Aufgabe B

Die wahre Liebe *True Love*

Jutta is telling Jürgen some home truths. Take the part of the long-suffering Jürgen, who replies that he already knows. For example:

Jutta   Du bist sehr faul! *You're very lazy!*
Jürgen Ich weiß, dass ich sehr faul bin. *I know that I am very lazy.*

1. **Jutta**   Du bist zu dick! *You're too fat!*
   Jürgen _____

2. **Jutta**   Deine ganze Kleidung ist alle altmodisch! *Your clothes are all old-fashioned!*
   Jürgen _____

3. **Jutta**   Du hast keine Hobbys! *You have no hobbies!*
   Jürgen _____

4. **Jutta**   Du machst nichts Vernünftiges! *You don't do anything sensible!*
   Jürgen _____

5. **Jutta**   Ich liebe dich sehr! *I love you very much!*
   Jürgen _____

Antworten

1. Ich weiß, dass ich zu dick bin. 2. Ich weiß, dass meine ganze Kleidung altmodisch ist. 3. Ich weiß, dass ich keine Hobbys habe. 4. Ich weiß, dass ich nichts Vernünftiges mache. 5. Ich weiß, dass du mich sehr liebst!

11 | TALKING ABOUT HABITUAL ACTIONS

11.1 Preliminary Note

To ask for and give information about habitual actions, for instance, *Do you get up early? I get up late*, you will need the present tense. When talking about personal body care and hygiene a reflexive verb is often used in German, where sometimes none would be used in English e.g. *I wash (myself), He shaves (himself), You don't clean (to yourself) your teeth*. These verbs can be either regular or irregular, separable or inseparable.

Talking about personal routine

Ich wiege mich einmal die Woche.	*I weigh myself once a week.*
Du wäscht dich nicht oft genug!	*You don't wash (yourself) often enough!*
Er rasiert sich jeden Morgen.	*He shaves (himself) every morning.*

Note If you wish to talk about washing or combing *your hair* or brushing or cleaning *your teeth*, the German structure is even more different from the English. Look at these examples and their translations:

Ich wasche mir täglich das Haar.	*I wash my hair daily* (literally, 'I wash to myself daily the hair').
Am besten putzt man sich nach jeder Mahlzeit die Zähne.	*It's best to clean your teeth after every meal* (literally, 'It's best one cleans to oneself the teeth').

Asking and answering questions about routine

Stehen Sie früh auf?	*Do you get up early?*
Nein, ich stehe spät auf.	*No, I get up late.*
Was machst du normalerweise am Abend?	*What do you normally do in the evening?*
Normalerweise lese ich.	*I normally read.*
Wie oft geht ihr ins Kino?	*How often do you go to the cinema?*
Zweimal die Woche.	*Twice a week.*

Relating a sequence of habitual actions

Zuerst wasche ich mich, dann ziehe ich mich an, esse schnell eine Scheibe Toast und gehe aus dem Haus.	*First of all I get washed, then I get dressed, quickly eat a slice of toast and leave the house.*
Zuerst grüße ich meinen Chef, dann lese ich die Post, spreche mit meiner Sekretärin und rufe meine Kunden an. Schließlich beginne ich mit der Arbeit!	*First of all I greet to the boss, then I read the post, talk to my secretary and phone my clients. Finally I start work.*

Asking for and giving more precise information about specific time

■ If you wish to say at exactly what time something will happen eg. at six o'clock, at half past ten, at 10.25 p.m., use the word **um**:

Der letzte Zug von Saarbrücken kommt **um** 22.15 auf Gleis 3 an.	*The last train from Saarbrücken arrives at 10.15 p.m. on platform 3.* (Notice that Germany uses the twenty-four-hour clock).

■ If you wish to say 'from six to seven o'clock' you can use **von ... bis** (*from ... till*):

Dr. Müller hat **von** neun **bis** zwölf Sprechstunde.

Dr. Müller's surgery (consulting hours) is from nine till twelve.

■ Use the preposition **zwischen** to translate 'between two and four o'clock':

Die Anmeldung ist zwischen zwei und vier Uhr.

Registration is between two and four o'clock.

Wie spät ist es? Wieviel Uhr ist es? *(What time is it?)*

Have a look at the following examples of times, paying particular attention to the way German expresses half past the hour:

Es ist genau acht Uhr	*It's exactly eight o'clock.*
Er kommt um dreizehn Uhr an.	*He's arriving at 1 p.m.*
Es ist eine Minute vor elf	*It's one minute to eleven (literally 'before eleven')*
Es ist zwei Minuten nach sieben.	*It's two minutes past seven (literally 'after seven')*
Die Schule beginnt um Viertel vor acht.	*School begins at a quarter to eight*
Es ist Viertel nach sechs.	*It's a quarter past six.*
Es ist halb fünf.	*It's half past four (i.e. 'half-way to five o'clock'.)*
Es ist fast halb neun.	*It's almost half past eight.*
Es war kurz vor Mittag.	*It was shortly before mid-day.*
Es war kurz nach Mitternacht.	*It was shortly after mid night.*
Ich komme um zwanzig Uhr.	*I'll come at eight in the evening.*

Notice two ways of saying It is 6.25:

Es ist fünfundzwanzig Minuten nach sechs or
Es ist fünf vor halb sieben.

Study the following questions and answers which give details of specific times:

Wann kommt der nächste Bus? Um elf Uhr.

When is the next bus? At eleven o'clock.

Wann beginnt die Tagesschau am Samstag? Um zwanzig Uhr.

When does the TV news start on Saturday? At 8 p.m. (20.00).

Wann beginnt die Schule am Montag? Um Viertel vor acht.

When does school begin on Monday? At a quarter to eight.

| Wann verlasst ihr das Haus? Um zwanzig vor acht. | *When do you leave home? At twenty to eight.* |
| Wann kommen wir in Interlaken an? Um halb drei. | *When do we arrive in Interlaken? At half past two ('half-way to three o'clock').* |

| Wann endet die Tagung am Freitag? Um Viertel nach fünf. | *When does the conference finish on Friday? At 5.15.* |
| Wann esst ihr am Sonntag? Punkt zwölf! | *When do you eat on Sunday? On the dot of twelve!* |

11.2 Grammar Summary

11.2.1 *Reflexive verbs (Reference Grammar 9.5)*

Reflexive verbs give the idea of doing something either for oneself, or to oneself e.g. *I wash myself, He has cut himself.* Their use in German is different from that in English. Reflexive verbs can be regular or irregular verbs, separable or inseparable. The reflexive verb consists of the normal verb form plus a reflexive pronoun (*myself, yourself, herself*, etc.)

11.2.2 *Reflexive verbs with an accusative reflexive pronoun (Reference Grammar 9.5.1)*

Many reflexive verbs use the pronoun in the accusative case, because the pronoun is the direct object of the verb. For example:

Sie wäscht sich nie mit Seife.	*She never washes herself with soap.*
Er wäscht sich im Badezimmer.	*He's washing himself in the bathroom.*
Ich ziehe mich jetzt um.	*I'll change* (my clothes) *now.*

Notice the word order in the question form:

| Rasierst du dich schon? | *Are you shaving* (yourself) *already?* |

---

sich waschen *to wash oneself*

Singular

ich wasche **mich** *I wash myself*
du wäschst **dich** *you wash yourself*
er wäscht **sich** *he washes himself*
sie wäscht **sich** *she washes herself*

Plural

wir waschen **uns** *we wash ourselves*
ihr wascht **euch** *you wash yourselves*
Sie waschen **sich** *you wash yourself*
sie waschen **sich** *they wash themselves*

11.2.3 Reflexive verbs with a dative reflexive pronoun (Reference Grammar 9.5.3)

When you wish to express an idea concerned with personal care such as *I wash my hair*, *He cleans his teeth*, *She washes her hands*, *They brush their teeth*, a reflexive verb with a dative reflexive pronoun is often used in German. You will notice that apart from the first and second person singular forms (**mir** and **dir**), these pronouns are the same as for **sich waschen**.

---

sich die Hände waschen *to wash your hands*

Singular

ich wasche **mir** die Hände	*I wash my hands*
du wäschst **dir** die Hände	*you wash your hands*
er wäscht **sich** die Hände	*he washes his hands*
sie wäscht **sich** die Hände	*she washes her hands*

Plural

wir waschen **uns** die Hände	*we wash our hands*
ihr wäscht **euch** die Hände	*you wash your hands*
Sie waschen **sich** die Hände	*you wash your hands*
sie waschen **sich** die Hände	*they wash their hands*

You will notice that instead of the possessive adjective *my, his, her, their*, etc, German uses a definite or an indefinite article:

Er putzt sich regelmäßig **die** Zähne.	*He cleans his teeth regularly.*
Ich muss mir **das** Haar waschen.	*I've got to wash my hair.*
Aber zuerst wäschst du dir **das** Gesicht, verstehst du!	*But, you'll wash your face first, you understand!*

11.2.4 Adverbs

Note: In the above examples about routine, notice that each sentence contains a word or phrase which shows frequency or time, e.g.

einmal die Woche *once a week*
zuerst *first of all*
nicht oft genug *not often enough*
jeden Morgen *every morning*
vor dem Abendessen *before supper/dinner*

This is known as an adverb or adverbial phrase, because it adds to the verb by enhancing or expanding its meaning.

11.3 Im Kontext

11.3.1 Read this extract from a letter from Thorsten in which he writes about his new life as a student.

Ich bin schon eine Woche hier in Heidelberg, und ich wohne mit vier anderen Studenten in einem Haus. Es ist ein bisschen eng aber es macht nichts. Ich stehe als Erster auf und zwar um halb acht. Ich wasche mich, aber ich rasiere mich nicht. Ich lasse mir einen Bart wachsen! Dann esse ich schnell eine Scheibe Brot und trinke eine Tasse Kaffee und fahre mit dem Bus zur Uni. (Ich glaube, ich kaufe mir ein Rad – dann spare ich Geld und ich bin schneller da.) Die erste Vorlesung beginnt um neun und dauert eine Stunde. Meistens habe ich zwei oder drei Vorlesungen pro Tag, aber am Freitag habe ich keine!

Zu Mittag esse ich in der Mensa und danach arbeite ich in der UB (Universitätsbibliothek). Am späten Nachmittag gehe ich im Park joggen, und nachher dusche ich mich. Am Abend koche ich manchmal eine Suppe oder Nudeln, oder ich kaufe eine Pizza und ich gehe erst spät ins Bett.

---

das Haus *house*
ein bisschen eng *a bit cramped*
es macht nichts (colloquial) *it doesn't matter*
auf/stehen *to get up*
Ich lasse mir einen Bart wachsen *I'm growing a beard* (literally, 'I'm letting a beard grow')
die Scheibe *slice*
das Brot *bread*
die Uni (Universität) *university*
das (Fahr)rad *bicycle*
Geld sparen *to save money*

die Vorlesung *lecture*
dauern *to last*
schneller *more quickly*
zu Mittag *at midday*
die Mensa *refectory*
die Universitätsbibliothek *university library*
sich duschen *to take a shower*
am Abend *in the evening*
manchmal *sometimes*
erst spät *not until late*
ins Bett gehen *to go to bed*

11.4 Machen wir weiter!

The use of **um...zu + infinitive**, *in order to...*

Look at these two examples, which both have the same meaning:

Ich muss fleißig arbeiten, **um**   *I must work hard in order to learn*
  Deutsch **zu lernen**.   *German.*

Um Deutsch zu lernen, muss ich fleißig arbeiten.

Did you notice the verb–comma–verb construction, i.e. **... lernen, muss** ..., in the second example?

Another similar construction is **ohne zu ... + infinitive**, *without + -ing*

Er verließ das Restaurant, **ohne**   *He left the restaurant without*
  zu bezahlen.   *paying.*

Ohne zu bezahlen, verließ er das Restaurant.

11.5 Jetzt sind Sie dran!

For the following exercise you will need to know numbers. Full details of cardinal numbers, used for showing quantity and in counting are to be found in Reference grammar 8.1.

Aufgabe A

At what time do the following activites take place?

Zum Beispiel

1 Wann beginnt der Film?

Antwort: Um fünfundzwanzig (Minuten) nach sechs. *At twenty five past six.*

2 Wann beginnt die Schule?

3 Wann fährt der nächste Zug nach Tübingen?

4 Wann wollt ihr losfahren?

 5 Wann essen wir?

6 Wann endet die Vorstellung (*performance*)?

 7 Um wieviel Uhr fährt der letzte Bus nach Raisdorf?

8 Wann soll ich da sein?

PARTY
Wann? Montag
2–3 Uhr
Wo? bei Effi

 9 Wann muss er sich anmelden?

10 Wann ist die Besuchszeit in der Klinik?

**KINDERKLINIK
BESUCHSZEIT:**
15–17 Uhr

Antworten

2 Um Viertel vor acht. 3 Um eine Minute nach elf. 4 Um zwölf Uhr.
5 Um acht Uhr abends. (zwanzig Uhr). 6 Um zehn nach elf abends
(dreiundzwanzig Uhr). 7 Um eine Minute nach Mitternacht. 8 Zwischen zwei und
drei Uhr. 9 Um halb elf. 10 Von fünfzehn bis siebzehn Uhr.

Aufgabe B

Complete the following sentences, using the appropriate part of the relevant reflexive verb.

1 Hans _____

2 Ich _____

3 Lieselchen _____

4 Karlchen _____

5 Wir _____

6 Sie _____

7 Thomas _____

8 Oma _____

9 Dr. Meyer _____

10 **Sie** _____

sich kämmen	*to comb one's hair*
sich ab/trocknen	*to dry oneself*
sich rasieren	*to shave oneself*
sich das Haar waschen	*to wash one's hair*
sich setzen	*to sit down*
sich die Zähne putzen	*to clean one's teeth*
sich um/ziehen	*to change one's clothes*
sich duschen	*to have a shower*
sich anziehen	*to get dressed*
sich wiegen	*to weigh oneself*

Antworten

1. Hans duscht sich. 2. Ich wiege mich. 3. Lieselchen kämmt sich. 4. Karlchen zieht sich an. 5. Wir ziehen uns um. 6. Sie trocknen sich ab. 7. Thomas rasiert sich. 8. Oma setzt sich. 9. Dr. Meyer putzt sich die Zähne. 10. Sie wäscht sich das Haar.

12 | EXPRESSING POSSESSION

Aims

In this unit you will learn how to:

■ Express possession; ■ Ask questions regarding possession

Grammar Content

■ Possessive adjectives; ■ preposition von to indicate possession
■ The verb gehören; ■ **wem?** ■ The genitive case

12.1 Preliminary note

There are many ways of expressing possession in German.

■ You may, for example, use words such as **mein** *my*, **dein** *your*, **sein** *his*, **ihr** *her*, **unser** *our*, **Ihr** *your*, **ihr** *their* as in '*my* house', '*your* car', '*their* career prospects', etc. These words are called possessive adjectives.

■ Phrases in English such as *Peter's friend, Anna's cat, Schubert's songs* can be expressed in a similar way in German: **Peters Freund, Annas Katze, Schuberts Lieder** (or **die Lieder Schuberts**), but note that no apostrophe is normally used in German. (One obvious exception is **Beck's Bier!**)

■ Later in this unit we shall also learn the fourth case, the genitive case, which is used to show possession, particularly in writing.

■ German also has another way of expressing possession using the word von, meaning *of*: **der Freund *von* Anna, die Stadtmitte** von **Hamburg, die Lieder *von* Schubert.**

First of all, have a look at the following sentences and their translations before going on to the Grammar Summary.

Expressing possession

Hier ist mein Chef.	*Here is my boss.*
Hier ist deine Tasche.	*Here's your bag.*
Unser Haus ist ein Einfamilienhaus.	*Our house is a detatched house.*
Unsere Kunden sind meistens aus Japan.	*Our customers are mostly from Japan.*
Er hat seinen Pass nicht bei sich.	*He doesn't have his passport on him.*
Es gibt sein neuestes Buch in der Bibliothek.	*His latest book is in the library.*
Die Mappe ist unter Ihrem Schreibtisch.	*The briefcase is under your desk.*
Ich koche lieber in meiner Küche.	*I prefer to cook in my own kitchen.*
Der Architekt arbeitet gerade in seinem Büro.	*The architect is just working in his office.*

12.2 Grammar Summary

You will notice how the form of the possessive adjective changes, depending on the gender of the noun it precedes and also the context in which it is used, which determines whether it is in the nominative, accusative dative or genitive case. In fact, possessive adjectives follow the same pattern in the singular form as **ein**, **eine**, **ein** (See 3.2.2, 3.2.3 and Reference Grammar 3.2).

Look at the chart showing all the possible forms for the word **mein** (*my*):

	M	F	N	Pl
Nom.	mein	meine	mein	meine
Acc.	meinen	meine	mein	meine
Dat.	meinem	meiner	meinem	meinen
Gen.	meines§	meiner	meines§	meiner

§ **-s** or **-es** is added to the masculine and neuter noun in the genitive singular

The basic forms of these possessive adjectives are:

mein *my*
dein *your* (singular familiar)
sein *his* or *its*
ihr *her* or *their*
unser *our*
eu(e)r *your* (plural familiar)
Ihr *your* (singular or plural formal)

Note:

1 Whenever you add an ending to **eu(e)r**, it drops the internal e (in brackets) for ease of pronunciation.

e.g. Wo sind eure Fahrkarten? *Where are your tickets?*

2 You will see that the possessive adjectives for *her* and *their* are identical, **ihr**. The context normally makes the exact meaning clear.

Wir kennen ihre Kinder nicht. *We don't know her/their children.*

12.3 Im Kontext

12.3.1 A young girl is describing her family and home:

Mein Vater ist Rechtsanwalt und arbeitet mit meinem Großvater in seiner Praxis. Meine Mutter ist Hausfrau und bleibt mit meinem kleinen Bruder zu Hause. Er ist drei Jahre alt und seine Lieblingsbeschäftigung ist Singen! Meine Schwester Anna ist älter als ich. Ihr Haar ist blond. Meins ist schwarz. Annas Augen sind blau. Meine sind braun. Ansonsten sind wir ähnlich. Unser Haus liegt am Waldrand, und es gibt viele Bäume in unserem Garten. Ein Teil von unserem Garten gehört der Gemeinde, aber das stört uns nicht. Es bedeutet nur, dass ein Gärtner von der Gemeinde unseren Garten mäht! Unsere Nachbarn sind alle sehr lieb.

der Rechtsanwalt *lawyer*	**das Singen** *singing*
der Großvater *grandfather*	**älter als** *older than*
die Praxis *(professional) practice*	**schwarz** *black*
die Hausfrau *housewife*	**blau** *blue*
bleiben *to stay*	**ansonsten** *otherwise*
zu Hause *at home*	**ähnlich** *similar*
der Bruder *brother*	**am Waldrand** *on the edge of a*
die Lieblingsbeschäftigung	*wood*
favourite occupation	**der Baum** *the tree*

der Teil *part* **die Gemeinde** (here) *local* *authority; parish* **stören** *to disturb, to bother* **bedeuten** *to mean*	**nur** *only* **der Gärtner** *gardener* **den Rasen mähen** *to mow the* *lawn* **der Nachbar** *the neighbour*

NB **Anna ist älter als ich** is an example of the comparative form of the adjective. For details of this, see Reference Grammar 5.3.1.

12.4 Machen wir weiter!

12.4.1 The use of the verb gehören, to belong to

It is possible to express possession or the idea of *belonging to* by using the verb **gehören** followed by either a noun or a pronoun, e.g. 'The chequebook belongs *to the man*' or 'The chequebook belongs *to him*'. The phrase *to the man* or *to him* is expressed in German by using the dative case of either the noun or the personal pronouns.

Der Koffer gehört dem Mann dort. *The case belongs to the man there.*

Die Handtasche gehört der Dame *The handbag belongs the the lady*
da vorne.   *at the front.*

Das Auto gehört den Eltern.   *The car belongs to the parents.*

12.4.2 The use of personal pronuns after gehören

After the verb gehören the following dative forms of the personal pronouns should be used:

mir	*to me*	uns	*to us*
dir	*to you*	euch	*to you*
ihm	*to him, to it*	Ihnen	*to you*
ihr	*to her*	ihnen	*to them*

Die spanische Villa gehört **mir** *The Spanish villa, unfortunately*
leider nicht.   *doesn't belong to me.*
Gehört **dir** diese Reisetasche?   *Does this travel bag belong to you?*
Der schwarze Mantel gehört **ihm**. *The black coat belongs to him.*

Gehören **ihr** diese Papiere?   *Do these papers belong to her?*
Gehört **Ihnen** dieser Regenschirm?   *Does this umbrella belong to you?*

12.4.3 Asking questions about ownership using **wem**?

In order to elicit any of the above answers you can simply use the question form used in the above examples or begin the question with the word **wem**? (*To whom?*)

Wem gehört der Koffer dort?   *Who does the case there belong to?*
Wem gehören diese Leinentaschen?   *Who do these linen bags belong to?*

12.4.4 The genitive case

To express possession in a formal way, often in writing, we use the genitive form of the definite article (see Unit 3): **des, der, des, der** (pl.), *of the,* or of the indefinite article: **eines, einer, eines,** *of a,* or of one of the possessive adjectives, e.g. **meines, meiner, meines, meiner** (pl.), *of* my.

Das ist das Motorrad des neuen   *That's the new vicar's motor bike*
  Pfarrers*.   (literally, 'That's the motorbike
                                         of the new vicar').

Am Anfang eines Migräneanfalls*   *At the beginning of a migraine*
  gehe ich gleich ins Bett.   *attack I go straight to bed.*
Hier ist ein Bild der alten Kirche.   *Here's a picture of the old church.*
Das Alter des Mädchens* ist   *The girl's age is not important.*
  nicht wichtig.

*Notice that a masculine or neuter noun (for example **der Pfarrer**, or **das Mädchen**) adds an **-s** or an **-es** ending in the genitive case, depending on which is easier to pronounce.

Now look at these further examples and their translations:

Die neue Sprechstunde unseres   *Our doctor's new consultation*
  Arztes ist am Dienstag.   *time is on Tuesday.*
Das Ziel seiner Reise ist Wien.   *The destination of his journey is*
                                        Vienna.

Das Landhaus ihrer Eltern ist   *Their parents' country house*
  riesengroß.   *is enormous.*

12.4.5 The use of von as a popular alternative to the genitive

As we saw in the preliminary notes, the preposition **von** is also used to show possession, and this is more common than the genitive.

■ If there is no definite or indefinite article in the phrase showing possession, then **von** is preferred to the genitive, for example:

Der Bau von Atomkraftwerken ist sehr umstritten.	*The building of atomic power stations is very controversial.*
Die Ankunft von noch mehr Truppen ist nicht willkommen.	*The arrival of even more troops is not welcome.*

■ The genitive case is generally avoided in speech, for example:

Das ist der Hut von meinem Vater.	*That's my father's hat.*
Dort steht das Fahrrad von ihrem Freund.	*There's her boyfriend's bike.*

In colloquial speech you are also likely to hear this curious structure to express possession:

Das ist dem Thomas seine Gitarre.	*That's Thomas' guitar.*
Das ist meiner Nichte ihr Taufkleid	*That's my niece's christening robe.*

You will see that this involves the nominative case + possessive adjective after the verb **sein** with the dative case in front of it (as you would use for an indirect object)

12.4.6 Possessive pronouns

Look at the following examples of possessive pronouns.

Hast du einen Bleistift? Ich finde meinen nicht.	*Have you a pencil? I can't find mine.*
Haben Sie meine Brille gesehen? Ich habe seine aber nicht deine gesehen.	*Have you seen my glasses? I've seen his but not yours.*
Hast du Bleistifte da? Meine sind kaputt.	*Have you any pencils (there)? Mine are broken.*
Mögen Sie Ihren neuen Wohnwagen? Wir mögen unseren sehr.	*Do you like your new caravan? We like ours a lot.*

12.5 Jetzt sind Sie dran!

Aufgabe A

Insert the correct form of the possessive adjective into each of the gaps in the following sentences:

1 Wo ist _____ Tasche? *Where is my bag?*
2 Wie heißt _____ Klassenlehrer? *What is his form teacher called?*
3 _____ Auto hat eine Panne. *Our car has broken down.*
4 Ist das _____ Haus? *Is that her house?*
5 Wo sind _____ Koffer? *Where are our suitcases?*
6 _____ Schwester heißt Silke. *His sister is called Silke.*
7 _____ Betten sind ungemacht. *Their beds are unmade.*
8 Wohnt _____ Sohn in Düsseldorf? *Does your* (singular polite) *son live in Düsseldorf?*
9 Hans, wo ist _____ Kreditkarte? (*Hans, where is your (singular familiar) credit card?*)
10 _____ Rucksäcke stehen draußen vor der Tür. *Your* (pl. familiar) *rucksacks are outside the door.*

Antworten

1. Wo ist meine Tasche? 2. Wie heißt sein Klassenlehrer? 3. Unser Auto hat eine Panne. 4. Ist das ihr Haus? 5. Wo sind unsere Koffer? 6. Seine Schwester heißt Silke. 7.Ihre Betten sind ungemacht. 8.Wohnt Ihr Sohn in Düsseldorf? 9. Hans, wo ist deine Kreditkarte? 10. Eure Rucksäcke stehen draußen vor der Tür.

Aufgabe B

Replace the **von** prepositional phrases in bold type with the equivalent phrase in the genitive, e.g.

Die Fenster **vom Rathaus** sind schmutzig. *The windows of the Town Hall are dirt*y. > Die Fenster **des Rathauses** sind schmutzig.

1 Das Schlafzimmer **von dem Kind** ist klein. *The child's room is small.*
2 Das Auto **von dem Pfarrer** ist alt. *The Vicar's car is old.*
3 Die Freundin **von meinem Bruder** kommt aus Österreich. *My brother's girlfriend comes from Austria.*
4 Ich nehme immer zwei Tabletten am Anfang **von einem Migräneanfall**. *I always take two tablets at the beginning of a migraine attack.*

5 Das Sprechzimmer **von unserem Arzt** ist immer kalt. *Our doctor's consulting room is always cold.*

6 Die Nachbarin **von meinen Eltern** ist verreist. *My parents' neighbour has gone away.*

7 Der Direktor **von dieser Schule** ist weltberühmt. *This school's head teacher is world famous.*

Antworten

1. Das Schlafzimmer des Kindes ist klein. 2. Das Auto des Pfarrers ist alt. 3. Die Freundin meines Bruders kommt aus Österreich. 4. Ich nehme immer zwei Tabletten am Anfang eines Migräneanfalls. 5. Das Sprechzimmer unseres Arztes ist immer kalt. 6. Die Nachbarin meiner Eltern ist verreist. 7. Der Direktor dieser Schule ist weltberühmt.

13 | GIVING DIRECTIONS AND INSTRUCTIONS

Aims

In this unit you will learn how to:

■ Ask and give directions; ■ Ask for and give instructions

Grammar Content

■ Imperative mood; ■ Use of the infinitive, the verb **lassen** and the passive as alternatives to the imperative

13.1 Preliminary note

Asking for directions

There are many ways of asking for directions. You will see from the following examples that most of them contain vocabulary and structures which we have already come across.

Entschuldigen Sie bitte, wie komme ich am besten zum Bahnhof?	*Excuse me please, what's the best way to the railway station?*
Wie kommen wir am besten zur Post, bitte?	*How do we best get to the post office please?*
Wo komme ich am besten in die Stadtmitte?	*What's the best way to the town centre?*
Sind wir hier richtig zur Sparkasse?	*Are we on the right way to the savings bank?*
Wir suchen die Sohststraße. Wissen Sie, wo sie ist?	*We're looking for Sohst Street. Do you know where it is?*

Wo ist die elektrische Abteilung bitte?	*Where is the electrical department please?*
Wo ist die Toilette, bitte?	*Where's the toilet, please?*
In welcher Richtung ist Flugsteig 28?	*(In) which direction is Gate 28?*

Giving directions

Gehen Sie hier geradeaus und an der Ampel nach links. Die Bank ist auf der rechten Seite.	*Go straight ahead and left at the traffic lights. The bank is on the right.*
Fahren Sie die Hauptstraße entlang bis zur Kaserne und dann biegen Sie nach links ab.	*Drive along the main street as far as the barracks and then turn left.*
Fahren Sie über die Kreuzung, und dann nehmen Sie die erste Straße rechts.	*Go over the crossing and then take the first street on the right.*
Fahren Sie mit dem Aufzug hoch bis zum zehnten Stock. Da befindet sich die Dachterrassenbar.	*Go up by lift to the tenth floor. That's where the rooftop bar is situated.*
Gehen Sie nach unten, und Sie finden das Fitnesscenter im Keller.	*Go downstairs and you will find the health club in the basement.*
Gehen Sie über die Brücke, und Sie finden den Zug nach Ulm auf Gleis zwei.	*Go over the bridge and you'll find the Ulm train on Platform 2.*

Asking for instructions

Was muss ich machen?	*What do I have to do?*
Wann muss man das machen?	*When do you have to do that?*
Soll ich das gleich machen?	*Should I do it straight away?*
Wo muss ich drücken?	*Where do I have to press?*

Giving instructions

Münzen zuerst einwerfen, Knopf drücken und warten!	*Put the coins in first, press the button and wait!*
Prüfen Sie zuerst den Reifendruck!	*First, check your tyre pressure*
Benutzen Sie den 1. Gang nur zum Anfahren.	*Only use first gear to get going.*

13.2 Grammar Summary

13.2.1 The Imperative mood (Reference Grammar 12)

You will notice from the examples that intructions are often given by using the imperative or command form. Because the instructions were given to strangers, the polite form (**Sie**) was always used. As you would expect, there are three main forms of the imperative, corresponding to the **du**, **ihr** and **Sie** forms of the verb.

13.2.2 The du imperative form

■ The familiar singular imperative is formed by dropping both the pronoun **du** and the ending from the **du** form of the verb (e.g. **du fragst**):

Frag deine Lehrerin zuerst!	*Ask your teacher first!*
Komm sofort hierher!	*Come here immediately!*
Trink bitte keinen Alkohol!	*Don't drink any alcohol, please!*
Geh sofort ins Bett!	*Go to bed immediately!*
Mach schnell!	*Do it quickly! Be quick!*

Note 1: If the verb adds an umlaut in the **du** form, (e.g. **ich laufe, du läufst**) the same rules apply, but the umlaut is also dropped:

Lauf nicht weg!	*Don't run away!*
Schlaf gut!	*Sleep well!*
Fahr doch langsam!	*Drive slowly!*

Note 2: If the verb stem changes its vowel in the **du** form, (e.g. **ich esse, du isst**) this vowel change is retained in the imperative mood:

Iss bitte langsamer!	*Please eat more slowly!*
Gib mir das Kleingeld, bitte!	*Give me the change, please!*
Sprich nicht so viel!	*Please don't talk so much!*

If the pronoun du is used with the imperative, it intensifies to command:

Mach *du* das!	You *do it!*

Note 3: You will sometimes find that an **e** is added to this imperative form. It can have the effect of making it sound a bit more formal or imperious, even though it is addressed to a child or a friend.

Nenne drei Flüsse!	*Name three rivers!*
Antworte mit ja oder nein!	*Answer yes or no!*

In these examples the extra **e** is added for ease of pronunciation, as we saw in Unit 5.

13.2.3 The ihr imperative form

The familiar plural imperative form is simply the appropriate **ihr** form of the verb, minus the pronoun **ihr**:

Raucht bitte nicht!	*Please don't smoke!*
Bleibt da!	*Stay there!*
Schwimmt rüber! (colloquial)	*Swim across!*
Setzt euch!	*Sit down!*

13.2.4 The Sie imperative form

As we have already seen, the polite singular and plural imperative form consists of the inverted form of the verb . You will realise that this is the same as the question form (see Unit 1), but the intonation in speech never leaves us in doubt as to whether the sentence is a question or a command. In the written language the sentence ends in a question mark or an exclamation mark.

Kommen Sie wieder nach Österreich!	*Come to Austria again!*
Setzen Sie sich!	*Take a seat!*
Wiederholen Sie das bitte!	*Please repeat that!*
Essen Sie doch!	*Do eat!*
Sprechen Sie bitte langsamer!	*Please speak more slowly!*
Tun Sie das bitte nicht!	*Please don't do that!*
Verzeihen Sie!	*Forgive (me)! Excuse (me)!*

13.2.5 The verbs sein and haben in the imperative form

Both of these verbs have an irregular imperative form:

sein		**haben**	
du: **sei** ruhig!		du: **hab** keine Angst!	
ihr: **seid** ruhig!	} Be quiet!	ihr: **habt** keine Angst!	} Don't be afraid!
Sie: **Seien** Sie ruhig!		Sie: **haben** Sie keine Angst!	

13.3 Im Kontext

13.3.1 Look at this memo from the boss, which a city worker finds on his desk when he returns from a lunch break:

Würden Sie bitte morgen spätestens um 10 Uhr in meinem Büro sein? Bringen Sie den Bericht mit, der wohl bis dann fertig sein wird. Eine weitere Bitte: Fertigen Sie auch die Dokumente über Projekt A47 an, die ich gern mit Ihnen diskutieren möchte!

---

morgen *tomorrow*
spätestens *at the latest*
der Bericht *report*
der wohl bis dann fertig sein
  wird *which will presumably be*
  ready by then
eine weitere Bitte *a further*
  request

die Dokumente an/fertigen *to*
  prepare the documentation
über *(here) about*
das Projekt *project*
diskutieren *to discuss*

13.3.2 Read through the following recipes:

Glühwein

Zutaten: *Ein Achtelliter Wasser, eine Flasche Rotwein, ein Teelöffel Zimt, fünf Nelken, 150 g (Gramm) Zucker, Schale einer Zitrone.*

Wasser mit Zucker, Gewürzen und Zitronenschale aufkochen, Rotwein dazugeben und bis zum Sieden erhitzen.

---

der Glühwein *mulled wine*
die Zutaten *ingredients*
das Achtel *one eighth*
die Flasche *bottle*
der Teelöffel *teaspoon*
der Zimt *cinnamon*
die Nelke *(here) clove (also*
carnation)

der Zucker *sugar*
das Gewürz *spice*
die Zitronenschale *lemon peel*
auf/kochen *to bring to the boil*
das Sieden *simmering*
erhitzen *to heat*

Machen wir weiter!

13.4 Commands involving the speaker

If the speaker is involved in the projected action, a **wir** imperative form can be used by inverting the normal verb form. In this usage the pronoun **wir** is retained as follows:

Fangen wir an!	*Let's begin!*
Gehen wir!	*Let's go!*
Essen wir zuerst!	*Let's eat first!*
Schlafen wir lieber!	*Let's rather sleep!*

13.4.1 The imperative using the verb lassen

The verb **lassen** (in the sense of '*to let*') can be used to express the imperative, as in the old usage in the church liturgy: **Lass(e)t uns beten!** *Let us pray!*:

Lass uns gehen!	*Let's go!*
Lasst uns alles vergessen!	*Let's forget it all!*
Lass ihn weitersprechen!	*Let him carry on speaking!*
Lassen Sie mich bitte ausreden!	*Let me finish (speaking), please!*

13.4.2 More general commands

Endstation. Alle aussteigen!	*Terminus. Everyone get out!*
Vorne einsteigen!	*Get in at the front!*
Bitte von links anstellen!	*Form a queue from the left, please!*
Leise sprechen!	*Talk quietly!*
Festhalten!	*Hold on tight!*
Aufmachen!	*Open (it) up!*
Hier öffnen!	*Open here!*
Nicht anfassen!	*Don't touch!*

13.4.3 The use of the passive to express the imperative

In spoken, colloquial speech the passive voice is also sometimes used to issue an energetic command:

Es wird hier nicht geraucht!	*No smoking here!*
Es wird hiergeblieben!	*Stay here!*

Es wird jetzt geschlafen!	*Now get to sleep!*
Zuerst wird aber gegessen!	*Eat first!*
Es wird jetzt getanzt!	*Let's dance now!*

From these examples you will see that the passive is formed by using the **es** form of the verb **werden**, plus a past participle at the end of the clause. This is a very limited use of the passive. For fuller details see Unit 19.

13.5 Jetzt sind Sie dran!

Aufgabe A

Read through the following conversation between a tourist and a local inhabitant and then decide if the statements that follow are right or wrong:

Tourist	Entschuldigen Sie! Wissen Sie bitte, wo die Wechselstelle ist?
Einwohner	Jawohl. Sie ist am Bahnhof.
Tourist	Oha! Wie komme ich bitte am besten zum Bahnhof?
Einwohner	Gehen Sie hier geradeaus bis zur Ampel. Nehmen Sie die erste Straße rechts und nach 100 Metern kommen Sie zur U-Bahnunterführung. Gehen sie dort nach unten (entweder auf der Treppe oder aber mit der Rolltreppe) durch die Unterführung und dann die Treppe wieder hoch. Sie müssen dann die Kochstraße überqueren, über den Bahnhofsplatz gehen und die Wechselstelle steht gleich an der Ecke neben dem Haupteingang. Aber beeilen Sie sich. Sie macht um 18 Uhr zu. Sie brauchen höchstens fünf Minuten dorthin.

entschuldigen Sie! *excuse me!*	**die Rolltreppe** *escalator*
die Wechselstelle *bureau de change*	**hoch/gehen** *to go up*
oha! *oh! (North German)*	**überqueren** *to cross*
der Bahnhof *railway station*	**gleich an der Ecke** *just at the corner*
die Straßenampel *traffic lights*	**der Haupteingang** *the main entrance*
nehmen *to take*	**sich beeilen** *to hurry*
die U-Bahn *underground (railway)*	**zu/machen** *to close*
die Unterführung *underpass*	**brauchen** *to need*
nach unten gehen *to go down*	**höchstens** *at the most*
entweder ... oder *either ... or*	
die Treppe *steps*	

Sind die folgenden Sätze richtig oder falsch?

		R	F
1	Der Tourist will wissen, wo die Wechselstelle ist	☐	☐
2	Der Einwohner weiß es nicht.	☐	☐
3	Der Tourist fragt dann nach dem Weg dorthin.	☐	☐
4	Er muss an der Ampel nach rechts abbiegen.	☐	☐
5	Die U-Bahnunterführung ist 100 Meter von der Ampel entfernt	☐	☐
6	Er kann nur mit der Treppe nach unten gehen.	☐	☐
7	Er muss dann nur die Kochstraße überqueren.	☐	☐
8	Die Wechselstelle befindet sich an der Ecke.	☐	☐
9	Die Wechselstelle schließt um 8 Uhr abends.	☐	☐
10	Man braucht fünfzehn Minuten, um die Wechselstelle zu erreichen.	☐	☐

Antworten: 1R, 2F, 3R, 4R, 5R, 6F, 7F, 8R, 9F, 10F

Aufgabe B

Respond to each of these requests with an appropriate imperative form, e.g.

Darf ich bitte meine Mutter anrufen? *Please may I telephone my mother?* (**Du**)

Ruf mal an! *Do phone!*

1 Darf ich bitte ein Fax schicken? *Please may I send a fax?* (**Du**)
2 Darf ich bitte rauchen? *Please may I smoke?* (**Du**)
3 Dürfen wir bitte hier bleiben? *Please may we stay here?* (**Ihr**)
4 Dürfen wir bitte hier warten? *Please may we wait here?* (**Ihr**)
5 Dürfen wir bitte eine Tasse Tee trinken? *Please may we have a cup of tea?* (**Ihr**)
6 Darf ich bitte schon beginnen? *Please may I begin?* (**Sie**)
7 Darf ich mich bitte hinsetzen? *Please may I sit down?* (**Sie**)
8 Darf ich bitte noch ein Glas Wein einschenken? *Please may I pour another glass of wine?*

Antworten

1 Schick mal ein Fax! 2. Rauch mal! 3. Bleibt bitte hier! 4. Wartet bitte hier! 5. Trinkt bitte eine Tasse Tee! 6. Beginnen Sie bitte! 7. Setzen Sie sich bitte hin! 8. Schenken Sie bitte nichts mehr ein!

14 | MAKING REQUESTS AND OFFERS

Aims

In this unit you will learn how to:

■ Make requests; ■ Reply to a request; ■ Make offers; ■ Reply to offers
■ Issue and accept invitations

Grammar Content

■ Direct and indirect objects; ■ Word order

14.1 Preliminary note

We can make requests and offers in a variety of ways in English, for example: *Will you help me, please? Can you give me directions, please? Shall I phone your boss? Can I take you home? Do you want a cup of coffee?* German also has a number of ways of making a request or offer. These involve some of the constructions learned in previous units.

Look at the following examples and their translations:

Prefacing requests

You could preface your request in one of the following ways:

Ich habe eine (große) Bitte (an Sie): Können Sie mich mitnehmen?

I have a (big) request (of you). Can you take me with you?

Ich hätte eine Bitte: Kannst du heute das Fax schicken?

I have a request. Can you send the fax today?

Ich möchte Sie etwas fragen: Können Sie mich mitnehmen?

I'd like to ask you something. Can you take me with you?

| Ich möchte/wollte/muss Sie um etwas bitten. | *I should like to/ wanted to/ must ask something of you.* |
| Könnt ihr mir bitte helfen? | *Could you help me please?* |

Making requests

Requests can be made by using some of the question forms which we came across in previous units, or the imperative form (see 13.2), or the verb **bitten**:

Using questions

Holst du mich von der Bushaltestelle ab?	*Will you pick me up from the busstop?*
Darf ich bitte sprechen?	*May I speak, please?*
Können Sie das bitte buchstabieren?	*Could you spell that, please?*
Könnten Sie das ins Englische übersetzen?	*Could you translate that into English?*
Wäre es möglich, dass ich meinen Hund mitbringe?	*Would it be possible for me to bring my dog with me?*

Using the imperative

Bitte, bleib bei mir!	*Please stay with me!*
Sei lieb zu mir!	*Be kind to me!*
Rufen Sie mich bitte an!	*Please phone me!*
Sprechen Sie langsamer, bitte!	*Please speak more slowly!*
Bringen Sie eine Flasche Wein mit!	*Bring a bottle of wine with you!*
Reservieren Sie bitte vier Plätze!	*Please reserve four seats!*

Using the verb bitten

You will probably have noticed how frequently the word **bitte** (*please*) occurs in requests. This is not surprising, as it is connected with the verb **bitten** (*to ask, beg, plead, beseech, invite*).

Look at the following examples of formal requests:

Darf ich zu Tisch bitten?	*May I ask (invite) you to come to the table?*
Wir möchten euch zum Abendessen bitten.	*We would like to ask (invite) you to supper.*
Ich möchte dich auf ein Glas Wein bitten.	*I'd like to ask (invite) you over for a glass of wine*

Darf ich um Verständnis bitten? *May I ask for understanding?*

Darf ich Sie um Ihren Namen bitten? *May I ask you for your name?*

Replying to a request or an offer

The following words and phrases can be used to accept requests and offers:

(aber) ja! *yes, that's fine!*

ja gern *yes, with pleasure!*

Ja (na) klar! *sure! of course!*

ja gut *yes, fine*

ja ist gut *yes, that's fine*

ja natürlich *yes, of course*

ja gewiss *yes, of course*

selbstverständlich! *of course; that goes without saying*

freilich *of course*

sicher *certainly*

jawohl! *certainly!*

okay! *OK!*

(Das) mache ich. *I'll do it.*

(na) klar! *of course!*

Das versteht sich (von selbst). *That goes without saying.*

logo! *sure!*

Refusing requests and offers

nein *no*

leider nicht *unfortunately not*

bestimmt nicht *certainly not*

natürlich nicht *of course not*

Leider geht das nicht. *Unfortunately that is not possible.*

Es tut mir leid, aber heute passt es nicht. *I am sorry but today it is not convenient.*

auf keinen Fall *on no account, no way*

Das kommt nicht in Frage! *That's out of the question!*

niemals! *never!*

Making offers using an/bieten (to offer), ein/schenken (to pour out), überreichen (to present, to hand over)

an/bieten (*to offer*)

Darf ich Ihnen eine Tasse Kaffee anbieten? *May I offer you a cup of coffee?*

Er bietet uns nur DM 5000 für unser Auto an. *He is offering us only DM 5000 for our car.*

ein/schenken (*to pour out*)

Darf ich dir noch ein Glas Wein einschenken?	*May I pour you some more wine?*
Ich schenke Ihnen noch eine Tasse Tee ein, oder?	*I'll pour you another cup of tea, shall I?*

14.2 Grammar Summary

14.2.1 Word order of direct and indirect object (Reference Grammar 14.2)

Let's have a closer look at the last example:

subject pronoun	verb	indirect object in dative case	direct object in accusative case	prefix of verb
Ich	**schenke**	**Ihnen**	**noch eine Tasse Tee**	**ein.**
I	*pour*	*you*	*another cup of tea.*	*out.*

You will see that there are two objects after the verb: first the indirect object, and then the direct object.

■ To find the direct object ask the question *who/what undergoes the action of the verb* i.e. here, what is being poured out? The answer to this question is the direct object of the sentence, and we know that this requires the accusative case.

■ To identify what is the indirect object , check by preceding the noun or pronoun with 'to' or 'for' (i.e. 'I pour a cup of tea for *you*')

Here are some other examples of verbs which can have both a direct and an indirect object :

Darf ich **Ihnen einen Scheck** im Wert von DM 1000 überreichen?	*May I present you with a cheque for DM 1000?*
Können Sie **mir ein gutes Restaurant** empfehlen?	*Can you recommend me a good restaurant?*

Der Chef schenkt **seiner Sekretärin** immer **Tulpen** zu Ostern.	*The boss always gives his secretary tulips at Easter.*

There are certain rules for word order when there is both a direct and an indirect object after the verb :

■ If both the direct and the indirect object are nouns, *the dative (indirect object) comes before the accusative (direct object),* as in the last example.

■ If there is a combination of noun and pronoun, *the pronoun comes before the noun*, regardless of case, e.g.

Der Chef schenkt **ihr Tulpen**.	*The boss gives her flowers.*
Der Chef schenkt **sie der Sekretärin**.	*The boss gives them to the secretary.*

■ If both the direct and indirect objects are pronouns, *the accusative pronoun comes before the dative pronoun*:

Der Chef schenkt **sie ihr**.	*The boss gives them to her.*

14.2.2 Requests and offers

The *subjunctive* is often used to give a request a more polite ring as the following examples show. (For further details, see Unit 21.)

Könnten Sie mir einen Gefallen tun? Könnten Sie diesen Scheck einzahlen?	*Could you do me a favour? Could you pay in this cheque?*
Ich wäre sehr froh, wenn Sie mich morgen anrufen könnten/würden.	*I'd be very happy if you could/ would phone me tomorrow.*
Wäre es möglich, dass Sie gleich hinfahren?	*Would it be possible for you to go there straight away?*
Hätten Sie gern etwas zu trinken?	*Would you like something to drink?*
Würden Sie gern mit nach Japan fahren?	*Would you like to come to Japan (with me/us?)*
Möchten Sie, dass ich den Rasen mähe?	*Would you like me to mow your lawn?*
Dürfte ich hier rauchen?	*May I (possibly) smoke here?*

14.3 Im Kontext

14.3.1 A plea for help

Liebe Silke!

Kannst Du mir einen riesigen Gefallen tun? Holst du bitte Günther heute Nachmittag um 3 Uhr vom Kindergarten ab? Aber bitte gib ihm nichts zu essen. (Wenn er Hunger hat, darf er die Karotten essen, die im Kühlschrank sind!) Oh, und noch eine Bitte! Kannst du den Wellensittich füttern? Heute Morgen habe ich das vergessen. Ich bin dir sehr dankbar,

Gruß und Kuss,

Dein Julius!

P.S. Ich bin um 5 Uhr wieder da!

---

einen Gefallen tun *to do a favour*
riesig *enormous*
heute Nachmittag *this afternoon*
ab/holen *to collect, pick up*
nichts *nothing*
Hunger haben *to be hungry*
die Karotte *carrot*
der Kühlschrank *fridge*
der Wellensittich *budgerigar*

füttern *to feed*
heute Morgen *this morning*
dankbar *grateful*
Gruß und Kuss Dein Julius *a jocular ending to a letter to a very close friend*
der Gruß *greeting*
der Kuss *kiss*

14.4 Machen wir weiter!

14.4.1 Other examples of requests:

Kaufst du mir das Kleid?	*Will you buy me the dress?*
Holst du mich bitte vom Bahnhof ab?	*Will you pick me up from the railway station, please?*
Kann ich deinen alten Rasenmäher haben?	*Can I have your old lawn mower*
Können Sie ihn bitte besuchen?	*Please could you visit him?*

The command form can also be used as a form of request:

Nehmen Sie mich bitte mit in die Karibik.	*Please take me with you to the Caribbean.*
Rauchen Sie doch lieber nicht.	*Please don't smoke.*

14.4.2 Other examples of making offers:

Wollen Sie heute Abend ins Theater gehen?	*Do you want to go to the theatre tonight?*
Brauchen Sie sonst noch etwas?	*Do you need anything else?*
Trinkst du etwas?	*Will you have something to drink?*
Wollen wir zusammen ins Kino gehen?	*Shall we go to the cinema together?*
Sollen wir lieber bis morgen warten?	*Would it be better for us to wait until tomorrow?*
Kann ich Ihnen helfen?	*Can I help you?*
Brauchen Sie (meine) Hilfe?	*Do you need (my) help?*
Darf ich Sie in die Oper einladen?	*May I invite you to the opera?*
Nimmst du auch noch ein Glas?	*Will you also have another glass?*

14.5 Jetzt sind Sie dran!

Aufgabe A

You have just had an operation and are impatient to resume your normal activities. Using the appropriate form of the modal verb **dürfen** to ask if you may do the following things, e.g.

May I please get up? Darf ich bitte aufstehen?

1 Ask if you may watch the television
2 Ask when you may drink a glass of beer
3 Ask if you may eat a piece of cake
4 Ask if you may go home tomorrow
5 Ask what you may do!

Antworten

1. Darf ich fernsehen? 2. Wann darf ich ein Glas Bier trinken? 3. Darf ich ein Stück Kuchen essen? 4. Darf ich morgen nach Hause gehen? 5. Was darf ich machen?

Aufgabe B

Can you replace the nouns in bold type in the following sentences with pronouns? Remember: the word order varies if pronouns are used. Refer back to 14.2 for help.

1 **Der Kellner** schenkt **meinem Vater ein Glas Wein** ein.   *The waiter pours my father a glass of wine.*

2 **Der Nachbar** empfiehlt **meinem Sohn ein gutes Restaurant**.   *Our neighbour recommends a good restaurant to my son.*

3 Jeden Tag zeigt **der Schüler der Lehrerin seine Hausaufgaben**.   *The pupil shows his homework to his teacher every day.*

4 **Der Arzt** gibt **der Frau eine Spritze**.   *The doctor gives the woman an injection.*

5 **Das Kindermädchen** liest **dem Kind eine Gutenachtgeschichte** vor.   *The nanny reads the child a bedtime story.*

Antworten

1. Er schenkt es ihm ein. 2. Er empfiehlt es ihm. 3. Jeden Tag zeigt er sie ihr. 4. Er gibt sie ihr. 5. Es liest sie ihm vor.

15 DESCRIBING PEOPLE, PLACES AND THINGS

Aims

In this unit you will learn how to:

■ Ask questions leading to the description of people, places and things;
■ Describe people, places and things; ■ Describe the weather

Grammar Content

■ Adjectives standing alone and in a noun phrase
■ Adjectives and verbs to describe the weather
■ **Aus** used to describe what things are made of

15.1 Preliminary Note

To describe people, places or things in general terms as, for example, *Hans is tall, Berlin is big, She's nice*, etc. German normally uses a verb such as **sein** (*to be*) followed by a word which describes the noun or pronoun. This describing word is called an adjective. It is also possible to put an adjective before a noun, resulting in a noun phrase such as *the red car, our old house*.

Asking questions leading to the description of people, places and things

To ask questions such as *What is he like?* or *What is it like in Berlin?* Use the word **wie?** (literally, 'how?', followed by a verb such as **sein** or **aus/sehen** (*to look like*):

Wie ist das Wetter?	*What is the weather like?*
Was für ein Mensch ist Christoph?	*What is Christoph like?* (literally, 'What sort of a person is Christoph?')
Wie sieht Inge aus?	*What does Inge look like?*

Describing people, places and things

Using an adjective after the noun and verb

Christoph ist sympathisch.	*Christoph is kind.*
Inge ist groß und blond.	*Inge is tall and blond.*
Der Verkäufer sieht krank aus.	*The salesman looks ill.*
Die Kuchen sehen sehr süß aus.	*The cakes look very sweet.*

Using an adjective before the noun

In the above examples the adjective always comes after the noun and verb (*the car is new*), but an adjective can also be used immediately before the noun (*the new car*), in a noun phrase. In this case it will need to add an ending to show that it agrees with the noun (i.e. is in the appropriate case).

Christoph ist ein sympathisch**er** Mann.	*Christoph is a kind man.*
Neumünster ist eine groß**e** Stadt.	*Neumünster is a large town.*
Der Mercedes ist ein schnell**es** Auto.	*The Mercedes is a fast car.*

The examples above illustrate a masculine, a feminine, and a neuter noun and adjective in the nominative case.

Now look at the following examples very carefully:

Inge hat ein**en** sehr sympathisch**en** Mann.	*Inge has a very kind husband.*
Die Regierung plant eine neue Stadt.	*The Government is planning a new town.*
Sein Lehrer hat **ein** alt**es** Auto.	*His teacher has an old car.*

The last three examples illustrate each of the genders using a noun (with the indefinite article) and adjective in the accusative case.

15.2 Grammar Summary

15.2.1 Adjectival endings (Reference Grammar 5.1)

You will have noticed from these examples that when the adjective is used immediately in front of a noun, the ending changes according to the gender and case of the noun.

Look at some examples of adjectival endings in the dative case:

Der Chef schreibt immer mit einem schwarzen Füller.	*The boss always writes with a black fountain pen.*
Das Kindermädchen kommt von einer guten Familie.	*The nanny comes from a good family.*
Wir essen am liebsten in einem italienischen Restaurant.	*Most of all we like eating in an Italian restaurant.*

Finally, look at these examples in the genitive case (for further details about the genitive case see Unit 12):

Die Hilfe eines starken Mannes beim Wohnungsumzug ist sehr viel wert.	*The help of a strong man when moving house is worth a lot.*
Der Preis einer möblierten Wohnung ist sehr hoch.	*The price of a furnished flat is very high.*
Vor dem Schlafengehen wirkt das Lesen eines guten Buches sehr entspannend.	*Reading a good book before going to sleep has a very relaxing effect.*

15.2.2 The following chart shows the adjectival endings which are used after **ein, eine, ein**.

	M	F	N
Nominative	-er	-e	-es
Accusative	-en	-e	-es
Dative	-en	-en	-en
Genitive	-en	-en	-en

These endings are also be used after **mein, dein, sein, ihr** etc. in the singular, for example:

Montag ist **ihr** erster Schultag.	*Monday is her first day at school.*
Meine neue Brille ist kaputt.	*My new glasses are broken.*

Unser zweit**es** Haus ist im Schwarzwald.	*Our second home is in the Black Forest.*

The same endings are used after **kein, keine, kein** (*not a*), for example:

Otto ist **kein** sympathisch**er** Mann.	*Otto is not a kind man.*
Liebburg ist **keine** schöne Stadt.	*Liebburg is not a nice town.*
Es gibt **keine** gut**e** Konditorei in Heikendorf.	*There's no good cake shop in Heikendorf.*
Wir erwarten **kein** gut**es** Wetter.	*We're not expecting good weather.*

There are two more charts of adjectival endings. Have a look at the charts in 15.2.3 and 15.2.4 before reading the remaining examples, and try to work out why each adjective ends as it does.

15.2.3 Adjectival endings after **der, die das, dieser, -e, -es** (*this*), **welcher, -e, es** (*which*):

	Singular			Plural
	M	F	N	
Nominative	**-e**	**-e**	**-e**	**-en**
Accusative	**-en**	**-e**	**-e**	**-en**
Dative	**-en**	**-en**	**-en**	**-en**
Genitive	**-en**	**-en**	**-en**	**-en**

Der grau**e** Schlafsack ist leider zu klein.	*The grey sleeping bag is unfortunately too small.*
Die weiß**e** Bluse ist zu teuer.	*The white blouse is too expensive.*
Das grün**e** Kleid passt dir am besten.	*The green dress suits you best.*
Die bunt**en** Schlipse sind im Moment modisch.	*The brightly coloured ties are fashionable at the moment.*
Ich möchte **den** schwarz**en** Mantel kaufen, bitte.	*I'd like to buy the black coat, please.*
Er mag **die** blau**e** Hose sehr.	*He likes the blue trousers very much.*
Ich kaufe lieber **das** rot**e** Hemd.	*I'd prefer to buy the red shirt.*
Diese Jacke passt gut zu **dem** braun**en** Rock.	*This jacket goes well with the brown skirt*
Ich nehme **die** gelb**en** Nelken.	*I'll take the yellow carnations.*

15.2.4 Adjectival endings used when the adjective stands alone before the noun (*black coffee revives you*) or after numbers (*three red buses*):

	Singular			Plural
	M	**F**	**N**	
Nominative	**-er**	**-e**	**-es**	**-e**
Accusative	**-en**	**-e**	**-es**	**-e**
Dative	**-em**	**-er**	**-em**	**-en**
Genitive	**-en**	**-er**	**-en**	**-er**

Schwarz**er** Kaffee schmeckt gut mit braun**em** Zucker. *Black coffee tastes good with brown sugar.*

Schnell**e** Züge verbinden Hamburg und München. *Fast trains connect Hamburg and Munich.*

Zwei dänisch**e** Vertreter kommen morgen an. *Two Danish sales reps are arriving tomorrow.*

Die Deutsche Bahn AG baut noch mehr schnell**e** Züge. *The German Federal Railways are building even more fast trains.*

15.3 Im Kontext

15.3.1 Describing someone:

A   Wer ist der Herr da drüben?
B   Er ist der neue Deutschlehrer.
A   Was für ein Mensch ist er?
B   Er ist sehr sympathisch, aber auch sehr streng.
A   Ist er aber ein guter Lehrer?
B   Oh ja! Er ist ein ausgezeichneter Lehrer.

aber	*but*
auch	*also*
streng	*strict*
ausgezeichnet	*excellent*

15.4 Machen wir weiter! *Let's continue!*

Describing the weather

There are various replies to the simple question **Wie ist das Wetter?** *What is the weather like?* (literally, 'How is the weather'?). The simplest answer uses **sein** plus an appropriate adjective:

Das Wetter ist schön.	*The weather is nice.*
Es ist sehr warm heute.	*It is very warm today.*
Der Wind ist kalt .	*The wind is cold.*
Es ist furchtbar windig.	*It's terribly windy.*

You can also use the phrase **es gibt** *there is, there are*. See Unit 3.

Es gibt jetzt wenig Schnee in Bayern.	*There is little snow in Bavaria just now.*
Es gibt viel Sonne in Spanien.	*There's a lot of sun in Spain.*
Es gibt oft Nebel in Hamburg.	*There's often fog in Hamburg.*
Es gibt heute Gewitter am Mittelmeer.	*There are thunderstorms in the Mediterranean today.*
Es gibt keinen Regen in Bonn.	*There's no rain in Bonn.*
Es gibt Sprühregen in Osnabrück.	*There's drizzle in Osnabrück.*

It is also possible to describe the weather by using a more specific verb:

Es friert, aber die Sonne scheint.	*It's freezing but the sun is shining.*
Es regnet oft im November.	*It often rains in November.*
Es blitzt und donnert im Norden.	*It's thundering and lightning in the North.*

(Note: 'thunder and lightning' appear in the reverse order in German.)

Es hagelt im Rheinland.	*It's hailing in the Rhineland.*
Es schneit noch nicht.	*It's not snowing yet.*
Die Temperatur liegt bei 26 Grad in der Schweiz.	*It's 26° in Switzerland.*
Das Klima an der Ostsee tut gut.	*The climate on the Baltic does (you) good.*

15.5 Jetzt sind Sie dran!

Aufgabe A

Wie ist das Wetter in Europa? *What's the weather like in Europe?*

Write a sentence describing the weather in each of the towns marked, for example:

In Paris scheint die Sonne.

Do you remember that the verb must be the second idea in a normal sentence? That's why the verb comes before the subject (**die Sonne**) when the sentence begins In Paris …

Wie ist das Wetter in Europa?

1 In London

....

2 In Madrid

....

3 In Oslo

....

4 In Porto

....

5 In Berlin

....

6 In Müchen

....

7 In Wien

....

8 In Zürich

....

9 In Rom

....

10 In Athen

....

Antworten

1. In London regnet es. 2. In Madrid gibt es Gewitter. 3. In Oslo schneit es. 4. In Porto ist es bedeckt. 5. In Berlin gibt es Sprühregen. 6. In München ist es neblig. 7. In Wien ist es windig. 8. In Zürich hagelt es. 9. In Rom ist es sehr heiß. 10. In Athen blitzt und donnert es.

Aufgabe B

Detektiv spielen *The amateur detective*

There has recently been a spate of burglaries in your area, and from your window you see two people acting supiciously. You phone the police to give a description of them. Use the following words to help you. Check that you are using the correct gender and case, and don't forget the adjectival ending if the adjective comes just before a noun!

Der erste Verdächtige *the first suspect*:

He's tall and thin and is wearing a black raincoat, small sunglasses and a big hat. He is carrying an old, brown, leather briefcase. His hair is long and blond. He looks young.

groß *tall, big*	**der Hut** *hat*
dünn *thin*	**alt** *old*
er trägt *he's wearing*	**die Aktentasche** *briefcase*
schwarz *black*	**das Haar** *hair*
der Regenmantel *raincoat*	**lang** *long*
klein *small*	**blond** *blond*
die Sonnenbrille *sunglasses*	**jung** *young*

Er ist ....

Er trägt ....

....

....

Er sieht .... aus.

Die zweite Verdächtige *the second suspect*:

She's short and fat and is wearing a red blouse, a green skirt and a blue hat, and is carrying a big, white handbag. Her hair is dark and curly. She looks very old and dirty.

Sie ist ....

Sie trägt ....

....

....

Sie sieht .... aus.

klein short	**die Handtasche** handbag
dick fat	**lockig** curly
die Bluse blouse	**dunkel** dark
der Rock skirt	**alt** old
rot red	**schmutzig** dirty
grün green	
blau blue	

Antworten

Der erste Verdächtige *the first suspect*:

Er ist groß und dünn, und er trägt einen schwarzen Regenmantel, eine kleine Sonnenbrille und einen großen Hut. Er trägt auch eine alte, braune Aktentasche aus Leder. Sein Haar ist lang und blond. Er sieht jung aus.

Die zweite Verdächtige *the second suspect*

Sie ist klein und dick. Sie trägt eine rote Bluse, einen grünen Rock, einen blauen Hut und eine große, weiße Handtasche. Ihr Haar ist dunkel und lockig. Sie sieht sehr alt und schmutzig aus.

16 REFERRING TO FUTURE PLANS AND EVENTS

16.1 Preliminary Note:

Future plans, such as *We're going to buy a new house, They're going to get married, The party will be on Tuesday at 9 o'clock, My mother-in-law will arrive on Friday*, can be expressed in more than one way in German.

Asking questions about future plans using the present tense

Hat Hans morgen Geburtstag?	*Is it Hans' birthday tomorrow?*
Fahren Sie nächstes Jahr nach Kanada?	*Are you will you be going to Canada next year?*
Kaufen sie im August ein neues Auto?	*Are they buying a new car in August?*

Asking questions about the future using the verb werden

Wann **wird** er wieder zu Hause sein?	*When will he be home again?*
Wann **wird** die Konferenz beginnen?	*When will the conference start?*
Werden Sie noch mehr Seide aus Thailand importieren?	*Will you be importing more silk from Thailand?*
Wo **werden** wir eine so gute Raumpflegerin finden?	*Where will we find such a good cleaner?*

Giving information about future plans using the present tense

Look first at these examples which use the present tense to express the future, before starting the Grammar Summary:

Heute Abend geht er in die Kneipe.	*He's going to the pub tonight.*
Ich komme nächsten Donnerstag.	*I'll come next Thursday.*

16.2 Grammar Summary

16.2.1 Use of the present tense to refer to a future event

Whenever it is clear that you are referring to the future the present tense can be used to express the idea of the future. In each of the following sentences you can see an expression of time, e.g. **morgen, nächsten Dienstag, nächstes Jahr**, or **bald**, which clearly sets the context in the future, or **zu Weihnachten, im August**, which could be referring to the future, depending on the context.

Ich gehe morgen ins Kino.	*I shall go to the cinema tomorrow.*
Bald sind wir zu Hause!	*We'll be home soon!*
Wir fahren nächstes Jahr nach Kanada.	*We're going to Canada next year.*

16.2.2 The future tense

The future tense is simply formed by using the appropriate part of the verb **werden** (used here as an auxiliary verb) plus an infinitive at the end of the

clause. **Werden** is an irregular verb, and it is worth learning it in full:
NB On its own **werden** means *to become*, e.g. **es wird bald dunkel**, '*It will soon become/get dark*', but it does not have this meaning when used to form the future tense.

Singular	*Plural:*
ich **werde**	wir **werden**
du **wirst**	ihr **werdet**
er **wird**	Sie **werden**
sie **wird**	sie **werden**
es **wird**	

The future tense is frequently used in the following situations:

■ when there is no adverb or adverbial phrase to make a clear reference to the future, e.g.

| Er wird hinfahren. | *He'll go (there).* |
| Wir werden weitermachen. | *We'll continue.* |

■ for more formal information, such as the timing of a function:

| Die Trauung wird in der Nikolaikirche stattfinden. | *The wedding will take place in St. Nicholas' Church.* |
| Der Bundeskanzler wird die Sitzung eröffnen. | *The Federal Chancellor will open the meeting.* |

■ To express a prediction:

| Du wirst dick werden! | *You'll get fat!* |
| Wir werden sehen. | *We shall see.* |

■ to express determination or intention

| Ich werde mitmachen. | *I'll join in.* |
| Er wird abnehmen. | *He will lose weight.* |

16.3 Im Kontext

16.3.1 Read the following press release:

Die Prinzessin wird schon morgen mit dem Hubschrauber ankommen. Ihre Kinder werden erst übermorgen ankommen. Die königliche Kapelle und der Posaunenchor werden sie begrüßen, und es ist erwartet, dass die Prinzessin eine Rede halten wird. Am Abend werden sich ungefähr 100 eingeladene Gäste in dem Schloss versammeln, wo ein Festessen stattfinden wird. Übermorgen werden die Schulkinder der Stadt für die Prinzessin auf dem Marktplatz tanzen.

die Prinzessin *princess*	**eine Rede halten** *to make a speech*
mit dem Hubschrauber *by helicopter*	**ungefähr** *approximately*
erst übermorgen *not until the day after tomorrow*	**ein/laden** *to invite*
königlich *royal*	**der Gast** *guest*
die Kapelle *band (also chapel)*	**sich versammeln** *to gather*
der Posaunenchor *brass band*	**das Schloss** *castle*
begrüßen *to welcome, to greet*	**das Festessen** *banquet*
erwartet *expected*	**tanzen** *to dance*

16.4 Machen wir weiter!

More verbs which express future intention:

planen *to plan*

Sie planen, nach Berlin umzuziehen.   *They're planning to move to Berlin.*

vor/haben *to intend*

Was haben Sie (für) morgen vor?   *What are are your plans for tomorrow? What do you intend doing tomorrow?*

Ich habe morgen nichts vor.   *I've nothing planned for tomorrow.*

die Absicht haben *to intend*

Ich habe die Absicht, diese Dame zu heiraten.   *I intend marrying this lady.*

wollen *to want to* (see also.7.2.1)

Die Regierung will in Zukunft mehr Krankenhäuser bauen.   *The Government intends to build more hospitals in the future.*

Adverbs or adverbial phrases which express the future

bald	*soon*
demnächst	*soon*
gleich	*at once, immediately, in a minute*
morgen	*tomorrow*
morgen früh	*tomorrow morning*
morgen Abend	*tomorrow evening*
übermorgen	*the day after tomorrow*
sofort	*immediately*
nächste Woche	*next week*
nächsten Monat	*next month*
nächstes Jahr	*next year*
in Zukunft	*in future*
in der nahen Zukunft	*in the near future*
zukünftig	*in future, from now on*

16.5 Jetzt sind Sie dran!

Aufgabe A

Gute Vorsätze zum Neujahr *New Year resolutions*

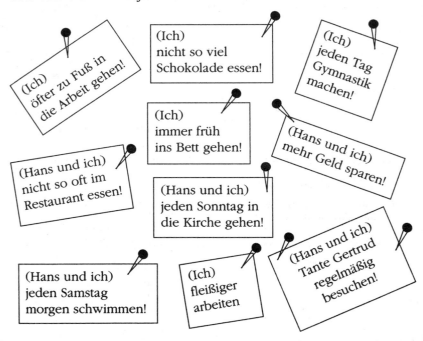

(Ich) öfter zu Fuß in die Arbeit gehen!

(Ich) nicht so viel Schokolade essen!

(Ich) jeden Tag Gymnastik machen!

(Ich) immer früh ins Bett gehen!

(Hans und ich) mehr Geld sparen!

(Hans und ich) nicht so oft im Restaurant essen!

(Hans und ich) jeden Sonntag in die Kirche gehen!

(Hans und ich) jeden Samstag morgen schwimmen!

(Ich) fleißiger arbeiten

(Hans und ich) Tante Gertrud regelmäßig besuchen!

Make a list of your new year resolutions using the notes you have made on your pinboard. Can you translate each full sentence into English?

1 Ich _____
  I _____
2 Ich _____
  I _____
3 Ich _____
  I _____
4 Ich _____
  I _____
5 Ich _____
  I _____
6 Wir _____
  We _____
7 Wir _____
  We _____
8 Wir _____
  We _____
9 Wir _____
  We _____
10 Wir _____
   We _____

Antworten

1 Ich werde nicht so viel Schokolade essen. *I shall not eat so much chocolate.*
2 Ich werde immer früh ins Bett gehen. *I shall always go to bed early.*
3 Ich werde fleißiger arbeiten. *I shall work harder.*
4 Ich werde öfter zu Fuß zur Arbeit gehen. *I shall walk more often.*
5 Ich werde jeden Tag Gymnastik machen. *I'll exercise every day.*
6 Wir werden nicht so oft im Restaurant essen. *We'll shall not eat out in a restaurant so often.*
7 Wir werden mehr Geld sparen. *We'll save more money.*
8 Wir werden jeden Samstagmorgen schwimmen. *We'll go swimming every Saturday morning.*
9 Wir werden jeden Sonntag in die Kirche gehen. *We'll go to church every Sunday.*
10 Wir werden Tante Gertrud regelmäßig besuchen. *We'll visit Aunt Gertrud regularly.*

Aufgabe B

Re-write the following notes in the future tense so that you can issue a press-release with details of a foreign president's visit:

Der Präsident und seine Berater kommen um 20 Uhr in Hamburg an und fahren direkt zum Hotel Atlantik. Sie ziehen sich schnell um, und der deutsche Botschafter begleitet sie in den Speisesaal. Nach dem Essen hält der Präsident eine Rede über die Dritte Welt. Anschließend gibt es einen Empfang im Goldenen Saal für alle Angestellten der Botschaft. Der Empfang ist um 24 Uhr zu Ende, und der Präsident und seine Gattin fahren gleich danach zum Hotel zurück. Eine weitere Pressemitteilung erscheint am Mittwoch.

der Berater	*adviser*
der Botschafter	*ambassador*
begleiten	*to accompany*
der Speisesaal	*dining-room*
eine Rede halten	*to make a speech*
die Dritte Welt	*the Third World*
anschließend	*afterwards, subsequently*
der Empfang	*reception*
der Goldene Saal	*the Gold Room*
die Angestellten	*employees*
die Botschaft	*embassy*
die Gattin	*wife* (more formal than **Frau**)
die Pressemitteilung	*press release*
erscheinen	*to appear*

Antwort

Der Präsident und seine Berater **werden** um 20 Uhr in Hamburg **ankommen** und **werden** direkt zum Hotel Atlantik **fahren**. Sie **werden** sich schnell **umziehen**, und der deutsche Botschafter **wird** sie in den Speisesaal **begleiten**. Nach dem Essen **wird** der Präsident eine Rede über die Dritte Welt **halten**. Anschließend **wird** es einen Empfang im Goldenen Saal für alle Angestellten der Botschaft **geben**. Der Empfang **wird** um 24 Uhr zu Ende **sein**, und der Präsident und seine Gattin **werden** gleich danach zum Hotel **zurückfahren**. Eine weitere Pressemitteilung **wird** am Mittwoch **erscheinen**.

17 DESCRIBING THE PAST

Aims

In this unit you will learn how to:

■ Describe states or actions which were habitual in the past
■ Describe events or activities which indisputedly belong to the past from the narrator's point of view; ■ Reported speech; ■ Describe states or actions which occurred before some past event; ■ Describe a past event or activity in writing

Grammar Content

■ The simple past tense; ■ Adverbs frequently used in the past; ■ The pluperfect tense

17.1 Preliminary Note

Describing states or actions which were habitual in the past

Look at the following examples of the simple past tense (often rendered in English as *used to*) which you may well hear spoken in Northern Germany, and will certainly find in written German throughout the country:

Er **fuhr** jedes Jahr nach Italien.   *He travelled to Italy every year.*
Sie **besuchten** uns jeden Sonntag.   *They used to visit us every Sunday.*

Describing events or activities which indisputedly belong to the past from the point of view of the narrator:

Unser Flugzeug **landete** mit 7 Stunden Verspätung	*Our plane landed seven hours late.*
Mein Bruder **hatte** Glück. Er **musste** nicht zum Militär.	*My brother was lucky. He didn't have to join up/do military service.*

Describing the past using other adverbs or adverbial phrases:

In den sechziger Jahren wohnte ich in der Ludwigstraße in München.	*In the Sixties I lived in Ludwigstraße in Munich.*
Mein Mann studierte **eine Zeitlang** in Marburg.	*My husband studied for a time in Marburg.*
Abends aßen wir immer in Georgios Taverne am Strand.	*In the evenings we always ate at Georgio's Taverna on the beach.*

17.2 Grammar Summary

17.2.1 The *simple past* (also known as the preterite, the imperfect or the narrative past) has only one form in German, for example **ich kaufte,** which can be translated into English as *I bought, I was buying* or *I used to buy*. It comprises the verb stem plus simple past endings.

The simple past tense is often used to describe an activity or event which indisputably belongs to the past from the point of view of the narrator, for example: I *asked* her to marry me.

In the next unit we will learn that the *perfect* tense is often used to refer to events in the recent past which are of relevance or interest in the present, for example: I *have asked* her to marry me (and now – at this present moment – I'm on tenterhooks to hear if she will accept).

This difference technically applies in German, but regional and stylistic variations mean that the simple past is often replaced by the perfect tense (See next unit). However, it is important to know and understand the simple past tense because it is frequently used in writing, and certain forms (especially: **ich war, ich hatte, ich blieb, ich ging, ich kam, ich sah, ich stand, es gab**) appear regularly in speech.

17.2.2 The formation of the simple past tense of regular verbs

The simple past tense of regular verbs is formed by adding the following endings to the verb stem:

kaufen *to buy*	
Singular	*Plural*
ich kauf**te** *I bought, I was buying, I used to buy*	wir kauf**ten** *we bought*
	ihr kauf**tet** *you bought*
du kauf**test** *you bought*	Sie kauf**ten** *you bought (s. and pl.)*
er kauf**te** *he bought*	
sie kauf**te** *she bought*	sie kauf**ten** *they bought*

Als Schüler **lernte** er nicht sehr viel in der Schule.	*As a school boy he didn't learn much at school.*
Sie **verkaufte** Töpferwaren auf dem Markt.	*She used to sell pottery on the market.*
Sie **tanzten** ausschließlich miteinander.	*They danced exclusively with each other.*

The simple past of verbs with stem ending in -d, -t, -m or -n preceded by a consonant

If the stem of regular verb ends in **-d**, **-t**, e.g. **red**en (*to speak*), **arbeit**en (*to work*), or a combination of **-m** or **-n** preceded by another consonant, e.g. **atm**en (*to breathe*), **regn**en (*to rain*), an **-e** is added before the following endings to form the simple past:

arbeiten *to work*	
Singular	*Plural*
ich arbeit**ete** *I worked, I was working, I used to work*	wir arbeit**eten** *we worked*
	ihr arbeit**etet** *you worked*
du arbeit**etest** *you worked*	Sie arbeit**eten** *you worked*
er arbeit**ete** *he worked*	sie arbeit**eten** *they worked*
sie arbeit**ete** *she worked*	
es arbeit**ete** *it worked*	

Look at the following examples and check the endings in the box above:

Sie blutete stark nach der Operation. *She bled heavily after the operation.*

Es regnete den ganzen Tag. *It was raining the whole day.*

Meine Frau begegnete dem Dieb im Flur. *My wife met the thief in the hall.*

Sie antworteten immer mit nein. *Their answer was always no.*

17.2.3 The formation of the simple past of irregular verbs

Unlike the regular verbs, it is not possible to work out what the simple past form of an irregular verb is. For the sake of simplicity no further subdivisions of verbs are named. All good dictionaries and course books include a verb list, which you should consult to find out the correct form. For guidance, there are now approximately 170 of these irregular verbs.

This is how such a verb list works:

infinitive	meaning	3rd person sing. present	3rd person simple past	3rd person perfect tense
bleiben	*to stay*	bleibt	blieb	ist geblieben
essen	*to eat*	isst	aß	hat gegessen
fahren	*to travel*	fährt	fuhr	ist gefahren
geben	*to give*	gibt	gab	hat gegeben
gehen	*to go*	geht	ging	ist gegangen

The choice of **ist** or **hat** in the final column is explained in Unit 18. For the full verb list see Reference Grammar 10.7.

The *third person singular* form is given in the column for the simple past tense. This is, in effect, the simple past *stem* to which endings are added to form the simple past as follows:

trinken *to drink*	
Singular	*Plural*
ich trank - I drank, I was drinking, I used to drink	wir trank**en** we drank
du trank**st** you drank	ihr trank**t** you drank
er trank - he drank	Sie trank**en** you drank
sie trank - she drank	sie trank**en** they drank
es trank - it drank	

There is no ending at all on the **ich** and **er, sie es** forms (which are identical to the one found in the verb list).

Früher **schlief** er gern im Freien
Previously he enjoyed sleeping in the open air.

Jeden Morgen **gingen** wir zusammen zur Schule.
Every morning we used to go to school together

Am Heiligen Abend **gab** es immer Karpfen bei uns zu Hause.
At home there was always carp (to eat) in on Christmas Eve

If necessary, refer to the complete verb list (Reference Grammar 10.7) as you look at the following examples:

Wir **flogen** nur mit Lufthansa.
We flew only with Lufthansa.

Jedes Jahr **schrieben** sie ihm einen netten Brief zum Geburtstag.
Every year they wrote him a nice letter on his birthday.

Damals **hielt** der Zug in Einfeld.
In those days the train stopped in Einfeld.

17.2.4

Perhaps you have noticed that some verbs have unpredictable forms in the simple past. In the next unit we will see that the past participles are equally unpredictable.

Look at the various tense forms of the following verbs :

Infinitive	meaning	3rd person sing. present	3rd person simple past	3rd person perfeit
brennen	*to burn*	brennt	**brannte**	hat gebrannt
bringen	*to bring*	bringt	**brachte**	hat gebracht
denken	*to think*	denkt	**dachte**	hat gedacht
kennen	*to know*	kennt	**kannte**	hat gekannt
nennen	*to name*	nennt	**nannte**	hat genannt

Look at the following examples of the above verbs:

Die Fabrik **brannte** die ganze Nacht hindurch.
The factory burned all through the night.

Wolfgang **brachte** uns Spätzle aus Schwaben.	*Wolfgang brought us spaetzle pasta from Swabia.*
Ihr Schwiegersohn **dachte** nicht daran, sie zu besuchen.	*Their son-in-law didn't think of visiting them.*
Man **nannte** ihn immer Fritzchen.	*They always called him Little Fritz.*

17.2.5 The verbs **haben** and **sein**

These two verbs are very frequently used. Here are their past forms:

infinitive	meaning	3rd person sing present	3rd person simple past	3rd person perfect
haben	*to have*	hat	**hatte**	hat gehabt
sein	*to be*	ist	**war**	ist gewesen

17.3 Im Kontext

17.3.1 Now look at memoirs of Kurt's schooldays before comparing it with the English translation.

Kurt **war** insgesamt sieben Jahre auf dem Schillergymnasium und **ging** jeden Tag mit Begeisterung hin. Seine Lieblingsfächer **waren** Geschichte und deutsche Literatur. Er **las** leidenschaftlich gern und **besuchte** Museen so oft wie möglich. Er **arbeitete** fleißig und **half** gern in der Schulbibliothek. Seine Schulkamaraden **nannten** ihn den kleinen Professor, denn er **hatte** nicht viele Hobbys. Sonntags **machte** er immer lange einsame Wanderungen. Er **schrieb** schon damals Kurzgeschichten und **wollte** unbedingt auf die Universität gehen. Seine Lehrer **schätzten** ihn sehr. Alles in allem **war** Kurt ein außergewöhnlicher Junge.

Kurt was at the Schiller Grammar School for seven years in all and he went there enthusiastically every day. His favourite subjects were history and German literature. He was a passionate reader and visited museums as often as possible. He worked hard and enjoyed helping in the school library. His schoolmates called him 'The Little Professor' as he didn't have many hobbies. On Sundays he used to go on long walks all by himself. Even then he was writing short stories and really wanted to go to university. His teachers held him in high regard. (literally, 'valued him very much'). All in all, Kurt was an extraordinary boy.

17.4 Machen wir weiter!

17.4.1 The past simple tense in reported speech

Sie sagte, sie liebte ihn damals nicht. *She said she didn't love him in
                                            those days.*
Er sagte, er studierte den ganzen Tag. *He said he was studying the
                                           whole day*

Note: As you will see in Unit 20 , the following subjunctive forms may
well be preferred:
Sie sagte, sie **liebe** ihn nicht.
Er sagte, er **habe** den ganzen Tag studiert.

17.4.2 The pluperfect tense

Describing states or actions which occurred before some past event

The pluperfect tense is used both in English and in German to refer to
events which took place before another event in the past. In fact it can *only*
be used in connection with a more recent event, even if this is simply
implied rather than stated in full, for example: 'Her son *had* already *told*
her about it' (when the doctor finally got round to mentioning it). '*I had
saved* enough money to buy a Mercedes' (when I decided to get married).

Note: The pluperfect tense can be translated into English as *I had saved* or
I had been saving.

The pluperfect tense is a compound tense formed by using the appropriate
form of either **haben** or **sein** (see 17.2.5) plus a past participle at the end
of the clause . You will not find this form given in the verb lists as you can
work it out by combining the past stem of **haben** or **sein** (from the simple
past column) with the past participle.

Die Studentin war todmüde, weil   *The student was dead tired*
   sie schlecht **geschlafen hatte**.   *because she had slept badly.*
Der Zug **war** schon **abgefahren**,   *The train had already set off*
   als sie am Bahnhof ankamen.   *when they arrived at the station.*

There are two clauses in each of the sentences above. The pluperfect tense
is used in one clause, and the simple past in the other.

17.4.3 *Examples of mixed usage of tenses in the past*

It is common in newspaper articles to find that the first sentence is written in the perfect tense (to arrest our attention, as it were) and is then followed by a detailed description in the simple past, for example:

Beim schwersten Unglück der
Luftfahrtgeschichte **sind** 349
Menschen ums Leben **gekommen**.
Die Absturzursache ist noch unklar.
In etwa 4 200 Metern Höhe
prallten zwei Flugzeuge zusammen
und **stürzten** ab.

*In the worst accident in aviation
history 349 people died. The
reason for the crash is still
unclear. At a height of
approximately 4,200 metres two
planes collided and crashed.*

If you look at the fairy tales of the Brothers Grimm you will find that they often start with the opening formula (**Es war einmal,** *Once upon a time*), and continue in the simple past until the closing formula:

Und wenn sie nicht gestorben sind,
dann leben sie noch heute.

*And they all lived happily ever
after* (literally, 'If they haven't
died, they're still alive').

17.5 Jetzt sind Sie dran!

Aufgabe A

Insert the appropriate form of the verb (given in brackets as an infinitive) into the gaps in the following sentences:

1. In den sechziger Jahren _____
   (**wohnen**) ich in Paris, wo ich
   an einer Universität _____
   (**studieren**).

   *In the sixties I lived in Paris,
   where I was studying at a
   university.*

2. Es _____ (**geben**) oft
   Demonstrationen in der
   Stadtmitte.

   *There were often demonstrations
   in the town centre*

3. Wir Studenten _____
   (**singen**) Protestlieder, und wir
   _____ (**tragen**) Transparente.

   *We students sang protest songs
   and carried banners.*

4. An jeder Straßenecke _____   *On every street corner groups of*
   (**warten**) Gruppen von Polizisten.   *police were wating. Suddenly they*
   Plötzlich _____ (**laufen**)   *ran towards us.*
   sie uns entgegen.

5. Ich _____ (**haben**) Glück.   *I was lucky. Thank God, I*
   Ich _____ (**kommen**), Gott   *escaped unharmed.*
   sei Dank, unversehrt davon.

Antworten

1. In den sechziger Jahren **wohnte** ich in Paris, wo ich an einer Universität **studierte**.
2. Es **gab** oft Demonstrationen in der Stadtmitte.
3. Wir Studenten **sangen** Protestlieder, und wir **trugen** Transparente.
4. An jeder Straßenecke **warteten** Gruppen von Polizisten. Plötzlich **liefen** sie uns entgegen.
5. Ich **hatte** Glück. Ich **kam**, Gott sei Dank, unversehrt davon

Aufgabe B

(N)Ostalgie *Nostalgia for old East Germany*

You are the secretary of an Anglo-German Society and have written to the elderly relative of a member to ask for his reminiscences about life in the former East Germany. Translate the contents of his letter into English for publication in the next newsletter:

                                                       Leipzig

Liebe Frau Lane,

      Vielen Dank für Ihren Brief. Also, Sie wollten wissen, wie es damals in der DDR war.

Vor der Wende war nicht alles schlecht, wissen Sie! Wir hatten alle Arbeit und konnten immer schöne Urlaubsreisen an die Ostsee oder in die Berge machen. Eintrittskarten für die Oper und das Theater waren sehr billig (Fahrkarten und Bücher auch). Wir mussten natürlich jahrelang auf unsere lieben Trabis warten, aber das waren doch gute Autos! Und es gab so viele gute Möglichkeiten für unsere Kinder. Plätze in Kindertagesstätten hatten wir genug, und es gab wunderbare Sportmöglichkeiten und Bibliotheken für unsere Jugendlichen. Wir bekamen frisches Gemüse aus dem Schrebergarten. Im Sommer machten wir lange Radtouren und schwammen in den herrlichen Seen. Abends saßen wir gerne zusammen und erzählten. Und wir hatten überhaupt keine Angst, nachts alleine durch die dunklen Straßen zu laufen. Übrigens schmeckten die Brötchen damals viel besser als heute.

Es ist schade, dass Sie nicht die Gelegenheit hatten, die DDR selber zu erleben!

Mit bestem Gruß,

Walter Trublich

Übersetzung (Translation):

Dear Mrs. Lane,

Many thanks for your letter. So, you wanted to know what it was like in the days of the GDR (German Democratic Republic). You know, it wasn't all bad before the Wall came down. We all had work and could take great holiday trips to the Baltic coast and to the mountains. Tickets for the opera and theatre were very cheap (as were tickets for public transport and books). Naturally we had to wait for years for our beloved Trabis (Trabant cars), but they were worth waiting for. And there were so many good opportunities for our children. We had enough kindergarden places, and there were wonderful opportunities for sport, and libraries for our young people. We got fresh vegetables from our allotment. In the summer we went on long cycle tours and swam in the beautiful lakes. In the evening we used to like to sit together and tell stories. And we weren't at all afraid of walking down dark streets at night. By the way, the bread rolls tasted much better than today.

It is a pity that you did not have the opportunity to experience the GDR for yourself!

Yours sincerely,

Walter Trublich

18 | TALKING ABOUT THE RECENT PAST

Aims

In this unit you will learn how to:

■ Talk about events in the past which are of relevance or interest to the present; ■ Talk about events which have happened on the recent past

Grammar Content

■ The pefect tense of regular and irregular verbs with **haben** or **sein**
■ The use of **seit** and **schon** with the present tense

18.1 Preliminary Note:

It is impossible to give hard and fast rules to explain how to talk about the recent past, because usage varies both regionally and stylistically, but here are some guidelines.

Referring to past events which are of relevance or interest to the present

Ich habe ihn immer ehrlich gefunden.

I've always found him honest (I still do, and recommend him for this job).

Ich habe die ganze Woche für die Deutschprüfung gepaukt.

I've been swotting for the German exam all week. (That's why I haven't phoned you.)

Er hat das Büro gerade verlassen.

He's just left the office (so he can't take your phone call).

Talking about events which have happened in the recent past

Look at the following examples of colloquial speech which refer to the recent past:

Sag mal, Uschi, was hast du in der Stadt gemacht?	*Tell me, Uschi, what did you do in town?*
Ich habe mir einen neuen Mantel gekauft und dann suchte ich neue Schuhe – vergebens. Ich habe Anna in der Hauptstraße getroffen, und wir sind zusammen ins Café gegangen. Sie hat Kaffee und Kuchen für uns beide bestellt. Hat das geschmeckt!	*I bought (myself) a new coat and then looked – in vain – for new shoes. I met Anna in the main street and we went to a café together. She ordered coffee and cakes for the two of us. Did that taste good!*
Was habt ihr beide gestern Abend gemacht?	*What did you two do last night?*
Wir sind ins Kino gegangen und haben den Film 'Die Spinne' gesehen. (Er hat uns gut gefallen.) Dann haben wir Inge besucht und sind zusammen in die Disko gegangen. Da haben wir getanzt, Cola getrunken, ein bisschen geredet und haben Inge gegen Mitternacht nach Haus' gebracht.	*We went to the cinema and saw the film 'The Spider'. (We liked it). Then we visited Inge and went to the disco together. There we danced, drank Coca Cola and talked a bit. We took Inge home towards midnight.*

18.2 Grammar Summary

18.2.1 The perfect tense of regular verbs

From the above examples we see that German has only one form of the perfect tense, for example: **er hat ... geschrieben** which can be translated as *he wrote, he did write, he has written* (and occasionally *he was writing*) or **ich bin ... gefahren**, which can be translated into English as *I travelled, I did travel, I have travelled* (and occasionally *I was travelling*).

The perfect tense is formed by using the appropriate part of either the verb **haben** or **sein** plus a past participle (e.g. **gekauft**, **getanzt**) at the end of the clause:

Ich **habe** einen neuen Mantel **gekauft.** *I bought a new coat.* (in a different context this could be translated as *I have bought, I did buy* or *I was buying*.

Wir haben **getanzt.** *We danced* (In different contexts this could be translated equally well as *we did dance* or *we have danced*.)

NB The past participle of most regular verbs is formed by first removing the **-en** from the infinitive (e.g. **kaufen**), giving us the stem of the verb (i.e. **kauf-**). Secondly, put **ge-** in front of the stem and **-t** after the stem , resulting in **gekauft** (*bought*). The past participle stands at the end of the clause.

Look at the following examples of verbs in the perfect tense, in which the past participle is formed in the same way:

Ich habe gerade eine Zwiebelsuppe **gekocht.**	*I have just made some onion soup.*
Der Schüler hat seine Hausaufgaben **gemacht.**	*The pupil has done his homework.*
Was **hast** du **gesagt**?	*What did you say?*

18.2.2 Formation of the past participle of separable verbs

To form the past participle of a separable verb, for example **ein/kaufen** (*to go shopping*), **auf/machen** (*to open*), **zu/machen** (*to close*), simply put the **ge-** between the two parts of the verb, forming a 'sandwich' past participle, e.g. **aufgemacht, eingekauft, zugemacht.** This is always written as one word.

Wir **haben** gestern bei Kaufhof **eingekauft.**	*We went shopping at Kaufhof yesterday.*
Er **hat** das Geburtstagsgeschenk noch nicht **aufgemacht.**	*He hasn't opened the birthday present yet.*
Die Hausfrau **hat** die Tür gleich **zugemacht.**	*The housewife closed the door immediately.*

You will find more examples of past participles of separable verbs in the section on irregular verbs below.

18.2.3 Formation of past participles from verbs whose stem ends in -d, -t, or -m or -n preceded by a consonant

If the stem of the verb ends in -**d**, -**t** or -**m** or -**n** preceded by a consonant an additional -**e** is added before the final -**t** in the past participle for ease of pronunciation, for example:

Oma **hat** im Toten Meer **gebad**e**t**.	*Grandma bathed in the Dead Sea.*
Es **hat** gestern viel **geregn**e**t**.	*It rained a lot yesterday.*
Sie **hat** nicht fleißig genug	*She didn't work hard enough.*
gearbeite**t**.	

18.2.4 Formation of the past participle of verbs beginning with be-, emp, ent-, er-, ge-, hinter-, miss-, ver- or zer-, or ending with -ieren.

If the infinitive begins with the prefixes listed above, or ends with -**ieren**, no **ge-** is required at the beginning of the past participles, e.g.

Wir **haben** nichts *be*merkt.	*We didn't notice anything.*
Der Archäologe hat ein Wikingerboot	*The archaeologist discovered a*
im Schlamm *ent*deckt.	*Viking boat in the mud.*
Er **hat** schon vier Jahre **stud**iert.	*He's already been studying for*
	four years.

18.2.5 The perfect tense of irregular verbs

Many verbs do not form their past participle in the way described above. The past participles of most irregular verbs end in -**en**, and many also undergo a vowel change from the infinitive form. There is no reliable way to work this out, and the verb list (see Reference Grammar 10.7, or any good German dictionary) should be consulted until individual forms of the various groups have been learned.

Look at the following examples of irregular verbs used in the perfect tense:

Er **hat** den ganzen Tag kein Wort	*He didn't speak a word all day*
gesprochen.	(**gesprochen** is the past participle of **sprechen**)
Ich **habe** zu viel *gegessen*.	*I've eaten too much* (**gegessen** is the past participle of **essen**)
Hast du dieses Buch schon *gelesen*?	*Have you already read this book?* (**gelesen** is the past participle of **lesen**)

Ein kleiner Scherz *A little joke*

Weißt du, was Tante Herta gestern gemacht hat? Sie hat versucht, den Kanal mit meinem Taschenrechner zu wechseln!! Das hat natürlich nicht geklappt, und sie musste den ganzen Abend Fussball sehen!

Do you know what Aunt Herta did yesterday? She tried to change the T.V. channel with my pocket calculator. Of course it didn't work and so she had to watch football all evening!

18.2.6 Verbs which form their perfect tense using sein

Nowadays we always use the verb *to have* plus a past participle to form the perfect tense in English e.g. 'I *have* come specially', 'You *have* ruined

my reputation', 'He *has* already paid the price', 'We *haven't* seen the
exhibition yet'). But in older English we can find examples of the verb *to
be* plus a past participle being used to form the perfect tense. In the King
James Bible, for example, we can still read 'I *am* come' rather than 'I *have*
come', but of course it sounds archaic. This is not so in German, where
the verb **sein** (*to be*) is still used to form the perfect tense of certain verbs.

A verb uses **sein** in the perfect tense

■ If the verb shows motion or movement from one place to another, for
example:

Ich **bin** mit dem Zug **gefahren**.	*I travelled by train.*
Ihr Mann **ist** um 2 Uhr morgens nach Hause **gekommen**.	*Her husband came home at 2 am.*
Bist du über Brüssel **geflogen**?	*Did you fly via Brussels?*

■ If the verb shows a change of state or condition:

Es **ist** dunkel **geworden**.	*It has got dark* (literally, 'It has become dark').
Ich **bin** schnell **eingeschlafen**.	*I fell asleep quickly.*
Meine Tante **ist** letzte Woche **gestorben**.	*My aunt died last week.*
Die Katze **ist** einfach **verschwunden**.	*The cat simply disappeared.*

■ Two exceptions which form the perfect tense using **sein** (and require the
dative case):

folgen (*to follow*)

Der Herr hat gerufen und der Hund **ist** ihm **gefolgt**.	*The master called and the dog followed him.*

begegnen (*to meet*)

Sie **ist** ihrem Ex-Mann im Restaurant **begegnet**.	*She met her ex-husband in the restaurant.*

■ Note: The verbs **sein** and **bleiben** also form their perfect tense using
sein:

Sie **ist** sehr krank **gewesen**.	*She has been very ill.*
Er **ist** in Rostock **geblieben**.	*He has stayed in Rostock.*

18.2.7 *Regional variations*

As suggested at the beginning of this unit, there are few hard and fast rules about the past tenses. For example, the verbs **sitzen**, **stehen** and **liegen** use **haben** to form their perfect tense in North Germany, but in Southern Germany, Austria and Switzerland **sein** is used. In theory this could result in confusion in some situations; for example, **sitzen** can mean either *to sit* or *to do time in prison*. Thus, **Er hat gesessen** could be ambiguous to someone in North Germany, meaning either *He has been sitting* or *He has been in prison*, but to a Southerner it could only mean *He has been in prison*.

A few other use either **haben** or **sein**, depending on the meaning:

Er **ist** nach Polen **gefahren**.	*He (has) gone to Poland.*
Er **hat** einen Mercedes **gefahren**.	*He was driving a Mercedes.*
Er **ist** den ganzen Nachmittag **geschwommen**.	*He swam the whole afternnoon.*
Er **hat** 1000 Meter in der Olympiade **geschwommen**.	*He swam the 1000 metres in the Olympics.*

From these examples we can see that the verb **sein** is often used to form the perfect tense of verbs which take no direct object (known as intransitive verbs.) If the verb clearly takes a direct object (i.e. there is a person or thing which undergoes the action of the verb), then the perfect tense is formed with **haben**. Such verbs are known as transitive verbs.

18.3 Im Kontext

18.3.1 Look at the following conversation, in which a doctor and a nurse are discussing a patient's progress over the last 24 hours.

Arzt	Hat er denn gut geschlafen?
Krankenschwester	Nein, überhaupt nicht. Er ist die ganze Nacht unruhig gewesen und hat manchmal laut geschrien. Er hat gestern Fieber gehabt und hat auch starke Schmerzen erlitten.
A	Hat er also nichts gegessen?
K	Doch, doch. Er hat eine Scheibe Toast 'runtergekriegt und hat ziemlich viel getrunken. Seine Frau hat ihm Apfelsaft gebracht.

A   Haben Sie schon den Blutdruck gemessen?

K   Das habe ich um 6 Uhr früh gemacht, aber seither habe ich keine Zeit dazu gehabt.

überhaupt nicht *on no account*	**die Scheibe** *slice*
unruhig *restless*	**'runter/kriegen** *to swallow, to get down* (colloquial)
manchmal *sometimes*	
laut schreien *to cry out loud*	**ziemlich viel** *rather a lot, quite a lot*
gestern *yesterday*	
Fieber haben *to have a temperature*	**den Blutdruck messen** *to take the blood pressure*
starke Schmerzen *severe pains*	
erleiden *to suffer*	**um sechs Uhr früh** *early on at six o'clock*
also *so, therefore*	
nichts *nothing*	**seither** *since then*
doch, doch (here) *oh yes, he has* (No was the expected answer).	**keine Zeit haben** *to have no time*

18.4 Machen wir weiter!

18.4.1 Use of the present tense to express something which began in the past and is still continuing

You will often find the word **seit** (*since, for*) + *dative* (see 4.2.3) or **schon** (*already*) in a German sentence which uses the present tense to express something which began sometime in the past and continues to be true, for example:

Seit wann **lernen** Sie Deutsch?   *How long have you been learning German?*

Enno **ist** seit seiner Kindheit kränklich.   *Enno has been sickly since childhood.*

Er **lernt** Klavier seit einem Jahr.   *He has been learning the piano for a year.*

Henning **wohnt** seit der Wende in Koblenz.   *Henning has been living in Coblence since Unification (literally, 'the Turn', i.e. the fall of the Berlin Wall in 1989).*

Mein Onkel **liegt** seit Weihnachten im Krankenhaus.   *My uncle has been in hospital since Christmas.*

Wie lange **warten** Sie schon?	*How long have you already been waiting?*
Waren Sie schon in Leipzig?	*Have you ever been to Leipzig?*

Use of the perfect tense to show the completion of an activity

When we want to show that an activity has been completed, rather than being in process, we use the perfect tense in German.

Look at the following pairs of sentences and see if you can understand the difference between them:

Sie nähte das Hochzeitskleid, als ich ankam.	*She was sewing her wedding dress when I arrived* (i.e. she was in the process of sewing it).
Weißt du, sie hat das Hochzeitskleid selbst genäht.	*Do you know, she made her own wedding dress* (i.e. it is now finished).
Er verdiente das Geld, das er für das Auto brauchte.	*He was earning the money he needed for the car.*
Er hat das Geld für das Auto verdient.	*He has earned the money he needed for the car.*

18.5 Jetzt sind Sie dran!

Aufgabe A

Now look at the following sentences and see if you can work out from which verb each past participle comes. If in doubt, check the verb list (Reference Grammar 10.7).

1. Die Direktorin hat an meinen Vater **geschrieben**.	*The Headmistress wrote to my father.*
2. Habt ihr gut **geschlafen**?	*Did you sleep well?*
3. Ich habe einen Schock **bekommen**.	*I got a shock.*
4. Ich habe meinen Ausweis immer noch nicht **gefunden**.	*I still haven't found my identity card.*
5. Sie haben den ganzen Abend im Biergarten **getrunken**.	*They were drinking the whole evening in the beer garden.*

6. Der Film hat spät **angefangen**.   *The film began late.*
7. Unser Dirigent ist heute von   *Our conductor flew from London*
   London nach Wien **geflogen**.   *to Vienna today.*
8. Pastor Scheurich ist nach dem   *Rev. Scheurich remained in*
   Mauerfall in Eisenach **geblieben**. *Eisenach after the fall of the*
                                        (Berlin) Wall.
9. Der Notarzt ist gleich zum   *The doctor on emergency call*
   Unfallort **gefahren**.   *immediately went to the scene of*
                                        the accident.
10. Er hat mein Deutsch sehr gut   *He understood my German very*
    verstanden.   *well.*

Antworten

1. schreiben; 2. schlafen; 3. bekommen; 4. finden; 5. trinken; 6. an/fangen; 7. fliegen; 8. bleiben; 9. fahren; 10. verstehen.

Aufgabe B

Would you use **haben** or **sein** to complete the following sentences?

1. Ilse ... Käsekuchen bestellt. *Inge ordered cheesecake.*
2. Du ... einen Fehler gemacht. *You've made a mistake.*
3. Der Zug ... um 12.15 abgefahren. *The train set off at 12.15.*
4. Wir ... sehr viel Deutsch gelernt. *We've learned a lot of German.*
5. Sie ... sehr müde geworden. *She's got (become)very tired.*
6. ... ihr ein neues Auto gekauft? *Have you bought a new car?*
7. Ich ... in Stuttgart ein Glas Wein getrunken. *I drank a glass of wine in Stuttgart.*
8. ... Sie Lotte im Krankenhaus besucht? *Have you visited Lotte in hospital?*
9. Hans ... so schnell gewachsen. *Hans has grown so quickly.*
10. Sevim ... noch nie in der Schweiz gewesen. *Sevim hasn't ever been to Switzerland.*

Antworten

1. Ilse hat Käsekuchen bestellt. 2. Du hast einen Fehler gemacht. 3. Der Zug ist um 12.15 abgefahren. 4. Wir haben sehr viel Deutsch gelernt. 5. Sie ist sehr müde geworden. 6. Habt ihr ein neues Auto gekauft? 7. Ich habe in Stuttgart ein Glas Wein getrunken. 8. Haben Sie Lotte im Krankenhaus besucht? 9. Hans ist so schnell gewachsen. 10. Sevim ist noch nie in der Schweiz gewesen.

19 | DESCRIBING PROCESSES AND PROCEDURES

Aims

In this unit you will learn how to:

■ Describe processes and procedures; ■ Ask questions regarding processes and procedures

Grammar Content

■ Passive and active sentences; ■ The use of **man** to avoid the passive

19.1 Preliminary note

To describe the various steps involved in a process such as *The grapes are picked by the students and are then taken to the storehouse. There they are immediately weighed by the foreman,* we use the passive. The passive sentence emphasises the process involved, whereas the active equivalent *The students pick the grapes and then take them to the storehouse. The foreman weighs them,* shows us more clearly who are the agents in the process.

Look at the following examples and their translations before reading the further explanation in the Grammar Summary:

Die Trauben **werden** meistens von Studenten mit der Hand **gepflückt.**	*The grapes are mostly picked by hand by students.*
Sie **werden** gleich in Körbe **getan** und **werden** dann mit dem Trekker zum Lagerhaus **gebracht**.	*They're immediately put into baskets and taken by tractor to the storehouse.*

Dort **werden** die Trauben **gewogen** und in große Gefäße **gekippt**, wo sie **gepresst werden**.	*There the grapes are weighed and put into large containers, where they are pressed.*
Am Ende der Weinernte **wird gefeiert**. Auf dem Winzerfest **wird** eine Weinprinzessin **gewählt**. In einigen Dörfern **wird** der Wein manchmal kostenlos vom Dorfbrunnen **angeboten**, aber in anderen Gegenden **wird** der Wein von Privathäusern aus **verkauft**.	*At the end of the wine harvest there are celebrations. At the wine festival a wine princess is chosen. In some villages wine is sometimes offered free of charge from the village fountain, but in other areas the wine is sold from private houses.*
Die Weinreben **werden** durch Frost oder Hagel oft **beschädigt**.	*The vines are often damaged by frost or hail.*
Sehr viel Wein **wird exportiert**.	*A great deal of wine is exported.*

19.2 Grammar Summary

19.2.1 The passive voice

The passive is formed by using the appropriate part of the verb **werden** (see 16.2.2) for other uses of this verb) plus a past participle at the end of the clause.

Let's analyse two sentences to learn more about the passive. First, let's look at an active sentence:

The students pick the grapes by hand.

■ *The students* are the subject of the sentence because they are carrying out the action of the verb, i.e. picking. In German the subject is put into the nominative case (see 3.2.2).

■ *pick* is the verb

■ *the grapes* are the direct object of the sentence because they are undergoing the action of the verb i.e. being *picked*. In German the direct object is put into the accusative case

■ *by hand* shows us the instrument used

Now let's compare this sentence with the passive equivalent:

The grapes are picked by hand by the students.

■ The grapes, the direct object in the active sentence, has become the subject of the passive sentence.

■ The students, the subject of the active sentence has become the agent by which the activity is carried out in the passive sentence.

■ *by hand* still represents the instrument used

Now have a look at the German version of the active sentence:

Die Studenten	pflücken	die Trauben	mit der Hand
Subject, therefore *nominative* case	verb	direct object, therefore *accusative* case	instrument in *dative* after preposition **mit**

Compare this with the passive equivalent:

Die Trauben werden von den Studenten mit der Hand gepflückt.

■ **Die Trauben**, the direct object of the active sentence, has become the subject of the passive sentence.

■ **Die Studenten**, the subject of the active sentence has become the agent by which the process is carried out in the passive sentence. In German the agent is expressed by using either **von** plus the *dative* case or **durch** plus the *accusative* case. Here **von** is used, and so **die Studenten** is changed into the dative plural (**von den Studenten**)

■ **mit der Hand,** the instrument, remains the same.

Now look at the same passive sentence in different tenses:

Die Trauben **wurden** von den Studenten mit der Hand **gepflückt.**	*The grapes were picked by hand by the students* (simple past tense)
Die Trauben **sind** von den Studenten mit der Hand **gepflückt worden.**	*The grapes have been picked by hand by the students* (perfect tense).
Die Trauben **waren** von den Studenten mit der Hand **gepflückt worden.**	*The grapes had been picked by hand by the students* (pluperfect tense).

Die Trauben **werden** von den Studenten mit der Hand **gepflückt werden.**	*The grapes will be picked by hand by the students* (future tense).

Now look at these different examples of the passive and check the formation of each sentence against the rules we have just learned.

Viele Autos werden importiert.	*Many cars are imported.*
Wir wurden von japanischen Kellnerinnen bedient.	*We were served by the Japanese waitresses.*
Sein Vater wurde durch den Brief gekränkt.	*His father was hurt by the letter.*

NB When the agent is inanimate, the preposition **durch** (*through*) is often used instead of **von.**

Viel Zeit wird von Kindern durch Computerspiele verschwendet.	*A lot of time is wasted by children on computer games.*
Sein letztes Buch wurde in Singapur gedruckt.	*His latest book was printed in Singapore.*
Das Kind ist schwer verletzt worden.	*The child has been badly hurt.*
Viele Flugblätter gegen das Atomkraftwerk sind gestern in der Stadtmitte verteilt worden.	*Many leaflets against the atomic power station were distributed in the town centre yesterday.*
Viele Zeitschriften werden immer noch in Hamburg veröffentlicht, aber bald werden die Verlagshäuser nach Berlin umziehen.	*Many magazines are still published in Hamburg, but soon the publishing houses will move to Berlin.*

(Notice the two different uses of the verb **werden** in this sentence, firstly as an auxiliary verb to form the passive, secondly as an auxiliary verb to form the future.)

19.3 Im Kontext

19.3.1 Now look at the following report which a social worker is helping a client threatened with eviction to compile:

Wir werden von allen asozial genannt. Es wird behauptet, dass nachts sehr laute Musik in unserem Haus gespielt wird, dass wilde Parties gehalten werden, wo zu viel Bier getrunken wird. Die Wahrheit ist, dass nachts Steine gegen unsere Fenster geworfen worden sind – ohne Grund! Es wird auch gesagt, dass Drogen bei uns zu finden sind. Wir werden Drogenhändler genannt. Wir werden von den Kindern vermieden und von den Erwachsenen verfolgt. Wir sind aber total unschuldig.

von allen by everyone	**das Fenster** window
asozial antisocial	**ohne** without
nennen to name, call	**der Grund** the reason
behaupten to maintain	**die Droge** drug
nachts at night	**zu finden sein** to be found
wild wild	**der Drogenhändler** drug dealer
eine Party halten to hold a party	**vermeiden** to avoid
zu viel too much	**verfolgen** to persecute
die Wahrheit the truth	**unschuldig** innocent
der Stein stone	

19.4 Machen wir weiter! *The use of* man *to avoid the passive*

The passive can often be avoided simply by using the indefinite pronoun **man**.

Compare the following sets of sentences. The first involves the passive, the second **man**. Both sentences have the same meaning.

Es wird oft gesagt, dass Albanien landschaftlich sehr schön ist.	*It is often said that Albania is scenically very pretty.*
Man sagt oft, dass Albanien landschaftlich sehr schön ist.	*They often say that Albania is scenically very pretty*
Im Moment werden sehr viele Aktien verkauft	*A lot of shares are being sold at the moment*
Im Moment verkauft **man** sehr viele Aktien.	*At the moment they're selling a lot of shares.*
Dieses Jahr ist mehr Bier denn je auf dem Oktoberfest getrunken worden.	*This year more beer than ever was drunk at the October Beer Festival.*
Dieses Jahr hat **man** mehr Bier denn je auf dem Oktoberfest getrunken.	*This year they drank more beer than ever at the October Beer Festival*

19.5 Jetzt sind Sie dran!

Aufgabe A

Einen schönen Feierabend allerseits! *Have a good evening, everyone!*

You want to help with the final tasks in the office, so that you can all leave early for the weekend. Unfortunately your offers of help come too late, as others are already doing the work. Change the active sentence into the present passive, e.g.

Darf ich den Brief tippen?

Der Brief **wird** schon **getippt.** *The letter is already being typed*:

1. Darf ich das Fax schicken? *May I send the fax?*

_____

2. Darf ich das Fenster zumachen? (*May I close the window?*)

_____

3. Darf ich den Papierkorb leeren? *May I empty the wastepaper basket?*

_____

4. Darf ich die Kaffeetassen abwaschen? *May I wash up the coffee cups?*

_____

5. Darf ich die Briefe unterschreiben? *May I sign the letters?*

_____

Antworten:

1. Nein, das Fax **wird** schon **geschickt.** 2. Nein, das Fenster **wird** schon **zugemacht.** 3. Nein, der Papierkorb **wird** schon **geleert.** 4. Nein, die Kaffeetassen **werden** schon **abgewaschen.** 5. Nein, die Briefe **werden** schon **unterschrieben.**

Another colleague comes into the office and asks the same questions (1–5). You refuse her help, saying that these tasks have just been done. You should use the perfect passive, e.g.

Darf ich den Brief tippen?

Nein, der Brief ist schon getippt worden.

1. Darf ich das Fax schicken? *May I send the fax?*

_____

2. Darf ich das Fenster zumachen? *May I close the window?*

_____

3. Darf ich den Papierkorb leeren? *May I empty the wastepaper basket?*

_____

4. Darf ich die Kaffeetassen abwaschen? *May I wash up the coffee cups?*

_____

5. Darf ich die Briefe unterschreiben? *May I sign the letters?*

_____

Antworten

1. Nein, das Fax **ist** schon **geschickt worden.** 2. Nein, das Fenster **ist** schon **zugemacht worden**. 3. Nein, der Papierkorb **ist** schon **geleert worden.** 4. Nein, die Kaffeetassen **sind** schon **abgewaschen worden**. 5. Nein, die Briefe **sind** schon **unterschrieben worden.**

Just as you are about to leave, your boss comes in and asks your colleague why she hasn't done various tasks. She replies that they had already been done when she offered. In response to the question with **warum**? Put the reply into the pluperfect passive:

Warum haben Sie den Brief nicht getippt?	*Why have you not typed the letter?*
Der Brief **war** schon getippt **worden**.	*The letter had already been written* (when I offered.)

1. Warum haben Sie das Fax nicht geschickt?

_____

2. Warum haben Sie das Fenster nicht zugemacht?

_____

3. Warum haben Sie den Papierkorb nicht geleert?

_____

4. Warum haben Sie die Kaffeetassen nicht abgewaschen?

_____

5. Warum haben Sie die Briefe nicht unterschrieben?

_____

Antworten

1. Das Fax **war** schon **geschickt worden.** 2. Das Fenster **war** schon **zugemacht worden.** 3. Der Papierkorb **war** schon geleert **worden.** 4. Die Kaffeetassen **waren** schon **abgewaschen worden.** 5. Die Briefe **waren** schon **unterschrieben worden.**

Aufgabe B

Rephrase the following passive sentences using the indefinite pronoun **man** and the active form of the verb.

1. Es wird oft gesagt, dass Zigaretten der Gesundheit schaden. _It is often said that cigarettes harm one's health._

   _____

2. Auf Bierfesten wird Bier oft aus Maßkrügen getrunken. _At beer festivals beer is often drunk out of one-litre steins._

   _____

3. Zu Weihnachten wird eine Gans nicht mehr so oft gegessen wie früher. _At Christmas, goose is not eaten as often as formerly._

   _____

4. Zu viel wird von Kleinkindern erwartet. _Too much is expected of toddlers._

   _____

5. Hier wird Deutsch gesprochen. _German is spoken here._

   _____

6. Der Reifendruck wird kostenlos geprüft. _Tyre pressure is checked free of charge._

   _____

7. Der Müll wird in fast jeder deutschen Küche getrennt. *Refuse is separated in almost every German kitchen.*

_____

8. Das Brot wird mit einer Schneidemaschine geschnitten. *Bread is cut with a slicing machine.*

_____

9. Immer mehr Geld wird bei den Sommerschlussverkäufen ausgegeben. *More and more money is being spent in the summer sales.*

_____

10. In dieser Schule wird nicht sehr viel gelernt. *Not very much is learnt in this school.*

_____

Antworten

1. Man sagt oft, dass Zigaretten der Gesundheit schaden.
2. Auf Bierfesten trinkt man Bier oft aus Maßkrügen.
3. Zu Weihnachten isst man eine Gans nicht so oft wie früher.
4. Man erwartet zu viel von Kleinkindern.
5. Hier spricht man Deutsch.
6. Man prüft den Reifendruck kostenlos.
7. Man trennt den Müll in fast jeder deutschen Küche.
8. Man schneidet das Brot mit einer Schneidemaschine.
9. Man gibt immer mehr Geld bei den Sommerschlussverkäufen aus.
10. In dieser Schule lernt man nicht sehr viel.

20 | REPORTING WHAT WAS SAID AND ASKED

Aims

In this unit you will learn how to:

■ Report who said and asked what

Grammar Content

■ Subjunctive 1

20.1 Preliminary Note:

When we say or ask something directly, we call this *direct speech* e.g. *"I've no money. Have you any?"* We use the normal form (or mood) of the verb, which you have learned so far in this book. This is known as the indicative mood.

If, however, we wish to report a statement or question to someone, and are not absolutely sure of the truth of the original statement, or wish in some way to distance ourselves from it, e.g. *He said he had no money and asked me whether I had any*, then a different mood of the verb is often used in German: the subjunctive. It indicates that we cannot be one hundred per cent sure that what is being reported is true.

There are very few remnants of the subjunctive left in English, mostly expressions such as *Be that as it may* or *So be it*, or, in the words of Topol's song, *If I were a rich man.*

Look at the following examples of direct speech (in the left column), and compare each one with the reported or indirect speech (in the right column). Please pay particular attention to the form of the verb in each example.

Direct speech	Indirect speech or, reported speech
1.My son's exact words to my husband this morning:	This same conversation as related to me by my husband:
Vati, ich bin krank. *Dad, I'm ill.*	Er sagte, er **sei** krank … *He said he was ill.*
Ich habe Kopfschmerzen. *I've got a headache.*	(Er sagte,) er **habe** Kopfschmerzen. *He said he had a headache.*
Ich kann nicht für meine Prüfung lernen. *I can't learn for my exam.*	(Er sagte,) er **könne** nicht für seine Prüfung lernen. *He can't learn for his exam.*
Ich muss ins Bett gehen. *I've got to go to bed.*	(Er sagte,) er **müsse** ins Bett gehen. *(He said) he had to go to bed.*
Ich brauche Ruhe. *I need (some) rest.*	(Er sagte,) er **brauche** Ruhe. *(He said) he needed (some) rest.*
Ich rufe lieber den Arzt an. *I'd better phone the doctor.*	(Er sagte,) er **rufe** lieber den Arzt an. *(He said) he'd better phone the doctor.*

2.Look at the comments my doctor made when she visited me this morning:	Now look at the way I pass these comments on to my boss:
Sie sehen nicht gut aus! *You don't look well!*	Die Ärztin sagte mir, ich **sähe** nicht gut aus. *The doctor told me I didn't look well.*
Aha! Sie haben Fieber! *Well! You've got a temperature.*	(Sie sagte,) ich **hätte** Fieber. *She told me I had a temperature.*
Sie sollen im Bett bleiben! *You should stay in bed.*	(Sie sagte,) ich **solle** im Bett bleiben. *She told me I should stay in bed.*

Sie müsssen viel trinken.   (Sie sagte,) ich **müsse** viel trinken.
You must drink a lot.   *She said I had to drink a lot.*

Sie dürfen nichts essen.   (Sie sagte,) ich **dürfe** nichts essen.
You're not allowed to eat   *She said I'm not allowed to eat*
anything.   *anything.*

Sie sind wirklich krank.   (Sie sagte,) ich **sei** wirklich krank.
You are really ill.   *She said I was really ill.*

Ich komme morgen wieder vorbei. (Sie sagte,) sie **komme** morgen
                                           wieder vorbei.
I'll call round again tomorrow.   *She said she would call round*
                                           again tomorrow.

3.Look at the questions   Now study the way the children
a policeman asks two little   later report these questions to
children who are lost in town: their parents:

Wie heißt ihr?   Er fragte uns, wie wir hießen.
What are you called?   *He asked us what we were called.*

Wie alt seid ihr?   Er fragte uns, wie alt wir seien.
How old are you?   *He asked us how old we were.*

Wo wohnt ihr?   Er fragte uns, wo wir wohnten.
Where do you live?   *He asked us where we lived.*

Sind eure Eltern zu Hause?   Er fragte uns, ob unsere Eltern
                                           zu Hause seien.
Are your parents at home?   *He asked us whether our parents*
                                           were at home.

Kommt ihr oft allein in die Stadt? Er fragte uns, ob wir oft allein in
                                           die Stadt kämen.
Do you often come to town alone? *He asked us whether we often*
                                           came to town alone.

Habt ihr Geld für den Bus?   Er fragte, ob wir Geld für
                                           den Bus hätten.
Have you money for the bus?   *He asked us whether we had*
                                           money for the bus.

The present tense (as used in the original speech) is normally used in indirect speech in German, whereas English prefers the past tense. However, when the Subjunctive 1 form is the same as the indicative, Subjunctive 2 is preferred (see Unit 21).

20.2 Grammar Summary

20.2.1 The subjunctive

■ There are two forms of the subjunctive in German, sometimes described as the present subjunctive and imperfect subjunctive. This can be misleading in that the subjunctive does not directly correspond to the tenses referred to, and so we shall use the terms Subjunctive 1 for the so-called present subjunctive and Subjunctive 2 for the so-called past subjunctive.

■ The two forms are sometimes interchangeable, and there is a trend in speech to avoid the subjunctive altogether by using the indicative.

■ Although one can very often avoid using it oneself, the subjunctive is still frequently used in newspapers and television news reports when reporting proceedings in parliament or details of negotiations, etc. (e.g. in the **Tageschau**, which is broadcast at 8 p.m. every evening). So you should at least be able to recognise how it is formed, even if you restrict usage to a few frequently used forms.

20.2.2 The formation of Subjunctive 1

By the very nature of reported speech, the 3rd person singular and plural forms (*he said that ..., she told me that ..., they related that ...*) are most frequently used. In fact, you are unlikely to come across some of the other forms – but you may well be interested to see what they are.

Subjunctive 1 is formed by adding the following endings to the stem of the verb:

haben	
Singular	*Plural*
ich habe	wir haben
du habest	ihr habet
er habe	Sie haben
sie habe	sie haben
es habe	

Notice that the **ich, wir, Sie** and **sie** forms are the same in the subjunctive as in the indicative for **haben**. In practice the Subjunctive 2 form is often substituted (see Unit 21).

können	
Singular	*Plural*
ich könne	wir können
du könnest	ihr könnet
er könne	Sie können
sie könne	sie können
es könne	

The verb **sein** is an exception in that it forms its present subjunctive as follows, without -**e** in the singular:

sein	
Singular	*Plural*
ich **sei**	wir **seien**
du **seiest**	ihr **seiet**
er **sei**	Sie **seien**
sie **sei**	sie **seien**
es **sei**	

This form will be familiar to you, as it is the same as the imperative mood of **sein** (see 13.2.5).

20.2.3 The use of dass in reported speech (see also 10.2.1)

The conjunction dass (*that*) is sometimes used in reported speech in the same way as in English, for example: *She told me she was hoping to change her job* or *She told me that she was hoping to change her job*. This tends to be a little more formal, and the subjunctive is normally used in reported speech which involves **dass**.

Sie sagte, **dass** sie krank **sei**.   *She said that she was ill.*
Er behauptete, **dass** er kein   *He maintained that he had no*
   Geld **habe**.   *money.*

Sie erzählten uns, **dass** sie in Dresden **wohne**.	*They told us that she lived in Dresden.*

20.2.4 The use of ob in reported questions

Ob means *whether* or *if*, and is frequently used in reported questions. It follows the same pattern as **dass** (see 10.2.1):

Er fragte mich, **ob** ich kommen **könne**.	*He asked me if I could come.*
Sie wollte wissen, **ob** ich genügend Geld **habe**.	*She wanted to know if I had enough money.*

Similarly, **ob** can also be used in indicative sentences, as follows:

Ich frage mich, **ob** es sich **lohnt**.	*I ask myself whether it's worth it.*
Er will wissen, **ob** der Anorak regendicht **ist**.	*He wants to know if the anorak is waterproof.*

20.3 Im Kontext

20.3.1 Read the following newspaper account of yesterday in Parliament:

Der Finanzminister versicherte, diese Sparmaßnahmen seien unvermeidlich. Er denke nur an die Zukunft und wolle alles Erdenkliche für Kinder machen. Er müsse also neue Geldquellen finden, um seine Pläne zu finanzieren. Er werde daher nächste Woche den Preis von

---

der Finanzminister *Minister of Finance*
versichern *to assure, affirm*
die Sparmaßnahme *economy measure*
denken an + accusative *to think of*
die Zukunft *the future*
alles Erdenkliche *conceivable, imaginable*
die Geldquelle *source of money*
der Plan *plan*
finanzieren *to finance*
daher *that is why*
nächste Woche *next week*

der Preis *price (also prize)*
erhöhen *to raise, increase*
ab *from*
das Benzin *petrol*
pro Liter *per litre*
ab sofort *with immediate effect*
jedoch *however*
das Kindergeld *child allowance*
die Eltern *parents*
erhältlich *available, obtainable*
ein zinsloses Darlehen *an interest-free loan*
der Student *student*

Zigaretten und Alkohol erhöhen, und ab Mitternacht werde Benzin 10 Pfennig pro Liter mehr kosten. Ab sofort sei jedoch mehr Kindergeld für Eltern erhältlich, und es gebe ein zinsloses Darlehen für Studenten.

20.4 Machen wir weiter!

You can further combine the Subjunctive 1 form of either **haben** or **sein** with a past participle to produce a perfect form such as:

Er sagte, er **habe** nichts getrunken.   *He said he **had** drunk nothing.*
Sie sagte, sie **sei** allein gekommen.   *She said she **had** come alone.*

20.5 Jetzt sind Sie dran!

Aufgabe A

Study the following examples of reported speech, and then write out what was actually said in the original conversation:

Zum Beispiel

Mein Chef sagte, er sei müde.   *My boss said he was tired.*
Der Chef sagt: "Ich bin müde".   *The boss says: I am tired.*

1 Das Mädchen meinte, sie habe Hunger. *The girl said she was hungry.*
   Das Mädchen sagt: "Ich ...."

2 Der Politiker meinte, er könne nichts mehr machen. *The politician said he couldn't do any more.*
   Der Politiker sagt: "Ich ...."

3 Der Arzt fragte, ob ich Tabletten habe. *The doctor asked whether I had any tablets.*
   Der Arzt fragt: "Haben Sie.."

4 Sein Freund fragte, was im Kino laufe. *His friend asked what was on at the cinema.*
   Der Freund fragt: "Was.."

5 Der Schaffner fragte den Schüler, ob er seinen Ausweis sehen dürfe. *The bus/tram conductor asked the schoolboy if he might see his identity card.*
   Der Schaffner fragt :"Darf.."

Antworten

1. "Ich habe Hunger". 2. "Ich kann nichts mehr machen!" 3. "Haben Sie Tabletten?" 4. "Was läuft im Kino?" 5. "Darf ich deinen Ausweis sehen?"

Aufgabe B

Look at the report of a recent study on sleep, and then write out what you think was actually said in the original findings of the report:

Laut einer Studie schliefen die Deutschen jetzt weniger als vor zwanzig Jahren. Heutzutage brauche man eine halbe Stunde weniger Schlaf als damals, aber dafür nähmen mindestens 30% aller Erwachsenen Schlafmittel. Stress am Arbeitsplatz sei der Grund dafür.

laut *according to* (plus the *dative* case)	**damals** *then*
die Studie *study*	**dafür** *to make up for that, for all that*
weniger als *less than*	**nähmen** *Subjunctive 2 of* **nehmen** *to take*
vor zwanzig Jahren *twenty years ago*	**die Erwachsenen** *adults*
heutzutage *nowadays*	**Schlafmittel nehmen** *to take sleeping pills*
brauchen *to need*	**mindestens** *at least*
eine halbe Stunde *half an hour*	**am Arbeitsplatz** *in the work place*
der Schlaf *sleep*	**der Grund dafür** *the reason for it*

Antwort

Text der Studie: Die Deutschen **schlafen** jetzt weniger als vor zwanzig Jahren. Heutzutage **braucht** man eine halbe Stunde weniger Schlaf als damals, aber dafür **nehmen** mindestens 30% aller Erwachsenen Schlafmittel. Stress am Arbeitsplatz **ist** der Grund dafür.

21 | EXPRESSING CONDITIONS

Aims

In this Unit you will learn to:

Express open conditions ■ Express remote conditions; ■ Express unfulfilled conditions

Grammar Content

Wenn followed by the indicative ■ **Wenn** followed by Subjunctive 2 ■ Other phrases expressing conditions

21.1 Preliminary note

To express conditions in German, we normally use the word **wenn** (*if, whenever, when*).

■ If we are talking about a real condition (i.e. if it is really likely to happen), for example: *If it stays fine, I shall play tennis this afternoon*, follow **wenn** with the indicative mood. This is called an open condition.

■ If you are talking about an unreal or hypothetical condition, for example: *If I were a rich man* or *If I were you*, follow **wenn** with Subjunctive 2. This is called a 'remote' condition. (It is one of the few examples of the subjunctive still heard in English, although some people replace it by the indicative.)

■ If we are reflecting on something which could have happened if circumstances had been different, for example: *If I had known in time, I would have gone to meet him* (but I didn't know, so I didn't go, and now it is too late), this is an 'unfulfilled' condition. It is expressed by Subjunctive 2 in the pluperfect.

Have a look at the following examples:

Expressing real conditions

Ich gebe ihr das Buch, wenn ich sie sehe.	*I'll give her the book when/if I see her.*
Wenn es morgen regnet, bleibe ich zu Hause.	*If it rains tomorrow, I'll stay at home.*
Wenn ich Zeit habe, rufe ich ihn an.	*If I have time I'll phone him.*

Expressing hypothetical conditions

Wenn ich mehr Platz hätte, würde ich euch alle einladen.	*If I had more room, I'd invite you all.*
Wenn er reich wäre, würde er sich ein Haus kaufen.	*If he were rich, he'd buy himself a house.*
Wenn ich das gewusst hätte, hätte ich nichts gesagt.	*If I had know that, I would have said nothing.*

21.2 Grammar Summary

21.2.1 The formation of Subjunctive 2

regular verbs:

The Subjunctive 2 form of regular verbs is the same as the imperfect indicative, for example **kaufte** in the sentence:

Wenn ich das **kaufte**, würde mein Mann lachen.	*If I bought that, my husband would laugh.*

irregular verbs

To form the Subjunctive 2 of irregular verbs, the following endings are added to the imperfect indicative (found in the verb list, Reference Grammar 10.7) In addition to these endings an umlaut must be added to the vowels **a, o** or **u** in the stem.

sein *to be*

The imperfect indicative
stem is **war**

Singular
ich **wäre**
du **wärest**
er **wäre**
sie **wäre**
es **wäre**

Plural
wir **wären**
ihr **wäret**
Sie **wären**
sie **wären**

haben *to have*

The imperfect indicative
stem is **hatte**

Singular
ich **hätte**
du **hättest**
er **hätte**
sie **hätte**
es **hätte**

Plural
wir **hätten**
ihr **hättet**
Sie **hätten**
sie **hätten**

---

gehen *to go*

The imperfect indicative
stem is **ging**

Singular
ich **ginge**
du **gingest**
er **ginge**
sie **ginge**
es **ginge**

Plural
wir **gingen**
ihr **ginget**
Sie **gingen**
sie **gingen**

You can further combine the Subjunctive 2 form of **haben** or **sein** with a past participle to produce a pluperfect form expressing unfulfilled conditions, as follows:

Wenn er das gewusst hätte, wäre er weggelaufen.	*If he had known that, he would have run away.*
Wenn ich das gehört hätte, hätte ich laut gelacht.	*If I had heard that, I would have laughed out loud.*
Wenn sein Chef das gesehen hätte, hätte er ihm gekündigt.	*If his boss had seen that he would have given him the sack.*

Hätte er uns rechtzeitig geschrieben, *Had he written to us in time,*
wäre dies nie passiert. *this would have never happened.*

21.2.2 As mentioned in Unit 20, there is a trend either to simplify or to
avoid the subjunctive in modern spoken German. In situations where a
subjunctive is clearly needed, a useful and simple formula **Ich würde +**
infinitive is often used, for example:

Ich **würde sagen**, dass es *I would say that it's*
unbedingt nötig ist. *absolutely necessary.*
Ich **würde** gerne **mitmachen**, aber *I'd love to join in but I*
ich habe keine Zeit. *have no time.*

This formula is not used with **sein**. The form **wäre** is preferred:

Ich **wäre** sehr dankbar, wenn Sie *I'd be most grateful if you*
das nicht weitersagen würden. *wouldn't pass this on.*

As we saw in the last unit, **wenn** sends the verb to the end of the clause.
If **wenn** starts the sentence it still sends the verb to the end of the clause,
but the verb in the next clause is also inverted, resulting in a so-called
verb–comma–verb construction:

Wenn du **willst, fahre** ich gerne mit. *If you want, I'll gladly come (with you).*

It is also possible to omit **wenn** and yet still express a conditional sentence
in the same way as in the English example: *Had I known that, I would
never have consented to it.* Although the word 'if' does not appear in this
sentence, it clearly has the meaning of *If I had known that, I would never
have consented to it.*

Now look at the following German examples of this:

Hätte ich das gewusst, **so hätte** ich *Had I known that, I would never*
nie 'ja' gesagt *have said yes.*
Wäre Norbert hier gewesen, **dann** *Had Norbert been here, then he*
hätte er uns sicher geholfen. *would certainly have helped us.*

You will notice from these examples that so (*so*) or **dann** (*then*) is added
in mid-sentence if **wenn** is omitted. This can also happen in examples
using the indicative:

Regnet es weiter, **dann** spiele *If it continues raining, I'll not*
ich nicht Tennis. *play tennis.*
Sollte es schön sein, **dann** bringe *Should it be nice (weather) I'll*
ich meine Mutter mit. *bring my mother.*

21.3 Im Kontext

21.3.1 Look at the following conversation in which two friends fantasise about winning the lottery.

Träumerei *(daydreaming)*

Jürgen Sag mal, Udo, was würdest du machen, wenn du die Lotterie gewonnen hättest?

Udo Ich würde nie wieder zum Dienst gehen. Ich würde mir ein großes Haus an der See kaufen und würde jeden Tag segeln. Das wäre was! Und du?

Jürgen Wenn ich über Nacht Millionär würde, würde ich alle meine Freunde zu einer Party in der Karibik einladen. Aber sollte der Gewinn nicht so groß sein, dann lade ich dich ein! Egal, wie wäre es, wenn wir jetzt ein Bier trinken würden? Wir könnten eins trinken, ohne in der Lotterie gewonnen zu haben!

In der Lotterie gewinnen *to win the lottery*		**in der Karibik** *in the Caribbean*	
zum Dienst gehen *to go to work*		**ein/laden** *to invite*	
an der See *by the sea*		**der Gewinn** *the win*	
jeden Tag *every day*		**egal** *all the same*	
segeln *to go sailing*		**ohne die Lotterie gewonnen zu**	
über Nacht *overnight*		**haben** *without having won the lottery*	

21.4 Machen wir weiter1

Other ways of expressing conditions

Ich bringe einen Regenschirm mit – im Falle eines Falles. *I'll bring an umbrella – just in case.*

Hier ist die Adresse des Hotels, **falls** du dich verläufst. *Here is the hotel address, **in case** you get lost.*

Er muss fleißig lernen, **sonst** besteht er die Aufnahmeprüfung nicht. *He's got to study hard, **otherwise** he won't pass the entrance exam.*

Bei Regen fällt die Theateraufführung im Freien aus. *In the event of rain the open air performance will be cancelled.*

Was? Du willst nicht hinfahren? Dann fahre ich auch nicht hin! *What? You don't want to go (there)? Then I shan't either.*

| Ohne seinen Klassenlehrer hätte er das Abitur nicht schaffen können. | *Without (the help of) his form teacher he would not have been able to manage das Abitur.* |

21.5 Jetzt sind Sie dran!

Aufgabe A

Link up each clause from the left column, beginning with a number, with one from the right column, beginning with a letter, to form sentences which make sense:

1. Wenn ich genug Geld habe,	A	werde ich alles erklären.
2. Wenn ich Millionär wäre,	B	hätte ich ihm keine Schokolade gegeben.
3. Wenn ich von seiner Zuckerkrankheit gewusst hätte,	C	kaufe ich mir ein neues Auto.
4. Wenn wir mehr Platz hätten,	D	können wir in den Bergen wandern.
5. Ich wäre Ihnen sehr dankbar,	E	würde ich nicht mehr arbeiten.
6. Wenn du willst,	F	würden wir euch alle zu Silvester einladen.
7. Wenn das Wetter morgen schön ist,	G	wenn Sie das nicht weitersagen.
8. Wenn ich sie sehe,	H	besuche ich dich.
9. Wenn es weiter regnet,	I	würde ich die Samstagsschule abschaffen.
10. Wenn ich Direktor dieser Schule wäre,	J	können wir nicht mehr im Garten arbeiten.

Antworten

1C, 2E, 3B, 4F, 5G, 6H, 7D, 8A, 9J, 10I

1. Wenn ich genug Geld habe, kaufe ich mir ein neues Auto. *If I have enough money I will buy myself a new car.*

2. Wenn ich Millionär wäre, würde ich nicht mehr arbeiten. *If I were a millionaire I would no longer work.*

3. Wenn ich von seiner Zuckerkrankheit gewusst hätte, hätte ich ihm keine Schokolade gegeben. *If I had known he had diabetes I would not have given him chocolate.*

4. Wenn wir mehr Platz hätten, würden wir euch alle zu Silvester einladen. *If we had more room we would invite you all for New Year.*

5. Ich wäre Ihnen sehr dankbar, wenn Sie das nicht weitersagen würde. *I would be grateful to you if you did not pass it on.*

6. Wenn du willst, besuche ich dich. *If you wish I will visit you.*

7. Wenn das Wetter morgen schön ist, können wir in den Bergen wandern. *If the weather is good tomorrow we can walk in the mountains.*

8. Wenn ich sie sehe, werde ich alles erklären. *If I see her (them) I shall explain everything.*

9. Wenn es weiter regnet, können wir nicht mehr im Garten arbeiten. *If it continues to rain we cannot work in the garden any more.*

10. Wenn ich Direktor dieser Schule wäre, würde ich die Samstagsschule abschaffen. *If I were head of this school I would abolish Saturday school.*

Aufgabe B

You have been asked to give advice as to what you would do in someone else's position. Re-phrase each recommendation, using the construction **ich würde** plus the appropriate infinitive, e.g.

Du solltest zum Arzt gehen.   *You ought to go to the doctor's.*
An deiner Stelle würde ich zum   *If I were you I would go to*
  Arzt gehen.   *the doctor.*

1. Du solltest ein neues Hobby finden. *You ought to find a new hobby.*

2. Du solltest früher ins Bett gehen. *You ought to go to bed earlier.*

3. Du solltest Diät machen. *You ought to go on a diet.*

4. Du solltest nicht so viel Geld ausgeben. *You ought not to spend so much money.*

5. Du solltest nicht rauchen. *You ought not to smoke.*

6. Du solltest fleißiger arbeiten. *You ought to work more diligently.*

7. Du solltest viel mehr lesen. *You ought to read far more.*

8. Du solltest den Rasen öfter mähen. *You ought to mow the lawn more often.*

9. Du solltest eine Ferienreise buchen. *You ought to book a holiday trip.*

10. Du solltest weniger Alkohol trinken. *You ought to drink less alcohol.*

Antworten

1. An deiner Stelle würde ich ein neues Hobby finden. **2.** An deiner Stelle würde ich früher ins Bett gehen. **3.** An deiner Stelle würde ich Diät machen. **4.** An deiner Stelle würde ich nicht so viel Geld ausgeben. **5.** An deiner Stelle würde ich nicht rauchen. **6.** An deiner Stelle würde ich fleißiger arbeiten. **7.** An deiner Stelle würde ich viel mehr lesen. **8.** An deiner Stelle würde ich den Rasen öfter mähen. **9.** An deiner Stelle würde ich eine Ferienreise buchen. **10.** An deiner Stelle würde ich weniger Alkohol trinken.

REFERENCE GRAMMAR

1 Pronunciation

1.1 The German alphabet

For those readers who need only to spell their name or give details of their car number plate or postal code, the names of the letters shown in this simple alphabet will be sufficient, without the more detailed explanation which follows.

a	ah	f	eff	k	kah	p	pay	u	ooh	x	iks
b	bay	g	gay	l	el	q	kuh	v	fau	y	ypsilon
c	tsay	h	ha	m	em	r	err	w	vay	z	tsett
d	day	i	ih	n	en	s	ess				
e	ay	j	yot	o	oh	t	tay				

1.2 Pronunciation and spelling

The following information about pronunciation starts with the German spelling system, and shows how the various letters or combination of letters are pronounced. The pronunciation is given in rough terms of comparison with English sounds and represents the standard pronunciation set out in *Duden 6 Aussprachewörterbuch*, 3rd edition, Mannheim 1990.

1.2.1 Vowels

- German has nine vowel letters: a, ä, e, i, o, ö, u, ü, y.
- These vowels can be pronounced both short and long but are always 'pure' vowels, as in Scottish English, as opposed to the 'double' or diphthongal sounds of southern English.
- They are usually short if they are followed by a double consonant or combination of consonants.

In the the following examples the vowels whose pronunciation is being illustrated are in bold type.

1.2.2 Short vowels

Ratte *rat*, pronounced as in northern English 'rat'
Bett *bed*, Gäste *guests*, both pronounced as in English 'bet'
bitte *please*, pronounced as in English 'bitter'
Motte *moth*, pronounced as in English 'bottle'
Götter *gods*, pronounced as in English 'better', but with rounded lips
Butter *butter,* pronounced as in northern English 'butter' (with u as in foot)
Mütter *mothers*, pronounced as in English 'bitter', but with rounded lips
mystisch *mystic*, pronounced as in English 'misty', but with rounded lips

- The letter **y** is only used in foreign words, usually from Latin and Greek, e.g. **Psychologie** *psychology*.
- The three umlaut vowels, **ä**, **ö**, **ü** occur chiefly in words which are derived in turn from other words containing **a**, **o**, **u**, e.g. the plural forms **Gäste** *guests*, **Götter** *gods*, **Mütter** mothers derived from the singular forms **Gast, Gott, Mutter**.
- Since the letters **e** and **ä** represent the same short vowel and **ü** and **y** also represent one vowel, the nine vowel letters represent seven short vowel sounds.

1.2.3 Long vowels

These same letters can also represent long vowels when they occur in certain positions in the word or are followed by certain letters.

1. Vowels are pronounced long when they occur before a single consonant, usually in the middle of a word:

baden *to bathe*, pronounced as in English 'rather'
Räder *wheels*, pronounced as in English 'cairn'
eben *even*, pronounced as in English 'neighbour'
Bibel *Bible*, pronounced as in English 'feeble'
oder *or*, pronounced as in English 'odour'
töten *to kill*, pronounced as in English 'patent', but with rounded lips
bluten *to bleed*, pronounced as in English 'moot'
Güte *goodness*, pronounced as in English 'beater', but with rounded lips

2. Vowels are pronounced long when they are followed by the letter **h**, and, in the case of **i**, when it is followed by **e**:

Biene *bee*, pronounced as in English 'keen'
Stuhl *chair*, pronounced as in English 'stool'
Bohne *bean*, pronounced as in English 'loner'
nahmen *took*, pronounced as in English 'calmer'
lehnen *to lean*, pronounced as in English 'gain'
Söhne *sons*, pronounced as in English 'retainer', but with rounded lips
Bühne *stage*, pronounced as in English 'bean', but with rounded lips
Mythos *myth*, pronounced as in English 'metres', but with rounded lips

3. Vowels are pronounced long when they are doubled:

Boote *boats*, pronounced as in English 'boats'
Saal *room*, pronounced as in English 'marl'
leeren *to empty*, pronounced as in English 'bearing'

■ The vowel letters **ä**, **ö**, **u**, **ü** never occur in a double combination. For example, the plural of **Saal** (*room*) is **Säle**, and the diminutive of **Boot** (*boat*) is **Bötchen** *little boat*.

1.2.4 Diphthongs

Combinations of vowel letters represent what are called diphthongs, 'double' sounds. In German these are represented by **ai**, **ei**, **au**, **eu**, **äu**. In English, diphthongs are very often spelt with a single letter, e.g. *mine*. The German diphthongs are pronounced as follows:

Main *(river) Main*, pronounced as in English 'mine'
fein *fine*, pronounced as in English 'fine'
Maus *mouse*, pronounced as in English 'mouse'
heute *today*, pronounced as in English 'hoity-toity'
Häuser *houses*, pronounced as in English 'noises'

■ The diphthong **ai** occurs only in a few words, e.g. **Kaiser** *emperor*, **Waise** *orphan*, **Kai** *quay*, **Saite** *string* (of an instrument).

■ The combination **äu** occurs only in words which are derived from another word which contains **au**, e.g. **Häuser** from **Haus**, **Fräulein** from **Frau**.

1.2.5 Consonants

To illustrate the pronunciation of consonants in German we will take the individual consonant letters and letter combinations and treat them together, again referring to English pronunciation.

b Bad *bath*, **Abend** *evening*, pronounced as in English 'bath', 'robing'

bb Krabbe *shrimp*, pronounced as in English 'lobby' (for the pronunciation of **b** at the end of words, see **p**)

ch Loch *hole*, **nicht** *not*, pronounced as in Scottish 'loch'

d Dieb *thief*, **laden** *to load*, pronounced as in English 'dove', 'laden'

dd Kladde *rough book*, pronounced as in English 'muddy' (for the pronunciation of **d** at the end of words, see **t**)

f fast *almost*, **schlafen** *to sleep*, v **Vogel** *bird*, pronounced as in English 'fast'

ff schaffen *manage*, pronounced as in English 'stuffy'

ph Philosphie *philosophy*, mostly in foreign words

g gehen *to go*, pronounced as in English 'get'

gg Egge *harrow*, pronounced as in English 'eggy' (for the pronunciation of **g** at the end of words, see **k**)

h Hand *hand*, pronounced as in English 'hand'

j ja *yes*, **Boje** *buoy*, pronounced as in English 'yam', (*never* as j in 'jam')

k Kind *child*, pronounced as in English 'kind'

ck Brücke *bridge*, **Blick** *glance*, pronounced as in English 'mucky', 'duck'

NB **g** at the end of words is also pronounced as **k**: **Tag** 'day'

l lachen *to laugh*, pronounced as in English 'laugh', (*never* as in 'ball')

ll Wille *will*, pronounced as in English 'lid'

m man *one*, pronounced as in English 'man'

mm Lamm *lamb*, pronounced as in English 'ram', 'swimming'

n nein *no*, pronounced as in English 'no'

nn nennen *to call,* pronounced as in English 'thinning'

ng singen *to sing*, **Gesang** *song*, pronounced as in English 'singing', 'sing', (*never* with the **g** sound as in' finger')

p Post *post*, pronounced as in English 'paper', 'up'

pp üppig *abundant*, pronounced as in English 'upper '

NB **b** at the end of words is also pronounced as **p**: 'dust', **Staub**

pf Pferd *horse*, **Apfel** *apple*, **Kopf** *head*, pronounced as **p** followed by **f**, cf. English 'cupful'

qu Quelle *source*, pronounced as in English 'quick'

r reisen *to travel*, **sparen** *to save*, **rar** *rare*, pronounced either as in French with a trill or roll at the back of the mouth, or else as in Scottish English with a trill or roll of the tongue tip against the teeth or gums

rr irren *to err*, pronounced as **r** above

NB **rh** in foreign words is pronounced as **r**: **Rhythmus** *rhythm*

s sein *to be*, **lesen** *to read*, pronounced as in English 'zeal', 'busy'

s las *read* (in final position), pronounced as in English 'boss'

ss dass *that*, **wissen** *to know*, after a short vowel, pronounced as in English 'kiss', 'kissing'

ß aß *ate*, **heiß** *hot* (after a long vowel or a diphthong), pronounced as in English 'dose', 'bias'

sch schon *already*, **waschen** *to wash*, pronounced as in English 'shine', 'washing'

NB **s** before **p** and **t** at the beginning of words is also pronounced **sch**: **spät** *late*, **stehen** *to stand*

t tun *to do*, **raten** *to guess*, **Rat** *advice*, pronounced as in English 'tone', 'rating', 'rat'

tt Mitte *middle*, pronounced as in English 'written'

NB **d** at the end of words is also pronounced as **t**: **Tod** *death*

dt is also pronounced as **t** in the frequently used word **Stadt** *town*

th in foreign words, e.g. **Thema** *topic*, is pronounced as **t**, (*never* as English *th* in 'thing')

tsch tschechisch *Czech*, **deutsch** *German*, pronounced as in English 'cheers', 'fetch'

w waschen *to wash*, **Möwe** *seagull*, pronounced as in English 'vast', 'even', (*never* as in 'wipe')

x Hexe *witch*, pronounced as in English 'six'

z Zeit *time*, **heizen** *to heat*, pronounced as in English 'bits'

tz sitzen *to sit*, **Platz** *square*, *place*, also pronounced as in English 'bits'

2 Nouns

A noun is a word used for naming a person, (**der Mensch**, *person*), place, (**die Stadt**, *town*), thing, (**der Tisch**, *table*) or abstract idea (**die Freiheit**, *freedom*). It is normally preceded by a determiner such as **der**, **ein**, **kein**, etc. or by a preposition (**in Ordnung** *in order*, *all right*; **in Zukunft** *in the future*). In German a noun always starts with a capital letter, irrespective of its position in the sentence. e.g. A German noun can be masculine (**der**), feminine, (**die**) or neuter (**das**).

2.1 Gender

German nouns have three genders, usually shown by the definite article, **der** (masculine), **die** (feminine) and **das** (neuter). (See Functional Grammar 1.2.4.) The allocation of gender is sometimes as one would expect, in that males, male roles and professions are mostly masculine, e.g. **der Mann, der Vater, der Sohn, der Onkel, der Neffe, der Kellner,** and females, female roles and professions are mostly feminine **die Frau, die Mutter, die Tochter, die Tante, die Nichte, die Kellnerin.** More often than not, however, gender is arbitary. There are a few helpful rules, but remember that there are always exceptions to the rule! Here are some guidelines on gender:

■ The following groups of nouns are masculine (**der**):

1. Nouns which end in *-er* and refer to a male: **der Lehrer** *teacher*, **der Pfarrer** *vicar/minister*, **der Schneider** *tailor*, **der Schweizer** *Swiss*

2. The days of the week: **der Sonntag** *Sunday*, **der Montag** *Monday*, **der Dienstag** *Tuesday*, **der Mittwoch** *Wednesday*, **der Donnerstag** *Thursday*, **der Freitag** *Friday*, **der Samstag** *Saturday* or **der Sonnabend**

3. The months of the year: **Januar** *January,* **Februar** *February*, **März** *March*, **April** *April*, **Mai** *May*, **Juni** *June*, **Juli** *July*, **August** *August*, **September** *September*, **Oktober** *October*, **November** *November*, **Dezember** *December*

4. The seasons of the year: **der Frühling** *spring*, **der Sommer** *summer*, **der Herbst** *autumn*, **der Winter** *winter*.

5. Many nouns connected with the weather: **der Frost** *frost*, **der Hagel** *hail*, **der Nebel** *fog*, **der Regen** *rain*, **der Schnee** *snow*, **der Wind** *wind*

6. The points of the compass: **der Norden** *north*, **der Süden** *south*, **der Osten** *east*, **der Westen** *west*

7. Nouns which end in *-ant, -eur, -ich, -ig, -ismus, -ist, -ling, -or*: **der Fabrikant** *manufacturer*, **der Ingenieur** *engineer*, **der Teppich** *carpet*, **der König** *king*, **der Atheismus** *atheism*, **der Jurist** *lawyer*, **der Lehrling** *apprentice*, **der Doktor** *doctor*

■ The following groups of nouns are feminine (**die**):

1. Nouns which end in *-age, -anz, -ei, -enz, -heit, -ie, -ik, -in, -ion, ität, -keit, -schaft, -ung, -ur:* **die Massage** *massage*, **die Toleranz** *tolerance*, **die Brauerei** *brewery*, **die Tendenz** *tendency*, **die Schönheit**

beauty, **die Kolonie** *colony,* **die Politik** *politics,* **die Religion** *religion,* **die Nationalität** *nationality,* **die Kindheit** *childhood,* **die Freundschaft** *friendship,* **die Teilung** *division,* **die Natur** *nature*

2. Many nouns which end in *-e*: **die Brücke** *bridge,* **die Kirche** *church,* **die Lampe** *lamp,* **die Rose** *rose,* **die Tulpe** *tulip*

   NB The exceptions to these are weak nouns. See 2.4.

3. Whole numbers under a hundred such as **die Eins, die Zwei, die Drei, die Vier** (for example, when referring to bus numbers)

4. Many European rivers (with the exception of **der Rhein** *Rhine*: **die Themse** *Thames,* **die Elbe, die Donau** *Danube,* **die Mosel** *Moselle,* **die Seine, die Oder.**

■ The following groups of nouns are neuter (**das**):

1. An infinitive used as a noun: **das Essen** *food,* from the verb **essen** *to eat*), **das Schwimmen** (*swimming*), **das Singen** (*singing*)

2. Nouns which end in *-chen, -ett , -ium, -lein, -ment*: **das Mädchen** *girl,* **das Ballett** *ballet,* **das Studium** *course, studies,* **das Fräulein** *young lady,* **das Klima** *climate,* **das Parlament** *parliament*

2.2 Compound nouns (see Functional Grammar 3.4.4)

Compound nouns are formed by combining two or more nouns.

A compound noun always takes the gender of the last element, e.g.

das Atom *atom* + **die Kraft** *power* + **das Werk** *plant, works, factory* = **das Atomkraftwerk** *atomic or nuclear power station*

Sometimes the compound noun is formed by joining a plural and a singular noun e.g.

die Kranken *sick people* + **der Wagen** *car* = **der Krankenwagen** *ambulance*

die Tage *days* + **das Buch** *book* = **das Tagebuch** *diary*

Sometimes a compound noun is formed by joining two nouns with a connecting **-s,** e.g.

der Staat + **das Examen** = **das Staatsexamen** *state examination* (often refers to the first university degree)

die Universität + **der Professor** = **der Universitätsprofessor** *university professor*

2.3 Noun plurals (see Functional Grammar 1.2.5)

There are many different ways in which nouns show that they are plural in German, and it is best to learn the plural of each noun with its gender. In dictionaries the plural is normally given in brackets after the noun, and any changes required for the plural are shown like this:

> **der Wagen (-)** *car*, i.e. the plural is **die Wagen**
> **der Vater** (⁻) *father* i.e. the plural is **die Väter**
> **die Schwester (-n)** *sister* i.e. the plural is **die Schwestern**
> **das Kind (-er** i.e. **die Kinder)** *child*
> **der Freund (-e** i.e. **die Freunde)** *male friend*
> **der Wald** (⁻ **er** i.e. **die Wälder)** *wood, forest*
> **der Autor (-en** i.e. **die Autoren)** *author*
> **das Hotel (-s** i.e. **die Hotels)** *hotel*

Some nouns change more radically in the plural:

Singular	Plural
die Firma *the firm*	**die Firmen**
das Bankkonto *bank account*	**die Bankkonten**
das Museum *museum*	**die Museen**
der Fachmann *expert*	**die Fachleute**

Some nouns are mainly used in the plural in German:

> **die Eltern** *parents*
> **die Ferien** *the holiday(s)*
> **die Lebensmittel** *food, provisions*
> **die Leute** *people*

2.4 Weak nouns

This group of masculine nouns is unusual in that an **-n** or **-en** is added to the noun in every case apart from the *nominative singular* e.g.

> **der Junge (-n, -n)**: Ich kenne den Jung**en**. *I know the boy.*
> **der Dirigent (-en, -en)**: Er sprach mit dem Dirigent**en**.
> *He spoke to* (literally, 'with') *the conductor*.

In many dictionaries and course books a weak noun is signalled by showing the weak noun endings in brackets, before the plural: **der Herr (-n, -en)**, *gentleman*, **der Präsident (-en, -en)** *president*.

Some masculine nouns which end in -e add an **n** to the noun in every case but the nominative singular: **der Brite** Briton, **der Franzose** *Frenchman,* **der Kunde** *customer,* **der Geologe** *geologist.*

Some other masculine nouns which end in a consonant add -**en** to the noun in every case but the nominative singular: **der Assistent** *assistant,* **der Kandidat** *candidate,* **der Philosoph** *philosopher,* **der Soldat** *soldier,* **der Christ** *the Christian,* **der Mensch** *person* (-male or female), **der Kommunist** *communist.*

In dictionaries these weak noun endings are shown in brackets just before the plural: **der Kollege (-n, -n)** *colleague,* **der Student (-en, -en).**

3 Declension of determiners

Nouns are normally preceded by a determiner i.e. the *definite* article, **der** *the,* the indefinite article **ein** *a/an,* or other words such as **dieser** *this,* **jeder** *each.*

The determiner declines or changes its form according to the function of the noun in the sentence.

There is no gender distinction in the plural, i.e. the nominative forms of **der, die, das** all change to **die** for the plural. The indefinite article **eine, eine, ein** disappears in the plural form, or is replaced by a higher numeral, e.g.

    ein Bus *one bus,* **Busse** *buses,* **zwei Busse** *two buses.*

3.1 Changes in the definite article.

This chart shows the changes in the definite article. The same pattern of changes applies to the demonstrative **dieser** *this/these,* and other determiners such as **jener** *that/those,* **jeder** *each/every,* **welcher** *which,* **mancher** *many a* and **solcher** *such a.* The plural also forms a pattern for **alle** *all.*

Masculine	*Singular*	*Plural*
Nominative:	**der** Vater	**die** Väter
Accusative:	**den** Vater	**die** Väter
Dative:	**dem** Vater	**den** Vätern‡
Genitive:	**des** Vaters§	**der** Väter

Feminine	*Singular*	*Plural*
Nominative:	**die** Mutter	**die** Mütter
Accusative:	**die** Mutter	**die** Mütter
Dative:	**der** Mutter	**den** Müttern‡
Genitive:	**der** Mutter	**der** Mütter

Neuter	*Singular*	*Plural*
Nominative:	**das** Kind	**die** Kinder
Accusative:	**das** Kind	**die** Kinder
Dative:	**dem** Kind	**den** Kindern‡
Genitive:	**des** Kindes§	**der** Kinder

‡Nouns in the dative plural end in -**n** unless the plural is -**s**, for example, **das Büro (-s)** *office*, **in den Büros**

§ -**s** or -**es** is added to the end of masculine and neuter singular noun in the genitive case

3.2 Changes in the indefinite article

This chart shows the changes in the indefinite article **ein**, which also provide the pattern for **kein** *not a* and the possessive adjectives **mein** *my*, **dein** *your*, **sein** *his*. NB As there is no plural for **ein**, the plural form is given using **mein** *my*:

	Masculine singular	Feminine singular	Neuter singular	Plural
Nom.	**ein** Mann	**eine** Frau	**ein** Kind	**meine** Kinder
Acc.	**einen** Mann	**eine** Frau	**ein** Kind	**meine** Kinder
Dat.	**einem** Mann	**einer** Frau	**einem** Kind	**meinen** Kindern
Gen.	**eines** Mannes	**einer** Frau	**eines** Kindes	**meiner** Kinder

4 Declension of Personal pronouns

You are familiar with the nominative form of the personal pronoun from the conjugation of verbs, but these pronouns also change or inflect when used in different cases:

Singular					Plural			
	1st	2nd	3rd			1st	2nd	2nd	3rd
Nom.	ich	du	er	sie	es	wir	ihr	Sie	sie
Acc.	mich	dich	ihn	sie	es	uns	euch	Sie	sie
Dat.	mir	dir	ihm	ihr	ihm	uns	euch	Ihnen	ihnen
Gen.	meiner	deiner	seiner	ihrer	seiner	unser	euer	Ihrer	ihrer

NB the genitive form is rarely used.

the **Sie** forms are polite singular as well as plural

5 Adjectives

An adjective is a word which gives more information about a noun or pronoun. When an adjective is used *after* the noun, e.g. **das Fahrrad ist neu** *The bicycle is new*, no ending is needed, but when the adjective comes *before* the noun, e.g. **das neue Rad** *The new bicycle*, the adjective itself must decline to agree with the gender, number and case of the noun.

5.1 Declension of adjectives (See Functional Grammar 15)

5.1.1 Adjectival endings

Adjectival endings can be divided into three groups:

Group 1 is used after **der** and all its forms, also after **dieser**, **jener**, **jeder**, **welcher**:

Der französische Koch wohnt uns gegenüber.	*The French chef lives opposite us.*
Ich kenne **die** beiden Ärzte gut.	*I know both the doctors well.*
Laut **dem** neuen Gesetz muss man das machen.	*According to the new law one has to do that.*
Der Sohn **des** alten Pfarrers ist der Minister für Gesundheit.	*The son of the old vicar is the minister of health.*

	Singular			Plural
	M.	F.	N.	
Nom:	-e	-e	-e	-en
Acc:	-en	-e	-e	-en
Dat:	-en	-en	-en	-en
Gen:	-en	-en	-en	-en

Group 2 is used in the singular after **ein** and all its forms, and in both the singular and the plural after kein and possessive adjectives **mein, dein, sein**, etc. e.g.

Sein neuer Chef ist sehr streng.	*His new boss is very strict.*
Er hat einen sehr großen Hund.	*He has a very big dog.*
Ich bleibe bei meiner alten Tante.	*I am staying with my old aunt.*
Er freut sich auf den Besuch eines reichen Onkels.	*He is looking forward to the visit of a rich uncle.*

	Singular			Plural
	M.	F.	N.	
Nom:	-er	-e	-es	-en
Acc:	-en	-e	-es	-en
Dat:	-en	-en	-en	-en
Gen:	-en	-en	-en	-en

Group 3 is used when the adjective stands alone in front of the noun:

Schwarzer Kaffee tut gut!	*Black coffee does you good!*
Er kauft seiner Frau nur rote Rosen.	*He buys only red roses for his wife.*
Ich schreibe immer mit schwarzer Tinte.	*I always write with black ink.*
Er ist immer guter Laune.	*He is always in a good mood.*

The plural endings in this group are also used after numbers, e.g. drei grüne Bleistifte *three green pencils* and after **einige** *some*, **ein paar** *a few*, **viele** *many*, **mehrere** *several, various*, **wenige** *few*:

	Singular			Plural
	M.	F.	N.	
Nom:	-er	-e	-es	-e
Acc:	-en	-e	-es	-e
Dat:	-em	-er	-em	-en
Gen:	-en	-er	-en	-er

Be careful! Never be tempted to use these endings with **kein, mein, dein, sein**, etc.

Adjectives formed from town names

If you wish to use the name of a town as an adjective you do not need to use the charts above. Simply add **-er** to the town name, irrespective of the gender, case and number of the noun it is describing, e.g.

Die Frankfurter Buchmesse ist weltberühmt.	*The Frankfurt Book Fair is world famous.*
Wir wollen den Kölner Dom besuchen.	*We want to visit Cologne cathedral.*
Ich habe den Artikel in dem Hamburger Abendblatt gelesen.	*I read the article in the Hamburg Abendblatt.*
Während der Kieler Woche sind die Hotels voll.	*The hotels are full during Kiel Week.*

5.2 Adjectival nouns

In German adjectives are frequently turned into nouns. To do this, the adjective is given a capital letter and it retains the gender and adjectival ending which is appropriate for the noun which it is replacing: **der Arme** *the poor man*, **die Arme** *the poor woman*, **die Armen** *the poor* (people).

The following examples (meaning *the* or *a German* (man), *the* or *a German* (woman) and *the Germans* or *Germans*) form a pattern for adjectival nouns:

	Masculine	Feminine	Plural
Nom:	der Deutsche	die Deutsche	die Deutschen
Acc:	den Deutschen	die Deutsche	die Deutschen
Dat:	dem Deutschen	der Deutschen	den Deutschen
Gen:	des Deutschen	der Deutschen	der Deutschen

	Masculine	Feminine	Plural
Nom:	ein Deutscher	eine Deutsche	Deutsche
Acc:	einen Deutschen	eine Deutsche	Deutsche
Dat:	einem Deutschen	einer Deutschen	Deutschen
Gen:	eines Deutschen	einer Deutschen	Deutscher

5.3 The comparative and superlative forms of adjectives

Adjectives can be used in various degrees of intensity:

- the normal (sometimes called positive) form, e.g. **der Mann ist alt** *the man is old* or **der alte Mann** *the old man.*

- the comparative form e.g. **der Mann ist älter** *the man is older* or **der ältere Mann** *the older man.*

- the superlative form, e.g. **der Mann ist der älteste** *the man is oldest* or **der älteste Mann** *the oldest man.*

  N.B. Where no noun is used, the form **am ältesten**, e.g. **Er ist am ältesten**, *He's the oldest*, is often used. This is in fact the superlative form of adverbs.

5.3.1 The formation of the comparative

In German the comparative is formed by adding **-er** to the normal adjective. Sometimes an umlaut is also added to an **a**, **o** or **u**. If the comparative adjective is used *after the verb* e.g. **der Mann ist älter**, no further adjectival ending is required. If, however, the comparative degree of the adjective is used in front of the noun, normal adjectival endings must be added, e.g. *der* **ältere Mann**, *ein* **älterer Mann**.

The following adjectives take an umlaut in the comparative and superlative forms:

alt – älter *old – older*
arm – ärmer *poor – poorer*
dumm – dümmer *stupid – more stupid*
grob – gröber *coarse – coarser*
groß – größer *big – bigger*
hart – härter *hard – harder*
kalt – kälter *cold – colder*
klug – klüger *clever – cleverer*
krank – kränker *ill – more ill*
kurz – kürzer *short – shorter*
lang – länger *long – longer*
oft – öfter *often – more often*
scharf – schärfer *sharp – sharper*
schwach – schwächer *weak – weaker*
schwarz – schwärzer *black – blacker*
stark – stärker *strong – stronger*
warm – wärmer *warm – warmer*

5.3.2 The formation of the superlative

The superlative is normally formed by adding -**st** to the adjective, and sometimes an umlaut (see list for comparative). Very occasionally, -**est** is added for ease of pronunciation, e.g. **der berühmt*este* Dirigent** *the most famous conductor*. If a superlative adjective is used in front of the noun, the appropriate adjectival ending must be added.

Frequently-used exceptions:

gut – besser *good – better*   der, die, das beste *the best*
hoch – höher *high – higher*   der, die, das höchste *the highest*
nah(e) – näher *near – nearer*   der, die, das nächste *the next, nearest*

6 The use of the cases (See Functional Grammar 3.2)

There are four cases in German: nominative, accusative, dative and genitive.

6.1 The nominative case

The nominative case is used:

- for the subject of the sentence and
- after the verb **sein** *to be*.

It is the form of nouns found in dictionaries.

6.2 The accusative case

The accusative case is used:

- to indicate the direct object of the sentence
- after the following prepositions:

bis *until*	Wir bleiben bis nächsten Dienstag.	*We'll stay until next Tuesday.*
durch *through*	Das Kind läuft durch den Eingang.	*The child runs through the entrance.*
für *for*	Das Geschenk ist für seinen Vater.	*The present is for his father.*
gegen *against*	Der Schüler stellt sein Fahrrad gegen den Zaun.	*The pupil puts his bicycle against the fence.*
ohne *without*	Sic ist ohne einen Regenschirm ausgegangen.	*She went out without an umbrella.*
um *around, round*	Der Taxifahrer fuhr schnell um die Ecke.	*The taxi driver drove quickly around the corner.*
wider *against*	Wir heirateten wider seinen Willen.	*We got married against his will.*

Entlang can be used with either the accusative or the dative. In the accusative, **entlang** often comes after the noun e.g.

Der Postbote kommt die Straße   *The postman comes along the*
  entlang.   *street.*

This is the more frequent usage.

- If the following prepositions are used in a context which shows motion or movement from one place to another:

in *to, into*	Wir gehen ins Kino.	*We're going to the cinema.*
an *on, onto*	Er klebt das Plakat an die Wand.	*He sticks the poster onto the wall.*

auf *on, onto*	Der Kellner legt den Teller auf den Tisch	*The waiter lays the plate on the table.*
über *above*	Sie hängt die Lampe über das Sofa.	*She hangs the lamp above the sofa.*
unter *under*	Sie schiebt ihren Koffer unter das Bett.	*She pushes her case under the bed.*
neben *next to*	Setzen Sie sich bitte neben den Bürgermeister!	*Please sit down next to the mayor!*
vor *in front of*	Der Polizist trat vor die Tür.	*The policeman stepped in front of the door.*
hinter *behind*	Der Junge geht hinter die Garage.	*The boy goes behind the garage.*
zwischen *between*	Der Hund läuft zwischen die Häuser und verschwindet.	*The dog runs between the houses and disappears.*

• for expressions of time which contain no preposition e.g.

Er kommt nächst**en** Sonntag.	*He's coming next Sunday.*
Jed**en** Winter fahren wir Ski.	*We go skiing every winter*
den viert**en** Juli	*the fourth of July.*

6.3 The dative case

The dative case is used:

■ to indicate the indirect object of the sentence

■ after the following prepositions:

aus *out of*	Der Dieb läuft aus dem Haus.	*The thief runs out of the house.*
bei *at, with*	Er wohnt bei seiner Freundin.	*He lives at his girlfriend's.*
laut *according to*	Laut dem Gesetz darf man den Jungen nicht nennen.	*According to the law the boy may not be named.*
mit *with*	Ich schreibe immer mit einem Kugelschreiber.	*I always write with a biro.*
nach *after*	Nach dem Film gehen wir zusammen in die Eisdiele	*After the film we go to the ice-cream parlour together.*
seit *since*	Meine Tante wohnt seit dem Krieg in Hamburg.	*My aunt has lived in Hamburg since the war.*

| **von** *from* | Der Brief ist von ihrem Ex-Mann. | *The letter is from her ex-husband.* |
| **zu** *to* | Ich muss schnell zur Post gehen. | *I must quickly go to the post office.* |

(Sometimes used in conjunction with **bis**, e.g. bis zum nächsten Mal *until the next time*)

| **gegenüber** *opposite* | Der Minister wohnt gegenüber dem Museum. | *The minister lives opposite the museum.* |

(**Gegenüber** sometimes appears after the noun, e.g. dem Museum gegenüber *opposite the museum*.)

■ If the following prepositions show position (as opposed to movement from one place to another):

in *in*	Er wohnt im einem Wohnwagen	*He lives in a caravan.*
an *on, at*	Wir haben ein Ferienhaus an der Küste.	*We have a holiday home on the coast.*
auf *on*	Das Essen ist schon auf dem Tisch.	*The food is already on the table.*
über *above*	Der Bäcker wohnt über der Bäckerei.	*The baker lives above the bakery.*
unter *under*	Als Experiment baut man Häuser unter der Erde	*As an experiment they are building houses underground.*
hinter *behind*	Direkt hinter ihrem Haus gibt es einen Wald.	*Directly behind their house is a wood.*
vor *in front of*	Das Taxi wartet vor dem Restaurant.	*The taxi is waiting in front of the restaurant.*
zwischen *between*	Zwischen den Bäumen steht die Mühle.	*The mill is between the trees.*
neben *next to*	Der Pfarrer wohnt neben der Kirche.	*The vicar/minster lives next to the church.*

■ after several verbs, e.g. **danken** *to thank*, **folgen** *to follow*, **gehören** *to belong to*, **gratulieren** *to congratulate*, **helfen** *to help*, **imponieren** *to impress*, **schaden** *to damage*.

6.4 The genitive case

The genitive case is used:

■ to show possession or ownership, the equivalent of the English (Peter's friends).

■ It is also used after the following prepositions:

außerhalb *outside*	Seine Freunde wohnen außerhalb der Stadt.	*His friends live outside the town.*
infolge *because of*	Infolge des Streiks bleibt die Fabrik heute geschlossen.	*Because of the strike the factory will remain closed today.*
(an)statt *instead of*	Statt eines Briefes schickte er mir eine Postkarte	*Instead of a letter he sent me postcard.*
trotz *in spite of*	Trotz des Regens spielen wir heute Tennis.	*In spite of the rain we will play tennis today.*
während *during*	Während des Krieges wohnten sie auf dem Lande	*During the war they lived in the country.*
wegen *because of*	Wir fahren erst am Sonntag wegen des Verkehrs.	*Because of the traffic we will not travel until Sunday.*

N.B In colloquial speech and some regional usage **trotz**, **wegen** and **laut** are sometimes followed by the dative case.

7 Adverbs

An adverb is a word or a group of words which tells us more about a verb. Adverbs do not normally inflect or change their form in any way. Very many well known words which we learn as simple items of vocabulary, such as **auch** *also*, **heute** today, **hier** *here*, **gern** *with pleasure*, **bald** *soon*, **fast** *almost*, **jetzt** *now*, **sofort** *immediately*, **oft** *often*, **schon** *already*, **vielleicht** *perhaps* are in fact adverbs.

• Some adverbs which are derived from other word classes end in -**weise**, e.g. **glücklicherweise** *fortunately*, **beispielsweise** *by way of example*, **teilweise** *partly*. **Stundenlang** *for hours*, **tagelang** *for days* are formed in a similar way, using -**lang** instead of -**weise**.

Sometimes the adverb is the same as the adjective, e.g.

Sie ist schön (adjective).	*She is beautiful.*
Sie singt schön (adverb).	*She sings beautifully.*
Seine Sicht ist nicht gut.	*His sight is not good.*
Er sieht nicht gut.	*He does not see well.*

7.1 The formation of the comparative of adjective-adverbs

Those adverbs which have the same form as adjectives are sometimes called *adjective-adverbs*, e.g. **schnell, heiß, klein**.

These form their comparative in the same way as the adjective – minus, of course, any additional adjectival ending, e.g.

Gabi läuft schnell**er** als Silke.	*Gabi runs more quickly than Silke.*
Hans singt schön**er** als Fritz	*Hans sings more beautifully than Fritz.*

Notice also:

Du singst genauso gut wie ich.	*You sing just as well as I do.*
Butter schmeckt nicht so gut	*Butter doesn't taste as good*
wie Margarine.	*as margarine.*

7.2 The formation of the superlative form of adverbs

German uses the form **am...-sten** to represent the superlative of adverbs, with the addition of an umlaut where necessary (as listed under the comparison of adjectives), e.g.

Er singt am schönsten.	*He sings the most beautifully.*
Wir fahren am schnellsten mit	*We will travel the fastest on*
der Bahn.	*the train.*
Am besten gehst du gleich ins Bett.	*It's best that you go to*
	bed immediately.

Frequently-used exceptions

gern – lieber – am liebsten *with pleasure, rather, best of all*
gut – besser – am besten *good, better, best*
hoch – höher – am höchsten *high, higher, highest*
nah(e) – näher – am nächsten *near, nearer, nearest/next*
viel – mehr – am meisten *much, more, most*

8 Numbers and dates

8.1 Cardinal numbers

null, (*nought, zero*)	sechzehn (16)
ein(s) (1)	siebzehn (17)
zwei (2)	achtzehn (18)
drei (3)	neunzehn (19)
vier (4)	zwanzig (20)
fünf (5)	einundzwanzig (21)
sechs (6)	zweiundzwanzig (22)
sieben (7)	dreiundzwanzig (23)
acht (8)	vierundzwanzig (24)
neun (9)	fünfundzwanzig (25)
zehn (10)	sechsundzwanzig (26)
elf (11)	siebenundzwanzig (27)
zwölf (12)	achtundzwanzig (28)
dreizehn (13)	neunundzwanzig (29)
vierzehn (14)	dreißig (30)
fünfzehn (15)	einunddreißig (31), etc.

vierzig (40)	achtzig (80)
fünfzig (50)	neunzig (90)
sechzig (60)	hundert *or* einhundert (100)
siebzig (70)	hunderteins *or* hundertundeins (101)
tausend or eintausend (1000)	tausendeins (1001)
zehntausend, eine Million (*a million*)	eine Milliarde (*thousand million*)
eine Billion (*billion*)	

- NB the unexpected spelling of **sechzehn** (no -s-), **siebzehn** (no -en-), **dreißig** (no -z-), **sechzig** (no -s-), **siebzig** (no -en-).
- Numbers under a million are normally written with a small letter. **Hundert** and **tausend**, however, can also be used as nouns, in which case they are written as **ein Hundert**, **ein Tausend**.
- **Eine Million**, **eine Milliarde** *thousand million* and **eine Billion** are only used as nouns.
- Apart from **eins** (which changes its form when used as an indefinite article before a noun or as a pronoun, e.g. **eine Katze** *a cat*) cardinal numbers are never declined.

- If cardinals under a hundred are used as a noun (e.g. referring to a bus number or a mark at school) they are feminine: **die Vier, die Sechs**.
- Telephone numbers are usually given in groups of two. For example, 96 48 37 is **sechsundneunzig achtundvierzig siebenunddreißig**.
- Commas are never used between thousands and hundreds. A space is simply left between them: **10 475**.
- A comma is used instead of a decimal point in German: **0,8 – null Komma acht**.
- The year is written simply as either **1999. (neunzehnhundertneunundneunzig)** *or* **im Jahre 1999**.
- Clock times use predominantly cardinals, e.g. **es ist zwei Uhr** (*2.00*), **es ist fünf (Minuten) nach eins**, (*1.05*) **es ist zwanzig vor zwölf** (*11.40*), **es ist dreiundzwanzig Uhr** (*11 p.m.*).

8.2 Ordinal numbers

These are, in effect, adjectives which are used specifically to show the order, position or arithmetical ranking of something or someone, e.g. **Mein erster Schultag** *my first day at school*, **Elisabeth die Zweite** *Elisabeth the Second*, **die Dritte Welt** *the Third World*.

- To form ordinals for the numbers from four up to and including nineteen, add **-t** to the cardinal number: **viert-**, **fünft-**, **sechst-** and then the appropriate adjectival ending.

  N.B. either **siebt-** or **siebent-** is possible for *seventh*, and **acht** requires only the adjectival ending, with no additional **-t**,
  e.g. **seine vierte Frau** *his fourth wife*, **der fünfte Versuch** *the fifth attempt*.
- To form ordinals for numbers for twenty upwards, add **-st** to the cardinal number, and then the appropriate adjectival ending, e.g. **sein fünfzigster Geburtstag** *his fiftieth birthday*.

8.3 Dates

Obviously, one of the most frequent uses of ordinals is to express dates e.g.

Silvester ist am einunddreißigsten Dezember.	*New Year's Eve is on December 31st.*
Mein Mann hat am dreizehnten Juni Geburtstag.	*My husband's birthday is on June 13th.*

Die Schulferien sind vom sechsten *The school holidays are from July*
Juli bis zum ersten September. *6th to September 1st.*

Usually numbers are used instead of words, and are always followed by a
full stop: **am 13. Juni** *on 13 June*, **vom 6. Juli bis zum 1. September**
from 6 July to 1 September.

To ask the date you can either ask: **Der wievielte ist heute?** (literally, 'the
how manyeth is it today?') The reply will be in the nominative **der erste
Mai**, (*1 May*) **der elfte März** (*11 March*).

You could also ask: **Den wievielten haben wir heute?** The reply will then
be in the accusative because it is the direct object: **den ersten Mai** or **den
1. Mai**; **den elften März** or **den 11. März** (This latter form is found at
the top of letters. The trend is to omit the definite article, e.g. **1. Mai** or
11. März.)

9 Verbs

A verb is a word or group of words which tells you what a person or thing
is doing or being, e.g. **Ich sammle Briefmarken** *I collect stamps*, **Sie
erwartete zu viel** *She expected too much*, **Es regnet viel im April** *It rains
a lot in April*. A verb can be used in various tenses, e.g. *I read, I was
reading, I have read, I had read, I shall read, I shall have read*. The present
tense is used to talk about an activity, action, state of affairs or event which
is happening just now. For further details, see Functional Grammar 5).

In dictionaries and course books verbs are listed in their infinitive form
which comprises the stem + the ending *-en*, e.g. **kauf + en**. Endings are
added to the stem according to person, number, and the tense of the verb.

There are three simple tenses in German:

1. present: **ich schreibe** *I write*
2. future: **ich werde schreiben** *I shall write*
3. past: **ich schrieb** *I wrote*

There are also three compound tenses formed with either the verb **haben**
or **sein** plus a past participle:

4. perfect: **ich habe geschrieben** *I have written*
5. pluperfect: **ich hatte geschrieben** *I had written*
6. future perfect: **ich werde geschrieben haben** *I shall have written*.

The last three are called compound tenses because they involve using two verbal forms, and so they do have a separate entry in the verb list.

9.1 The present tense

9.1.1 The present tense of regular verbs

The verb **kaufen** *to buy* is a regular verb. It consists of the stem **kauf-** plus various endings, shown below in italics. This provides the pattern for other verbs in the present tense.

Singular	
ich kauf**e**	*I buy, I am buying, I do buy*
du kauf**st**	*you buy*, etc.
er kauf**t**	*he buys*, etc.
sie kauf**t**	*she buys*, etc.
es kauf**t**	*it buys*, etc.
Plural	
wir kauf**en**	*we buy*, etc.
ihr kauf**t**	*you buy*, etc.
Sie kauf**en**	*you buy*, etc. (polite singular and plural)
sie kauf**en**	*they buy*, etc.

If the stem of a regular verb ends in **d, t,** (e.g. **reden** *to speak,* **arbeiten** *to work*), or a combination of **m** or **n** preceded by another consonant (e.g. **atmen** *to breathe,* **regnen** *to rain*), endings including an **e** are added to form the present tense of the **du, er, sie, es** and **ihr** forms, for ease of pronunciation. For example: **ihr antwort*et* nicht.** *You are not answering;* **er red*et*** *he is speaking;* **sie atm*et*** *she is breathing;* **du zeichn*est*** *you are drawing*); **es regn*et*** *it's raining.*

9.1.2 The present tense of irregular verbs

Although we noticed some slight variations in the endings of the regular verbs above to ease pronunciation, the stem was always based on the infinitive form.

Some verbs , however, change their stem vowel in the second (**du**) and third (**er, sie, es**) person singular so that these forms differ from the stem and thus also from the infinitive, e.g.

geben (*to give*):

	Singular		Plural
ich gebe	*I give*	wir geben	*we give*
du gibst	*you give*	ihr gebt	*you give*
er, sie, es gibt	*he, she, it gives*	Sie geben	*you* (polite) *give*
		sie geben	*they give*

essen – *to eat* – er **isst**
fahren – *to travel* – er **fährt**
laufen – *to run, to go* – er **läuft**
lesen – *to read* – er **liest**
schlafen – *to sleep* – er **schläft**
treffen – *to meet* – er **trifft**

We cannot predict these changes and have to refer to the verb list (Reference Grammar 10.7) to be sure of the correct form.

Furthermore, some verbs do not change their stem in the present tense, but in the past: **gehen** – **geht** – **ging** – **gegangen**. Even a cursory glance at a verb list will reveal further variations, which can be described and subdivided more fully. But for the purposes of this grammar only the distinction between regular and irregular verbs is made.

9.2 Modal verbs (See Functional Grammar 7, 8 and 9)

There are six irregular verbs:

> **dürfen** *to be allowed to, may*
> **können** *to be able to, can*
> **mögen** *to like*
> **müssen** *to have to, I must*
> **sollen** *to be supposed to 'ought'*
> **wollen** *to want to*

which belong to a group of verbs known as modal verbs. They reflect the mood of the speaker in that they express a wish, sense of obligation, volition, liking, ability or possibility.

These six verbs share several common features:

■ they are often followed by an infinitive at the end of the clause

■ with the exception of **sollen**, the singular form has a different vowel from the plural

- the first and third person singular have no endings
- the first and third person plural and second person polite form is always the same as the infinitive

dürfen	können	mögen
ich darf	ich kann	ich mag
du darfst	du kannst	du magst
er/sie/es darf	er/sie/es kann	er/sie/es mag
wir dürfen, etc.	wir können, etc.	wir mögen, etc.

müssen	wollen	sollen
ich muss	ich will	ich soll
du musst	du willst	du sollst
er/sie/es muss	er/sie es will	er/sie/es soll
wir müssen, etc.	wir wollen, etc.	wir sollen, etc.

9.3 Separable and inseparable verbs

The infinitive of some verbs begins with a *prefix* such as **an-**, **ab-**, **be-**, **über-**, **zu-** etc. If the prefix moves to the end of the clause when used as a finite verb, the verb is known as a *separable* verb, e.g. **an/kommen**:

Der Zug **kommt** um 9 Uhr **an**.   *The train arrives at 9.00 am.*

If the prefix always remains in front of the verb when used as a finite verb, it is known as an inseparable verb, e.g. **bekommen**:

Wir **bekommen** kein Kindergeld   *We do not receive the child*
   mehr.   *allowance any more.*

9.3.1 Separable verbs

- A prefix can be added to the infinitive of many frequently used verbs such as **fahren** *to travel to go*, **kommen** *to come*, **machen** (*to make, to do*.
- The addition of such a prefix has the effect of changing the meaning of the verb e.g. *ab/***fahren** *to depart*, *an/***kommen** *to arrive* *auf/***machen** *to open*.
- The prefix is always at the front of the verb in the infinitive form.

- When the verb is used (in the normal second position in the main clause), the prefix separates from the verb and is placed at the end of the clause, e.g.

Der Zug **fährt** um 2 Uhr von Gleis 5 **ab**. *The train will depart from platform 5 at 2 o'clock.*

- In a subordinate clause (when a subordinating conjunction has sent the verb to the end of the clause) the prefix is reattached to the front of the verb and is written as one word

Ich warte, bis der Zug **abfährt**. *I'll wait until the train departs.*

- The past participle of separable verbs is written as one word, with the prefix coming before the past participle of the basic verb e.g. **ab**g**eholt** *collected*, **an**g**erufen** *telephoned*.

- Verbs starting with the following prefixes are separable: **ab-, an-, auf-, aus-, bei-, ein-, fest-, fort-, her-, hin-, los-, mit-, vor-, weg-, zu-, zurück-, zusammen-**.

- the emphasis or stress in the infinitive of a separable verb is always on the prefix e.g. *ab*/**biegen**, *an*/**ziehen**.

- In this book, as in many others, the separable verb is signalled by a diagonal slash between the prefix and the verb e.g. **zu/machen** *to shut*. In dictionaries the verb is sometimes identified as separable by *sep* written after the verb .

NB Not all verbs which start with a prefix are separable! (See next section.)

9.3.2 Inseparable verbs

- The following prefixes remain always at the beginning of inseparable verbs: **be-, emp-, ent-, er-, ge-, miss-, ver-, zer-**. For example:

Er bekommt erst nächste Woche sein Zeugnis. *He will not receive his school report until next week.*

Mein Arzt verschreibt mir Penizillin. *The doctor is prescribing penicillin for me.*

- the past participle of inseparable verbs *never* starts with **ge-**:

Er hat sein Zeugnis letzte Woche bekommen. *He received his school report last week.*

Der Arzt hat mir Penizillin verschrieben. *The doctor prescribed penicillin for me.*

- The emphasis or stress in inseparable verbs is always on the verb itself, never on the prefix.

■ In dictionaries inseparable verbs are normally shown by *insep* written after the verb.

9.3.3 Separable or inseparable?

Some verbs can be either separable or inseparable, depending on their meaning. This should not daunt us too much as we are used to it from such English verbs as to *overtake* and *to take over*.

■ verbs which start with the following prefixes can be either separable or inseparable, according to meaning: durch-, hinter-, über-, um-, unter-, voll-, wieder-, wider-:

übersetzen	*to translate*
über/setzen	*to take across, to ferry across*
unterhalten	*to entertain, to maintain*
unter/halten	*to hold underneath*
umfahren	*to drive around, to bypass*
um/fahren	*to run over, to knock down*

9.4 Verbs associated with particular prepositions

Just as some verbs are followed by a particular case, e.g. dative, so other verbs are followed by a particular preposition. This information is usually found in a good dictionary. The following are examples of some frequently used verbs and their prepositions.

Angst haben vor + dative	*to be frightened of*
an/kommen in + dative	*to arrive at, to arrive in*
bitten um + accusative	*to ask for, to request*
denken an + accusative	*to think of something or someone, to have something or someone in mind*
denken über + accusative	*to think about, to have an opinion about*
halten von + dative	*to think of, to rate*
sich erinnern an + accusative	*to remember*
fragen nach + dative	*to ask about, to enquire about*
sich freuen auf + accusative	*to look forward to*
sich freuen über + accusative	*to be happy about*
schreiben an + accusative	*to write to*
vorbei/fahren an + dative	*to go past*
warten auf + accusative	*to wait for*

9.5 Reflexive verbs (See Functional Grammar 11)

Reflexive verbs express the idea of doing something either for oneself or to oneself e.g. *I wash myself, I astonish myself*. Their use in German is different from that in English. Reflexive verbs can be regular or irregular verbs, separable or inseparable. The reflexive verb consists of the normal verb form plus a reflexive pronoun (*myself, yourself, herself*, etc.).

9.5.1 Reflexive verbs with an accusative reflexive pronoun

Many reflexive verbs use the pronoun in the accusative case, because the pronoun is the direct object of the verb, for example:

sich wiegen *to weigh oneself*

Singular	*Plural*
ich wiege *mich* I weigh myself	wir wiegen *uns* we weigh ourself
du wiegst *dich* you weigh yourself	ihr wiegt *euch* you weigh yourself
er wiegt *sich* he weighs himself	Sie wiegen *sich* you weigh yourself
sie wiegt *sich* she weighs herself	sie wiegen *sich* they weigh themselves

Note the word order:

1. in the question form:
   Wiegen Sie sich regelmäßig?   *Do you weigh yourself regularly?*

2. in the command form:
   Wiegen Sie sich regelmäßig!   *Weigh yourself regularly!*

9.5.2 Other reflexive verbs with an accusative reflexive pronoun:

sich an/ziehen	*to get dressed*
sich aus/ziehen	*to get undressed*
sich um/ziehen	*to get changed*
sich ärgern	*to get annoyed*
sich aus/ruhen	*to rest, to have a rest*
sich beeilen	*to hurry up*
sich entschuldigen	*to apologise*
sich erinnern an + acc.	*to remember*
sich erkälten	*to catch a cold*
sich freuen auf + acc	*to look forward to*

sich freuen über + acc	*to be pleased about*
sich hin/legen	*to lie down*
sich hin/setzen	*to sit down*
sich kämmen	*to comb one's hair*
sich konzentrieren	*to concentrate*
sich rasieren	*to shave*
sich verabschieden	*to take one's leave*
sich verletzen	*to hurt oneself*
sich waschen	*to have a wash, to wash oneself*

9.5.3 Reflexive verbs with a dative reflexive pronoun

The idea of doing something for one's own benefit e.g. **Ich kaufe mir ein Haus** *I am buying a house (for myself)* is often expressed with a reflexive verb. In this usage the reflexive pronoun is in the dative case, because it is the indirect object of the sentence and it is followed by the direct object in the accusative case:

Ich (*I*)	kaufe (*buy*)	mir (*myself*)	ein Haus (*a house*)
subject pronoun (nominative)	finite verb	reflexive pronoun as indirect object (dative)	direct object (accusative)

sich die Hände waschen *to wash one's hands*

Singular

ich wasche **mir** die Hände I wash my hands
du wäscht **dir** die Hände you wash your hands
er wäscht **sich** die Hände he washes his hands
sie wäscht **sich** die Hände she washes her hands

Plural

wir waschen **uns** die Hände we wash our hands
ihr wäscht **euch** die Hände you wash your hands
Sie waschen **sich** die Hände you wash your hands
sie waschen **sich** die Hände they wash their hands

Other reflexive verbs with a dative reflexive pronoun:

sich das Haar waschen	*to wash one's hair*
sich die Zähne putzen	*to clean one's teeth*

9.5.4 The idea of getting something done for oneself using the verb *lassen*

The same reflexive pronouns as in the last example are also used in the expression **sich etwas tun lassen** *to have something done* or *to get something done*):

Ich lasse mir das Haar schneiden.	*I'm having my hair cut.*
Sie lässt sich einen Hotelprospekt schicken.	*She is having a hotel brochure sent (to her).*
Er lässt sich einen Zahn ziehen.	*He is having a tooth out.*
Wir lassen uns ein Haus bauen.	*We're having a house built.*
Ihr müsst euch untersuchen lassen.	*You must get yourself examined.*
Sie müssen sich operieren lassen.	*You must have an operation.*

10 Tenses

10.1 The formation of the simple past tense of regular verbs

The simple past tense of regular verbs is formed by adding the following endings to the verb stem:

kaufen *to buy*			
Singular		*Plural*	
ich kauf **te**	*I bought,* *I was buying,* *I used to buy*	wir kauf **ten**	*we bought*
du kauf **test**	*you bought*	ihr kauf **tet**	*you bought*
er kauf **te**	*he bought*	Sie kauf **ten**	*you bought*
sie kauf **te**	*she bought*	sie kauf **ten**	*they bought*

If the stem of regular verb ends in **-d, -t,** , e.g. **reden** *to speak*, **arbeiten** *to work*, or a combination of **m** or **n** preceded by another consonant, e.g. **atmen** *to breathe*, **regnen** *to rain*, an **e** is added before the past tense endings, e.g. **ich arbeit***e***te, du arbeit***e***test** etc.

10.2 The formation of the simple past of irregular verbs

Unlike the regular verbs, it is not possible to work out what the simple past form of an irregular verb is. All good dictionaries and course books include a verb list which you should consult to find out the correct form.

You will notice that in most verb tables the third person singular form is given in the column for the simple past tense. This is in effect the simple past stem, to which endings are added to form the simple past as follows:

Singular		*Plural*	
ich trank	*I drank*	wir trank**en**	*we drank*
	I was drinking,		
	I used to drink		
du trank**st**	*you drank*	ihr trank**t**	*you drank*
er trank	*he drank*	Sie trank**en**	*you drank*
sie trank	*she drank*	sie trank**en**	*they drank*

There is no ending at all on the **ich** and **er**, **sie es**, forms, which are thus identical to the one found in the verb list.

Separable and inseparable prefixes can be added to these verbs, and change the meaning, e.g.

schreiben *to write,*
beschreiben *to describe,*
verschreiben *to prescribe;*
kommen *to come,*
ankommen *to arrive,*
auskommen *to get by,*
umkommen *to die.*

You will not find the form with the prefix in the verb list (10.7). Always look up the basic verb and then add the prefix.

10.3 The perfect tense (Functional Grammar 18)

10.3.1 The formation of the perfect tense of regular verbs (Functional Grammar 18.2.2)

The perfect tense is formed by using the appropriate part of either the verb **haben** or **sein**, plus a past participle at the end of the clause, e.g.

Ich **habe** einen neuen Mantel **gekauft**.   *I bought a new coat.*
Wir **haben getanzt**.   *We danced.*

The perfect tense in German, for example, **er hat … geschrieben** can be translated into English as *he wrote, he was writing, he did write, he has written*. **Ich bin … gefahren** can be translated as *I travelled, I was travelling, I did travel* and *I have travelled*.

10.3.2 Formation of the past participle

The past participle of most regular verbs is formed by firstly removing the -en from the infinitive (e.g. **kaufen**), giving us the stem of the verb (**kauf**). Secondly we put **ge-** in front of the stem and -t after the stem , resulting in **gekauft** *bought*. You will have noticed that the past participle is sent to the end of the clause .

- To form the past participle of a separable verb (for example **ein/kaufen** *to go shopping*, **auf/machen** *to open*, **zu/machen** *to close*, simply put the **ge-** between the two parts of the verb, for example:

    Wir haben gestern bei Kaufhof   *We went shopping at*
    ein*ge***kauft**.   *Kaufhof yesterday.*

- If the stem of the verb ends in -**d**, -**t**, -**m** or -**n**, an additional e is added before the final **t** in the past participle for ease of pronunciation, for example:

    Oma hat im Toten Meer gebad**et**. *Grandma bathed in the Dead Sea.*

    If the infinitive begins with **be-**, **ge-**, **ent-**, **er-**, **ver-**, **zer-**, or ends with -**ieren**, no **ge-** is required at the beginning of the past participle:

    Wir haben nichts bemerkt.   *We didn't notice anything*

- Many verbs do not form their past participle in the way described for regular verbs. The past participles of most irregular verbs end in -**en** and many undergo a vowel change from the infinitive form e.g. **gehen – gegangen**, **schreiben – geschrieben**, **sprechen – gesprochen**. As already noted, a few verbs change the stem vowel of their infinitive in the past tense and past participle and also add **t** like regular verbs, e.g. **kennen** *to know*, – **kannte, gekannt**. The verb list (10.7) or any good German dictionary should be consulted until individual forms of irregular verbs have been learned.

10.3.3 Verbs which form the perfect tense using *sein*

(Functional Grammar 18.2.6)

■ If the verb shows motion or movement from one place to another the perfect tense is formed by using the appropriate part of the verb **sein** plus a past participle at the end of the clause:

fahren *to travel*
Ich **bin** mit dem Zug gefahren.   *I travelled by train.*

kommen *to come*
Ihr Mann **ist** um 2 Uhr morgens   *Her husband came home at 2 am.*
nach Hause gekommen.

fliegen *to fly*
Bist du über Brüssel geflogen?   *Did you fly via Brussels?*

ab/fahren *to depart, set off*
Mein Nachbar **ist** gestern   *My neighbour set off yesterday.*
abgefahren.

an/kommen *to arrive*
Der Zug aus Paris **ist** mit zwei   *The train from Paris arrived*
Stunden Verspätung angekommen.   *two hours late.*

folgen *to follow* NB this verb requires the dative case!
Der Herr hat gerufen und der   *The master called and the*
Hund **ist** ihm gefolgt.   *dog followed him.*

■ If the verb shows a change of state or condition:

Es **ist** dunkel geworden.   *It has got* (literally 'it has
become') *dark.*

Note: The verbs **sein** and **bleiben** also form their perfect tense using **sein**:

Sie **ist** sehr krank **gewesen**.   *She has been very ill.*
Er **ist** in Rostock **geblieben**.   *He has stayed in Rostock.*

10.4 The pluperfect tense

(See Functional Grammar 17.4.2)

The pluperfect tense is a compound tense, formed by using the appropriate form of the simple past tense of either **haben** or **sein**, plus a past participle at the end of the clause. You will not find this form given in the verb lists as you can work it out: combine the past stem of **haben** or **sein** (from the simple past column) with the past participle:

Er **hatte** schon zwei Liter Bier **getrunken**, bevor er mit dem Wagen nach Hause fuhr.	*He had already drunk two litres of beer before he drove home by car.*
Vor der Hochzeit **war** sie noch nie in einer Kirche **gewesen**.	*She had never been in a church before the wedding.*

10.5 The future tense

The future tense is another compound tense. It is formed by using the appropriate part of the present tense of the verb **werden** plus an infinitive at the end of the clause. On its own **werden** means *to become*, but when used to form the future tense, it is used merely as an auxiliary verb:

Wir **werden** acht Monate in Kanada **verbringen**.	*We shall spend eight months in Canada.*

It is an irregular verb, and its present tense is shown in 16.2.2.

The future is also often expressed in German by the present tense plus an adverb:

Ich fahre nächste Woche nach Ulm.	*I am/shall be going to Ulm next week.*

10.6 The future perfect tense

The future perfect is a compound tense formed by using the appropriate part of the present tense of the verb **werden** plus two other verbal forms: the past participle of the main verb, plus either **haben** or **sein**:

Er wird schon daran gedacht haben.	*He will already have thought of that.*
Sie werden schon in Afrika angekommen sein.	*They will already have arrived in Africa.*

NB The future perfect tense is very rarely used.

10.7 List of irregular verbs with simple past and perfect forms

Infinitive	Meaning	3rd person Sing. present	3rd person simple past	3rd person perfect tense
backen	*to bake*	backt	backte/buk	hat gebacken
befehlen	*to order*	befiehlt	befahl	hat befohlen
beginnen	*to begin*	beginnt	begann	hat begonnen
beißen	*to bite*	beißt	biss	hat gebissen
bergen	*to save*	birgt	barg	hat geborgen
bewegen	*to move*	bewegt	bewog	hat bewogen
biegen	*to turn*	biegt	bog	hat gebogen
bieten	*to offer*	bietet	bot	hat geboten
binden	*to bind*	bindet	band	hat gebunden
bitten	*to ask*	bittet	bat	hat gebeten
blasen	*to blow*	bläst	blies	hat geblasen
bleiben	*to remain*	bleibt	blieb	ist geblieben
braten	*to fry*	brät	briet	hat gebraten
brechen	*to break*	bricht	brach	hat gebrochen
brennen	*to burn*	brennt	brannte	hat gebrannt
bringen	*to bring*	bringt	brachte	hat gebracht
denken	*to think*	denkt	dachte	hat gedacht
dürfen	*to be allowed to*	darf	durfte	hat gedurft
empfehlen	*to recommend*	empfiehlt	empfahl	hat empfohlen
essen	*to eat*	isst	aß	hat gegessen
fahren	*to travel*	fährt	fuhr	ist/hat gefahren
fallen	*to fall*	fällt	fiel	ist gefallen
fangen	*to catch*	fängt	fing	hat gefangen
finden	*to find*	findet	fand	hat gefunden
fliegen	*to fly*	fliegt	flog	ist geflogen
fliehen	*to flee*	flieht	floh	ist geflohen
fließen	*to flow*	fließt	floss	ist geflossen
frieren	*to freeze*	friert	fror	ist gefroren
geben	*to give*	gibt	gab	hat gegeben
gehen	*to go*	geht	ging	ist gegangen
gelingen	*to succeed*	gelingt	gelang	ist gelungen

gelten	*to be valid*	gilt	galt	hat gegolten
genießen	*to enjoy*	genießt	genoss	hat genossen
geschehen	*to happen*	geschieht	geschah	ist geschehen
gewinnen	*to win*	gewinnt	gewann	hat gewonnen
gießen	*to pour*	gießt	goss	hat gegossen
gleiten	*to glide*	gleitet	glitt	ist geglitten
graben	*to dig*	gräbt	grub	hat gegraben
greifen	*to grab*	greift	griff	hat gegriffen
haben	*to have*	hat	hatte	hat gehabt
halten	*to hold*	hält	hielt	hat gehalten
hängen	*to hang*	hängt	hing	hat gehangen
heben	*to lift*	hebt	hob	hat gehoben
heißen	*to be called*	heißt	hieß	hat geheißen
helfen	*to help*	hilft	half	hat geholfen
kennen	*to know*	kennt	kannte	hat gekannt
kneifen	*to pinch*	kneift	kniff	hat gekniffen
kommen	*to come*	kommt	kam	ist gekommen
können	*to be able*	kann	konnte	hat gekonnt
kriechen	*to crawl*	kriecht	kroch	ist gekrochen
laden	*to load*	lädt	lud	hat geladen
lassen	*to let, leave*	lässt	ließ	hat gelassen
laufen	*to walk, run*	läuft	lief	ist gelaufen
leiden	*to suffer*	leidet	litt	hat gelitten
leihen	*to lend*	leiht	lieh	hat geliehen
liegen	*to lie*	liegt	lag	ist/hat gelegen
lügen	*to tell a lie*	lügt	log	hat gelogen
meiden	*to avoid*	meidet	mied	hat gemieden
messen	*to measure*	misst	maß	hat gemessen
mögen	*to like*	mag	mochte	hat gemocht
nehmen	*to take*	nimmt	nahm	hat genommen
nennen	*to call*	nennt	nannte	hat gennannt
pfeifen	*to whistle*	pfeift	pfiff	hat gepfiffen
preisen	*to praise*	preist	pries	hat gepriesen
raten	*to advise*	rät	riet	hat geraten
reiben	*to rub*	reibt	rieb	hat gerieben
reißen	*to tear*	reißt	riss	hat gerissen
rennen	*to run*	rennt	rannte	hat gerannt
reiten	*to ride*	reitet	ritt	ist geritten

riechen	*to smell*	riecht	roch	hat gerochen
rufen	*to call*	ruft	rief	hat gerufen
schaffen	*to create*	schafft	schuf	hat geschaffen
scheiden	*to separate*	scheidet	schied	hat geschieden
scheinen	*to shine*	scheint	schien	hat geschienen
schieben	*to push*	schiebt	schob	hat geschoben
schießen	*to shoot*	schießt	schoss	hat geschossen
schlafen	*to sleep*	schläft	schlief	hat geschlafen
schlagen	*to hit*	schlägt	schlug	hat geschlagen
schließen	*to close*	schließt	schloss	hat geschlossen
schmeißen	*to throw*	schmeißt	schmiss	hat geschmissen
schmelzen	*to melt*	schmilzt	schmolz	ist geschmolzen
schneiden	*to cut*	schneidet	schnitt	hat geschnitten
schreiben	*to write*	schreibt	schrieb	hat geschrieben
schreien	*to scream*	schreit	schrie	hat geschrien
schreiten	*to step*	schreitet	schritt	ist geschritten
schweigen	*to be silent*	schweigt	schwieg	hat geschwiegen
schwimmen	*to swim*	schwimmt	schwomm	ist/hat geschwommen
sehen	*to see*	sieht	sah	hat gesehen
sein	*to be*	ist	war	ist gewesen
senden	*to send*	sendet	sandte	hat gesandt
singen	*to sing*	singt	sang	hat gesungen
sinken	*to sink*	sinkt	sank	ist gesunken
sitzen	*to sit*	sitzt	saß	ist gesessen
sollen	*ought to*	soll	sollte	hat gesollt
sprechen	*to talk*	spricht	sprach	hat gesprochen
springen	*to jump*	springt	sprang	ist gesprungen
stechen	*to sting*	sticht	stach	hat gestochen
stehen	*to stand*	steht	stand	ist/hat gestanden
stehlen	*to steal*	stiehlt	stahl	hat gestohlen
steigen	*to climb*	steigt	stieg	ist gestiegen
sterben	*to die*	stirbt	starb	ist gestorben
stinken	*to stink*	stinkt	stank	hat gestunken
stoßen	*to push*	stößt	stieß	hat gestoßen
streichen	*to stroke, paint*	streicht	strich	hat gestrichen
streiten	*to quarrel*	streitet	stritt	hat gestritten

tragen	to carry	trägt	trug	hat getragen
treffen	to meet	trifft	traf	hat getroffen
treiben	to drive, push	treibt	trieb	hat getrieben
treten	to step	tritt	trat	ist getreten
trinken	to drink	trinkt	trank	hat getrunken
tun	to do	tut	tat	hat getan
verderben	to spoil	verdirbt	verdarb	hat verdorben
vergessen	to forget	vergisst	vergaß	hat vergessen
verlieren	to lose	verliert	verlor	hat verloren
verschwinden	to disappear	verschwindet	verschwand	ist verschwunden
wachsen	to grow	wächst	wuchs	ist gewachsen
waschen	to wash	wäscht	wusch	hat gewaschen
weisen	to point	weist	wies	hat gewiesen
wenden	to turn	wendet	wandte	hat gewandt
werden	to become	wird	wurde	ist geworden
werfen	to throw	wirft	warf	hat geworfen
wiegen	to weigh	wiegt	wog	hat gewogen
wissen	to know	weiß	wusste	hat gewusst
wollen	to want to	will	wollte	hat gewollt
verzeihen	to pardon	verzeiht	verzieh	hat verziehen
ziehen	to pull	zieht	zog	hat gezogen
zwingen	to force	zwingt	zwang	hat gezwungen

11 The Subjunctive

There are two forms of the subjunctive in German, which are sometimes described as the present subjunctive and imperfect subjunctive. This can be misleading in that the subjunctive does not directly correspond to the tenses referred to, and so we shall use the terms Subjunctive 1 for the so-called present subjunctive and Subjunctive 2 for the so-called imperfect subjunctive .

11.1 The use of the subjunctive

The subjunctive is used for: a few short, set phrases, often expressing hopes or wishes:

Gott sei dank!   *Thank God!*
Es lebe der König!   *Long live the King!*

sei es gut, sei es schlecht | *whether it be good or bad*
Das wär's! | *That's all, that's it!*

(often used at the end of an order in shops.)

Subjunctive 2 is used

- after **als ob** *as if*: Sie sah aus, als ob sie nicht geschlafen hätte. *She looked as if she had not slept.*

- for conditional hypothetical sentences:

Wenn ich reich wäre, würde ich | *If I were rich, I would buy a*
mir ein neues Haus kaufen. | *new house.*
Wenn ich das gewusst hätte, wäre | *If I had known that, I would have*
ich sofort nach Hause gegangen. | *gone home immediately.*

- For indirect speech. As a general rule, the subjunctive verb is put into the same tense as was used in the indicative speech, e.g.: From the direct statement: Der Lehrer sagte: „Ich bin müde." *The teacher said, "I am tired"* we can form the Indirect speech: Der Lehrer sagte, dass er müde **sei**/Der Lehrer sagte, er **sei** müde. *The teacher said he was tired.*

- For indirect questions. From the direct question: Er fragte: Hat das Auto eine Stereoanlage? *He asked, "Does the car have a stereo system?"* we can form the indirect question: Er fragte, ob das Auto eine Stereoanlage **habe**. *He asked if the car had a stereo system.*

However, units 20 and 21 show wide variations in usage.

11.2 The formation of the subjunctive

11.2.1 The formation of Subjunctive 1

(See Functional Grammar 20)

Subjunctive 1 is formed by adding the following endings to the stem of the verb:

> ich kauf**e**, du kauf**est**, er kauf**e**, sie kauf**e**, es kauf**e**,
> wir kauf**en**, ihr kauf**et**, Sie kauf**en**, sie kauf**en**

The **ich**, **wir**, **Sie** and **sie** forms are the same in the subjunctive as in the indicative for this verb.

By the very nature of reported speech the 3rd person singular and plural forms are most frequently used. In fact, you are unlikely to come across some of the other forms but we have shown them here for reference.

In practice the Subjunctive 2 form and/or the auxiliary **würde** plus infinitive is often substituted for Subjunctive 1 in reported speech, e.g.

Sie sagten, sie hätten keine Zeit.   *They said they had no time.*
Er sagte, er würde sich ein neues   *He said he would buy a new car.*
Auto kaufen.

The Subjunctive 1 of irregular and modal verbs is formed in exactly the same way as that of the regular verbs, i.e. from the stem plus the same endings:

---

ich fahre, du fahrest, er, sie, es fahre,
wir fahren, ihr fahret, Sie fahren, sie fahren

ich könne, du könnest, er, sie, es könne,
wir können, ihr könnet, Sie können, sie können

Even **haben** (*to have*) forms its Subjunctive 1 in the same way as a regular verb:

---

ich habe, du habest, er, sie, es habe,
wir haben, ihr habet, Sie haben, sie haben

Sein is an exception in that it forms its present subjunctive as follows, without -**e** in the singular:

---

ich **sei**, du **seist**, er, sie, es **sei**,
wir **seien**, ihr **seiet**, Sie **seien**, sie **seien**

This form will be familiar to you as it is the same as the imperative mood of **sein**. (See Unit 13)

11.2.2 The formation of Subjunctive 2

(See Functional Grammar 21)

Regular verbs:

The Subjunctive 2 form of regular verbs is the same as the imperfect indicative, for example **kaufte** in the sentence:

Wenn er das **machte**, würde ich weinen. *If he did that, I would cry.*

Irregular verbs:

■ To form the Subjunctive 2 of irregular verbs, the following endings are added to the imperfect indicative (found in the verb list, see 10.7). Using **kommen** *to come* as an example:

The imperfect stem is **kam**

> ich käme, du kämest, er, sie, es käme,
> wir kämen, ihr kämet, Sie kämen, sie kämen

■ As you can see, in addition to these endings an umlaut must be added to the vowels **a**, **o** or **u** in the stem.

■ If the stem vowel is not **a**, **o**, **u** then it does not change. The imperfect indicative stem from **gehen** *to go* is **ging**, and the Subjunctive 2 forms are:

> ich ginge, du gingest, er, sie, es ginge,
> wir gingen, ihr ginget, Sie gingen, sie gingen

■ The Subjunctive 2 forms of **sein** *to be* and **haben** *to have* are formed in the same way.

sein	**haben**
The imperfect indicative	The imperfect indicative
stem is **war**	stem is **hatte**
ich wäre	ich hätte
du wärest	du hättest
er, sie, es wäre	er, sie, es hätte
wir wären	wir hätten
ihr wäret	ihr hättet
Sie wären	Sie hätten
sie wären	sie hätten

■ You can further combine the Subjunctive 2 form of either **haben** or **sein** with a past participle to produce a pluperfect form expressing unfulfilled conditions, as follows:

Wenn er das gewusst hätte, *If he had known that, he would*
wäre er weggelaufen. *have run away.*

■ There is also a trend either to simplify or to avoid the subjunctive in modern spoken German. In situations where a subjunctive is clearly needed, a useful and simple formula **Ich würde** plus an infinitive is often used, for example:

Ich **würde sagen**, dass es *I would say that it's absolutely*
unbedingt nötig ist *necessary.*

Ich **würde** gerne **mitmachen**, *I'd love to join in but I have*
aber ich habe keine Zeit. *no time.*

NB This formula is not used with the verb **sein**. The form **wäre** is preferred:

Ich wäre sehr dankbar, wenn Sie *I'd be most grateful if you*
das nicht weitersagen würden. *wouldn't pass this on.*

The most commonly used forms of Subjunctive 2 are:

> ich wäre, bräuchte, dürfte, ginge, käme, könnte, möchte,
> müsste, sollte, wollte, wüsste

For example:

Das **wäre** gar nicht schlecht! *That wouldn't be at all bad!*
Wenn ich nur **wüsste,** was ich *If only I knew what I ought to do.*
machen sollte

12 The Imperative mood

The du imperative form

(See Functional Grammar 13.2.2)

■ the familiar singular imperative is formed by dropping both the pronoun **du** and the ending from the **du** form of the verb, e.g.: **du fragst**):

Frag deine Lehrerin zuerst! *Ask your teacher first!*

Note 1: You will sometimes find that an **e** is added to this form. It can have the effect of making it sound a bit more formal or imperious, even though it is addressed to a child or a friend.

Note 2: If the verb adds an umlaut in the **du** form, (eg. **ich laufe, du läufst**) the same rules as above apply, but the umlaut is dropped:

Lauf nicht weg!	*Don't run away!*
Schlaf gut!	*Sleep well!*

The ihr imperative form

(Functional Grammar 13.2.3)

■ The familiar plural imperative form simply comprises the appropriate **ihr** form of the verb minus the pronoun **ihr**:

Raucht bitte nicht!	*Please don't smoke!*

The Sie imperative form

(See Functional Grammar 13.2.4)

Setzen Sie sich!	*Take a seat!*

The imperative forms of verbs sein and haben

(See Functional Grammar 13.2.5)

sein	haben
du: **sei** ruhig! *Be quiet!*	**Hab** keine Angst! *Don't be afraid!*
ihr: **seid** ruhig! *Be quiet!*	**Habt** *keine Angst!* Don't be afraid!
Sie: **Seien Sie** ruhig! *Be quiet!*	**Haben Sie** keine Angst! *Don't be afraid!*

Commands involving the speaker (Functional Grammar 13.4)

If the speaker is involved in the projected action, a **wir** imperative form can be used by inverting the normal verb form. In this usage the pronoun **wir** is retained as follows:

Fangen wir an!	*Let's begin!*
Gehen wir!	*Let's go!*

13 The passive voice (Functional Grammar 19)

The passive voice is used in a construction which shows the subject of an equivalent active sentence undergoing or suffering the action of the verb, e.g. The workmen are felling the tree outside the gym > **The tree** outside the gym **is being felled** by the workmen.

The passive voice is formed by using the appropriate part and tense of the verb **werden** as an auxiliary verb, plus a past participle at the end of the clause .

Compare the following two sentences, which both have the same meaning but a different emphasis:

Present active voice: Die Gemeinde baut einen neuen Sportplatz. *The local authority is building a new sports ground.*

Present passive voice: Ein neuer Sportplatz wird von der Gemeinde gebaut. *A new sports ground is being built by the local authority.*

- In the passive sentence more emphasis is given to the process which is being carried out by the local authority (i.e what is being built)
- the direct object of the active sentence has become the subject of the passive sentence, and has therefore changed from the accusative to the nominative case.
- the agent by whom or which the activity is carried out is expressed by **von** + dative case

Simple past passive: Ein neuer Sportplatz **wurde** von der Gemeinde gebaut. *A new sports ground was built by the local authority.*

Perfect passive: Ein neuer Sportplatz **ist** von der Gemeinde **gebaut worden**. *A new sports ground has been built by the local authority.* NB The **ge-** is dropped from the past past participle of **werden** when used next to another past participle.

Pluperfect passive: Ein neuer Sportplatz **war** von der Gemeinde **gebaut worden**. *A new sports ground had been built by the local authority.*

Future passive: Ein neuer Sportplatz wird von der Gemeinde gebaut werden. *A new sports ground will be built by the local authority.*

Additional notes:

1. The means by which something is or was done is expressed by the preposition **durch** + accusative case:

Meine Sonnenblumen sind **durch** den Wind zerstört worden.	*My sun flowers have been destroyed by the wind.*

2. The object or instrument used to carry out an action is expressed by the preposition **mit** + dative case:

Der Brief wurde **mit** der Hand geschrieben.	*The letter was written by hand.*

3. If the object of the verb in the active sentence is in the dative e.g. Der Lehrer hilft **dem Kind.** *The teacher is helping the child*, then it must remain in the dative in the passive version: **Dem Kind** wird von dem Lehrer geholfen. *The child is being helped by the teacher.* Compare:

Die Firma Braun hat ihm eine Stelle angeboten. – Ihm ist eine Stelle von der Firma Braun angeboten worden.	*Braun and Company has offered him a job – He has been offered a job by Braun and Company.*

4. There are several ways of avoiding the passive, most notably by using the indefinite pronoun **man**:

Auf Bierfesten wird oft zu viel getrunken. – **Man** trinkt oft zu viel Bier auf Bierfesten.	*Often too much is drunk at beer festivals. – People often drink too much at beer festivals.*

5. There are sometimes very close similarities between sentences with an adjective or past participle after the verb **sein** *to be* and passive sentences. Compare, for example:

Die Haustür ist nach 22 Uhr geschlossen.	*The front door is closed after 10 pm.*

and

Die Haustür wird um 22 Uhr geschlossen.	*The front door is closed at 10 pm.*

Das Mittagessen ist serviert.	*Lunch is served.*

and

Das Mittagessen wird serviert.	*Lunch is being served.*

14 Word order

14.1 Main clauses

In a main clause (i.e. one which can stand independently as a sentence) which is not a question or command, the finite verb is the second element or 'idea' (See Functional Grammar 3.4.1). An element or idea is not necessarily only one word, as the following translations of the English sentence *I'm going to the cinema this evening* demonstrate:

1	2	3	4
Ich	**gehe**	heute Abend	ins Kino.
subject pronoun	finite verb	adverbial phrase	adverbial phrase

or

1	2	3	4
Heute Abend	**gehe**	ich	ins Kino.
adverbial phrase	finite verb	subject pronoun	adverbial phrase

This rule seems strange to an English speaker, but there are still relics of this 'verb second' practice in the English language, for example: 'Scarcely had I finished speaking', or 'Here endeth the first lesson'.

If a subordinate clause begins the sentence, it also counts as the first idea and the finite verb of the main clause comes next, i.e. in second position:

1	2	3	4
Wenn die Sonne heute Nachmittag scheint,	**spiele**	ich	Tennis.

The occurrence of the two finite verbs next to each other in the middle of the sentence, separated by only a comma, is often called a verb – comma, – verb construction. This happens whenever a subordinate clause begins the sentence, as a subordinating conjunction sends the verb to the end of the clause:

Als ich jung **war**, **spielte** ich die Gitarre.	*When I was young, I played the guitar.*

■ In terms of word order, interjections are not counted as an idea or element.

Ach, ich wollte Gabi anrufen.	*Oh bother, I wanted to phone Gabi.*

■ If **ja** or **nein** is used at the beginning of a sentence it is usually followed by a comma, and has no effect on subsequent word order:

Ja, man kann nur hoffen	*Yes, you can only hope.*

The same applies if a name or a word such as **also** *so*, *therefore* is followed by a comma at the beginning of a sentence:

Also, wir können endlich essen.	*Well then, we can eat at long last.*

■ In questions and the imperative, the finite verb begins the sentence:

Trinken Sie viel Tee?	*Do you drink a lot of tea?*
Trinken Sie viel Tee!	*Drink a lot of tea!*

14.2 The position of the direct and indirect object

■ Sometimes the direct object appears *before* the verb in German, especially if you wish to give it extra stress:

Den Mann möchte ich kennen lernen.	*I would like to get to know that man.*

■ Sometimes the direct object appears later in the sentence:

Ich bekam erst letzten Freitag **den Brief**.	*I did not get the letter until last Friday.*

■ If there are two nouns after the verb, (i.e. a direct object and an indirect object), the dative comes before the accusative:

Er schickte dem Direktor (dative) einen langen Brief (accusative).	*He sent a long letter to the Head Teacher.*

■ If there is a pronoun and a noun, the pronoun comes before the noun:

Er schickte ihm (pronoun) einen Brief (noun).	*He sent him a letter.*

or:

Er schickte (pronoun) ihn dem Direktor (noun).	*He sent it to the Head Teacher.*

■ If there are two or more pronouns after the verb , the order is

1) *nominative,* 2) *accusative,* 3) *dative*:

Ich (nom.) gebe es (acc.) ihr (dat.) jetzt. *I am giving it to her now.*
or:

Jetzt gebe ich (nom.) es (acc.) ihr (dat.). *Now I am giving it to her.*

14.3 The position of other elements in the main clause

14.3.1 Adverbs and adverbial phrases

When several adverbs or adverbial phrases are used after the finite verb the normal order for these is:

1) *time,* 2) *manner,* 3) *place* – i.e. answers to the questions 1) **wann?** *when?* **wie?** *how?* **wo?/wohin?/woher?** *where?/where to?/where from?*:

Ich fahre (**wann?**) nächste Woche   *I am going to Geneva*
(**wie?**) mit dem Zug (**wohin?**)   *by train next week.*
nach Genf.

14.3.2 Past participles

The normal position for the past participle is at the end of the main clause:

Ich habe ihn zwei Wochen   *I have not seen him for two weeks.*
lang nicht gesehen.

14.3.3 The infinitive after modal or auxiliary verbs

The normal position for the infinitive after a modal or auxiliary verb is at the end of the clause:

Er will nächsten Sommer nach   *He wants to travel/go to*
Australien **fahren**.   *Australia next summer.*
Wir werden meinen Onkel in   *We will visit my uncle in Mexico.*
Mexiko **besuchen**.

14.3.4 The position of separable prefixes

The normal position for the separable prefix of a finite verb is at the end of the clause:

Er rief mich gestern Abend **an**.   *He telephoned me yesterday evening.*

15 Subordinate clauses (Functional Grammar 10.2.1)

A subordinate clause is an add-on element to a main clause. It does not make full sense in its own right. It can appear *either* before *or* after the main clause and always starts with a subordinating conjunction, which sends the verb to the end of the clause:

> Ich bleibe heute im Bett (main clause), *I am staying in bed today*
> weil ich krank bin (subordinate clause). *because I am ill.*

If the subordinating conjunction begins the sentence, a verb – comma – verb construction appears in the middle, linking the two clauses:

> Weil ich krank bin (subordinate clause), *Because I am ill, I am*
> bleibe ich heute im Bett. *staying in bed today.*

When a separable verb is used in a subordinate clause, the verb goes to the end of the clause, complete with the prefix:

> Ich warte auf dem Bahnsteig, *I'll wait on the platform until*
> bis der Zug ankommt. *the train arrives.*

The subordinating conjunctions are:

als *when*	**bevor** *before*
bis *until*	**da** *as, since, seeing that*
damit *so that, in order that*	**dass** *that*
ehe *before* (cf. old-fashoned English ere)	
falls *in case*	**indem** *while, whilst*
nachdem *after*	**ob** *whether, if*
obgleich *although*	**obschon** *although*
obwohl *although*	**seit/seitdem** *since*
so dass *so that*	**während** *while, whereas*
weil *because*	**wenn** *if, whenever*

All of these send the verb to the end of the clause when used as a conjunction.

Note: Beware! These subordinating conjunctions are easily confused with other word classes, for example with the prepositions **vor** *in front of*, **bis** *until*, **nach** *after*, **seit** *since, for*, **während** *during*, e.g.

> Ich warte, **bis** er kommt. *I am waiting until he comes.*
> **Seit** ich Deutsch lerne, bin ich *Since I have been learning German*
> sehr glücklich *I have been very happy.*

Während sie warteten, lasen sie die Zeitungen.	*While they were waiting they read the newspapers.*

Prepositions do not, of course, send the verb to the end of the clause. The conjunction **als**, (Als ich sie besuchte, ging es ihr viel besser. *When I visited her she was much better*), is also used in the comparative of adverbs and adjectives; and the conjunction **damit**, (Er trinkt weniger Alkohol, damit er gesund wird. *He is drinking less alcohol in order to become healthy*), can be an adverbial preposition (see 10.4).

When interrogatives (wo? wann? warum? etc) are used at the beginning of subordinate clauses, they act like a conjunction and send the verb to the end of the clause:

Ich weiß nicht, **wo** mein Hausschlüssel **ist**.	*I don't know where my door key is.*
Können Sie bitte erklären, **warum** er das **macht**?	*Can you please explain why he does that?*

15.1 The occasional omission of conjunctions

■ In conditional clauses the subordinating conjunction **wenn** is sometimes omitted, and so the verb is not sent to the end of the clause. Compare:

Wenn er das gesagt **hätte**, (so) wäre ich nicht gekommen.	*If he had said that, I would not have come.*
Hätte er das gesagt, (so) wäre ich nicht gekommen.	*Had he said that, I would not have come.*

■ In indirect (reported) speech the conjunction **dass** is sometimes omitted, with the result that the verb does not go to the end of the clause. Compare:

Er sagte, **dass** er am Wochenende nach Hause **fahre**.	*He said that he was going home at the weekend.*
Er sagte, er **fahre** am Wochenende nach Hause.	*He said he was going home at the weekend.*

■ The expression **als ob** *as if* is normally followed by Subjunctive 2. **Ob** is sometimes omitted, in which case the verb is not sent to the end of the clause. Compare:

Sie sah aus, **als ob** sie krank **wäre**.	*She looked as if she were ill.*
Sie sah aus, **als wäre** sie krank.	

15.2 Relative clauses (See Functional Grammar 5.4.3)

Relative clauses are a sort of subordinate clause, and give us more information about the noun in the main clause. These clauses normally begin with a relative pronoun (occasionally with **welcher**). The relative pronoun must be preceded by a comma, and sends the verb to the end of the clause:

Sie heiratet den Mann, der sie liebt.   *She is marrying the man who*
loves her.

Relative pronouns show the following changes of form:

	Singular			*Plural*
	masculine	feminine	neuter	m.f.n.
Nominative	der	die	das	die
Accusative	den	die	das	die
Dative	dem	der	dem	denen
Genitive	dessen	deren	dessen	deren

- The relative pronoun agrees in number and gender with the word it refers back to. In **Sie heiratet den Mann, der sie liebt**, the relative pronoun **der** is masculine singular because it refers to the noun **der Mann**, which is masculine singular.

- The case of the relative pronoun is determined by the role which it plays in the relative clause, e.g.

    Sie heiratet den Mann, **der** die   *She is marrying the man,*
      Versicherungsgesellschaft **besitzt**. *who owns the insurance company.*

    The relative pronoun **der** is nominative because it is the subject of the relative clause. In the sentence **Sie heiratet den Mann, den sie liebt** *She is marrying (whom) she loves*, the relative pronoun **den** is accusative masculine because it is the direct object of the verb **liebt** in the relative clause. The subject of the relative clause is **sie**.

- If there is another verb in the sentence after the relative clause, a verb – comma – verb construction is required:

    Der Mann, den sie **heiratet**, **besitzt**   *The man (whom) she is marrying,*
      die Versicherungsgesellschaft.   *owns the insurance company.*